# Preaching Politics

# Studies in Rhetoric and Religion 3

# Preaching Politics

## The Religious Rhetoric of George Whitefield and the Founding of a New Nation

JEROME DEAN MAHAFFEY

BAYLOR UNIVERSITY PRESS

*Cover design* by Donna Habersaat, dh design
*Cover image:* Illustration of George Whitefield preaching. @ Bettman Corbis
DEC377-31. Used by permission.


Library of Congress Cataloging-in-Publication Data

Mahaffey, Jerome Dean.
  Preaching politics : the religious rhetoric of George Whitefield and the
founding of a new nation / Jerome Dean Mahaffey.
    p. cm. -- (Studies in rhetoric and religion ; 3)
  Includes bibliographical references.
  ISBN 978-1-932792-88-1 (alk. paper)
  1. Whitefield, George, 1714-1770. 2. Rhetoric--Political aspects--United
States--History--18th century. 3. United States--History--Colonial period,
ca. 1600-1775. I. Title.

  BX9225.W4M34 2007
  269'.2092--dc22

                              2007026450



Printed in the United States of America on acid-free paper with a minimum
of 30% pcw content.

# CONTENTS

# PREFACE

My interest in George Whitefield began in 1993 when I heard a couple of stories about him in a history class with John Corrigan at Arizona State University. While telling the anecdotes about how Whitefield could make audiences tremble by his pronunciation of the word "Mesopotamia," and that the famous actor David Garrick would give a hundred guineas just to say "O" like Whitefield, the taciturn Dr. Corrigan could not contain his mirth and let a chuckle escape. I was intrigued. How could someone "clothe words with emotion" as Corrigan had explained Whitefield did? The question haunted me for a couple of years until, during a break in classes in my M.A. program in Syracuse, I pulled out a book from Corrigan's class and began reading a Whitefield sermon. I was strangely moved in a climactic section near the end, feeling what I have since come to recognize as an indicator of an exceptional rhetorical passage. I suspected there was more than vocal inflection involved in Whitefield's effect on people. Although I had not yet studied enough rhetoric to recognize what made the section so powerful, I was surprised that a text written over two centuries earlier could reach forward and touch my soul in that way. I was further intrigued and reread all the other sources on Whitefield I had in my possession.

Two more years of graduate school passed, and I was sitting in John Angus Campbell's office chatting about dissertation ideas. Our conversation drifted into homiletics, and I told John a couple of the Whitefield anecdotes, becoming somewhat animated in the telling. John smiled and said, "I think we have found our dissertation topic." I immediately knew he was right.

With John's guidance I began to study Whitefield seriously at this point, seeking to understand what made him so successful and striving to recreate in my imagination the oratorical voice that might produce the effects described by his biographers. I quickly recognized that many historical sources were colored with admiration and produced a rather two-dimensional figure. I instinctively recognized there was a deeper person buried under the images created by evangelical writers. I also was not discovering in these works the source of his eloquence or any explanations for how his homiletic practice operated, not at least until I read Harry Stout's book *The Divine Dramatist*. Here at last was a missing piece of the puzzle and an honest portrayal of Whitefield's life from which a more robust character emerged.

Seeking to understand him more deeply, I began reading Whitefield's sermons. As my graduate education progressed, I received sufficient training in rhetorical criticism to identify the persuasive action and forces present in the texts. I found in Whitefield a person who understood the art of persuasion, considered his audiences, and produced just the right kind of discourse to meet his goals. Surprised that nothing I had read to that point delved deeply into his extant sermon texts, I believed that my dissertation could provide a new perspective on Whitefield, one that analyzed his sermons to describe the rhetorical action that blended with features other scholarship had discovered.

The focus of previous Whitefield studies has been largely contextual, discussing events of his life and his responses as recorded in his *Journals* and other primary sources penned by his contemporaries. Explanations for his eloquence have been posited that include his solid character, dramatic acting ability, marketing skills, public relations efforts, and even a spiritual anointing. However, these studies seldom investigated the substance of his preaching and the logic of his arguments. Successful persuasion will always contain a component of logic.

Sermonic evidence has been used sparingly to exemplify particular features of his ministry. But there are one hunderd and ten extant sermons and pamphlets, each between five thousand and six thousand words—a treasure trove of primary data. Whitefield wrote very little to explain his preaching strategies or views on persuasion. I believe that one reason for this is that he knew everything was embedded in his sermon texts or otherwise available from studying the classical sources on persuasion. Accordingly, this study reads the sermonic writings and tries to recreate his ministry from within the texts. Perhaps preachers can learn the most by reading his sermons and analyzing the persuasive strategies, but those with other interests can learn much as well. Whitefield's art, at a structural level, relied on principles that can be used in multiple contexts in any era. At a fundamental level, or from a psychological perspective, people have not changed much over time and, motivational or persuasion tactics tend to be stable. And we can learn much about the business of persuasion by studying those who do it well.

As my dissertation research and writing progressed, and as John Campbell and I discussed facets of Whitefield's life, John pointed out that there was more going on here than just an evangelist converting a lot of people to Christianity. There was clearly a political agenda embedded in Whitefield's enterprise. All of the solid secondary scholarship pointed to this facet as well. So I was forced to return to the history texts and learn more about the political currents of his age, in America as well as Britain, in order to understand the interplay between politics and religion in Whitefield's mind. Other writers had posited connections, albeit contested ones, between the revival years of the 1740s and the American Revolution, and these theories provided some powerful explanations for curious aspects of Whitefield's ministry. Thus, as my research evolved out of my dissertation over the next six years, the story that unfolded drifted further into politics and the development of the American people. Whitefield's persuasive efforts were "constitutive," directed at the development of a Christian community—his parish—that was both ecumenical and expansive. His messages centered on identity and the duties and privileges that came with inclusion in this community.

While I am passionate about the field of rhetoric, my interest in Whitefield is admittedly grounded in my own personal religiosity. Ideally, researchers are able to distance their personal feelings far enough from their topics so as to avoid bias. Yet, the passion one feels for a topic empowers the researcher to wade through tedious tasks that would otherwise mire a project and possibly end it altogether. This work is not intended as a hagiography but designs to present as honest a view of Whitefield as possible. Yet, my own interest and passion likely shows through the text in a few places. I ask the purist researcher's pardon on this account.

The story in the following pages probably does not add much to the events and facts of Whitefield's life. Other able historians have attended to that task more expertly than I could have done. But my hope is that my research will reveal a missing element of Whitefield's ministry by closely examining his sermons to understand the essences

of his messages, to uncover the logic with which he persuaded his hearers, and to learn about the audiences themselves from Whitefield's perspective. The title of the book, *Preaching Politics,* seeks to foreshadow the image of Whitefield contained therein as a politically minded minister with great influence. The subtitle, *The Religious Rhetoric of George Whitefield and the Founding of a New Nation,* emphasizes the angle of the book, the frame in which the image is placed.

I owe many debts that were incurred in the consummation of this project. First to John Corrigan (though he probably doesn't recall me), who inspired me with an image of a genuine scholar, immersed in books and knowledge, writing up his findings in an engaging, clear style. My rhetoric professor at Arizona State, Lesley DiMare, managed to get me hooked on the discipline and encouraged me to apply to graduate school. Our conversation and her subsequent recommendation changed my life. John Charles Adams directed my Master's thesis and helped me mature into a scholar, treating me as a colleague and friend while I was still a student. He led me into the postmodern world, guiding me into a deeper level of understanding of myself and certainly the business of rhetoric. John Angus Campbell continued that intellectual development, opening my eyes to the limitations and flaws of postmodernism and guiding me to a balance between raw knowledge, *phronesis,* and faith. I met Karlyn Korhs Campbell at a conference in 1998 where she graciously gave my paper a close edit, affirmed my fledgling feminist scholarship, and encouraged me to work more diligently on my writing—advice I took to heart and I hope bore some fruit in this publication.

Although a necessary part of the publishing process, putting your heart and soul out for display to receive criticism and comment is always difficult. I am immensely grateful to colleagues who have read the manuscript in various stages of production. As the book took form, my history colleague George Blakey read this manuscript, provided helpful editorial comments, and steered my historical research into the mainstream. I also am very thankful to an anonymous reviewer whose scathing rebuke helped me mature and write with less hubris and pointed to some genuine weaknesses in my argument. As Socrates advised, those who point out our faults are great friends. In addition to helpful reviews, I have received other encouragements from editors at two presses who were unable to offer a publication contract. I thank Barry Blose and Joanna Craig for taking the work of a young scholar seriously, pointing to areas that needed improvement, and confirming my research as worthwhile. This kept me diligent in my pursuit of a publisher. Marty Medhurst, at Baylor University Press, has continued the mentoring process in rhetoric, helping to condense and prioritize the comments of four diverse external reviews. I thank Beth Slattery and Rachel Ramer for reading the manuscript in various stages, finding my errors, and pointing out my grammatical issues.

Most of all I thank my family, who have partially sacrificed a father and husband to the demands of scholarship. Their forbearance has made my research possible. To Lainey, Isaac, and Anna, I express my deepest gratitude. Thank you all!

CHAPTER 1

# THE QUEST FOR AMERICAN ORIGINS

The entire man is, so to speak, to be seen in the cradle of the child.

—Alexis de Tocqueville*

If ever a diverse people occupied one land, they were the Euro-American colonists in the decades before the American Revolution. Consisting of various cultures, speaking different languages, adhering to dissimilar religions, and accustomed to the authoritarian rule of monarchs, it was unlikely that from 1735 to 1775 these colonists would find sufficient common ground upon which to construct a popular revolt against the British crown. Clearly, some manner of transformation occurred, likely rooted in the identity of the people, that built bridges between them and homogenized their divergent political sentiments. The nature of this transformation in the minds and hearts of the Revolutionary generation is emerging from the mists of time, but precisely how it traversed conceptual spheres, how it permeated towns, parishes, and ultimately encompassed thirteen of the British colonies warrants further investigation to deepen our understanding of America's nascent period.

With respect to American origins, Thomas Kuhn's assertion that perception requires the existence of an appropriate paradigm (a conceptual system) pointedly illuminates the heart of the question: How did colonial Americans develop into an "interpretive community" that allowed republicanism and notions of independence to even occur, let alone proliferate? What common experiences supplied American colonists with the vocabulary, grammar, and hermeneutical lenses that facilitated patterns of thought leading to independence? What kind of radical conceptual shift in the American mind enabled people, accustomed for centuries to a vertically structured, authoritarian society (in both religion and politics), to conclude logically that resisting British

1

oppression and forming a horizontally structured, democratic society were the right things to do? One might as well ask modern Americans to eschew our current republican government in favor of reinstituting a monarchy with strict religious hegemony!

The aim of this book is to examine key sites in the historical record closely to uncover rhetorical forces that fused American colonists more closely in their attitudes, beliefs, and values to form what is now recognized as "the American spirit." By using the term "rhetorical forces," we presume that societal change is fueled by ideas and that ideas are disseminated and propagated by people who employ the art of rhetoric. The thesis offered here is that a particular group of colonial leaders introduced a constitutive rhetoric that worked to unify American colonists into a cohesive whole at a deep structural level. In particular, one person is consistently found actively promoting this rhetoric at pivotal points in American evolution. The pages that follow trace the origins of that rhetoric and the role of this particular individual, George Whitefield, and then follow the trajectory and influence of these constitutive rhetorical forces up to the point where the American Founding Fathers declared independence from Great Britain.

A hefty barrier to colonial unification was the pervasive human tendency to form relationships with like-minded people, to bond in family and cultural groups with a spatial orientation, and to create an identity for each community member linked to, and formed from, the mores of the group. But this process was disrupted in colonial America by the disassociation of people from their traditional homelands. Michael Warner explained that many colonists expressed an identity anxiety rooted in the geography of conflicting European and American ways; they were strangers in a foreign world attempting to preserve their European heritage.[1] "The colonies were populated by individuals and groups," wrote Sydney Ahlstrom, "immigrants all, who were always beginning anew, even if they had left Europe in tears and with a determination to perpetuate its ways."[2] America would resist the imposition of European ways and instead shape those who came here according to her own unique conditions. Ambiguities regarding cultural identity among colonists prepared the colonial mind for an identity-establishing rhetoric that could resolve geographic and cultural tensions as "American ways" disrupted the social stability of immigrant colonists.

So how did American colonists develop a sufficient sense of identification with one another in order for the unifying rhetoric of Revolutionary-era leaders to be intelligible on a widespread scale? The present inquiry shall look at discourse prior to the Revolution that enacted community and identity-building functions, discourse that weakened the cultural glues of nationality and physical proximity, replacing them with a more powerful cohesive agent, while it introduced a "neutral space" in which colonists reformulated similar identities and founded an American community.

An emerging perspective that affords understanding into the evolution of an American ideology is the premise that assigns responsibility for social order to religion through its dogmatic assertions of "first principles." Religion and culture are intimately bound. As Alexis de Tocqueville, in the context of America's first fifty years, specifically wrote, "Men cannot do without dogmatical belief; and it is much to be desired that such belief should exist among them." Explaining what he meant, Tocqueville continued: "The first object, and one of the principal advantages, of religion is to furnish to each of these fundamental questions a solution which is at once clear, precise, intelligible . . . and lasting."[3] Fundamental beliefs of a culture are warranted and articulated by its predominant religious institution, compacted and symbolically coded into doctrines, rituals, liturgies, stories, and music to provide repetitive reminders of what people ought to believe and how they ought to behave. Religious scripts ultimately guide performances of culture by providing a "conceptual system"—an index of social and cultural values—that establishes "first principles" for social identity and community understanding.[4] Precisely defined, a conceptual system consists of a set of axioms about "knowledge and truth," about what "is," about the essence of "things," and about "how we ought to respond" to our world. The axioms that make up our conceptual system serve as the foundation for reasoning; they are inherited from "culture" and in the case of American colonists, the conceptual system was mediated through alterations in its dominant religion. In Western societies today, the disciplines of science have provided the elements of the conceptual system. Even in colonial America, "enlightened" thinkers, who put their faith in scientific explanations for phenomena rather than in God, were increasingly exerting an influence. But for the commoners of that day (indeed in any period of history), the latest scientific or philosophical thought was more distant. The people that form the masses of any culture cling to old prejudices, slowly relinquishing them over the course of decades, not years or months, often requiring two generations for seminal ideas to imbue social praxis. Modernity was slower to infiltrate the rugged colonial world and, until it did, the clergy held far more influence than the Royal Society, whose scientific authority would not be fully appreciated by the wider society until after the Revolution. Yet, inasmuch as educated clergy were gathering Enlightenment-influenced religious views, the colonists were soon to be offered those perspectives. Corrigan demonstrated how a number of Puritan clergy encouraged their congregants to develop positive emotional responses to "the beauty of unity and order found in nature, society and in God."[5]

No person can ever hope to fully develop a workable conceptual system independently—it would take a lifetime of trial-and-error learning. It must be taught; dogmatically at first. And collective identity is inherently bound to the dominant conceptual system of a society. In colonial America, through a circular process of influence between religion and society, religious identity brought its resources to bear on the formation of national identity. By providing first principles for a society, religion guided the possibilities of thought into specific molds. Nevertheless, society was also able to influence the development of its religion through the education of its future religious leaders, exemplified by the Enlightenment influence on evolving Protestant theology and later by the republican influences that shared a vocabulary with the religious sphere.[6] This give-and-take of influence occurs primarily in the youth since older people tend to hold stubbornly to their beliefs. As colonial American religion served its role in identity formation, the Great Awakening of 1739–1745 (a period of intense religious interest) introduced profound identity suggestions that quickly found receptive individuals in America, especially among the youth.

## RELIGION AND AMERICAN HISTORY

Specific to this study is the contribution of religious ideas to the evolving ideologies of the Revolutionary generation. To what extent, if at all, did their religious belief system inform their political sentiments? Scholars have posited answers to this question ranging from very little to considerable influence. Nearly every scholarly book or article addressing the topic provides its own perspective. The debate, if it may be called one, has ranged from a high degree of interplay to a low degree and seemingly back again. Multiple studies have established a solid perspective of political and religious culture of the period. A brief look at this relevant scholarship will help outline the broader influences with which this inquiry is concerned.

Beginning with those who lived through it, clergy, historians, and observers have speculated on the antecedents of the American Revolution. A range of influences have emerged: an evangelical influence, the effect of Enlightenment rationalism on the society, the contagion of republican political ideologies. All of these explanations possess merit, each bringing an essential perspective to the question and each able to shape the identity of the colonists in profound ways.

Initially, the record of American publications preceding the Revolution suggests a heavy religious influence. Newspaper articles, pamphlets, and books addressing theological issues comprised nearly half of New England publications, a quarter in the Middle colonies, a tenth in the South, and more than a third overall.[7] While the balance of secular or religious topics varied according to current events, religion always returned as a topical theme after any displacement.

Eschewing the Protestant hermeneutic that may have distorted the nation's history up through the 1900s, Progressive-era historians began to favor the explanatory power of Enlightenment rationalism as a catalyst for shifting modes of thought.[8] The advent of new knowledge provided by the natural sciences and philosophy affected every sphere of society—especially among the educated leaders on both sides of the Atlantic, which included the clergy. Yet, rationalism did not contend with religious theology for hegemony. Rather the theologians and scientists worked to reconcile scientific findings with theology. Many "enlightened" clergy composed and published essays describing how each new discovery supported biblical interpretations of truth. Rationalism provided an extremely fruitful perspective for explanations and theories about the intellectual and religious climate of colonial America. Most of the influential theologians in America possessed a number of influential books in their personal libraries that linked elements of their thought back to European writers, providing ideas that trickled down to their parishioners through weekly sermons.

For a number of years in the writing of American history, the influence of religion was subordinated to rationalism as the historiographical pendulum swung the other direction.

Beginning in the 1960s, several historians began reincorporating
religion in addition to Enlightenment influences as a vibrant component of the evolution of colonial America. Carl Bridenbaugh's research
explained how the struggle over establishment of an Anglican episcopacy in America exacerbated tensions in the midst of the Stamp Act
crisis.[9] A few years later, Alan Heimert described the evolving nuances
in doctrine and ideology that sculpted the contours of the intellectual and religious landscape of colonial America, locating the ideological innovations of Revolutionary thought in Protestantism of the
Great Awakening period.[10] A year later Heimert and his mentor Perry
Miller suggested a straight line of ideological development from shifts
in religious theology to republican expressions of liberty: "What was
awakened in 1740 was the spirit of American democracy."[11] Yet, their
work failed to convince many scholars of the strength of connections
and the direct cause-and-effect relationship between the Awakening
and the Revolution.[12] Well grounded in scholarship, their return to a
Protestant hermeneutic provided some needed insights yet still seemed
to be missing some important elements.

Working concurrently with Heimert, and publishing his ideas a
year later, Bernard Bailyn demonstrated the preponderance of republican ideology laced throughout the literature and oral narratives of
the period. A political ideology that had been in circulation in British
society since the Cromwellian revolution, republicanism was fueled
by and was ostensibly a natural extension of Enlightenment rationalism into the political realm. Adding the notion of "republicanism"
as a profitable hermeneutical perspective, Bailyn argued that the primary goal of the Revolution was not to transform society, but simply
to maintain the "political liberty threatened by the apparent corruption" of British constitutional government.[13] His seminal study built
upon the rationalist view and proceeded to identify "the radical social
and political thought of the English Civil War and of the Common-
wealth period" as the central mind-shaping force in the mid-eighteenth century.[14] Republican ideas gradually entrenched themselves
in the colonial mind as the eighteenth century proceeded, surfacing in
the vocabulary of speakers and writers as ideographs such as "liberty,"
"virtue," or "natural rights" in Revolutionary polemics. Although Bai-

lyn's work primarily explores republican influences, he does not completely ignore the role of religious sentiments, explaining the import of the Anglican episcopacy issue.

While not all historians seem fully convinced of any direct ideological connections between the Awakening and the Revolution, many have sensed the relationship and posited their own accounts. Cushing Strout rejects Heimert's thesis without naming him, but sketches the development of religiously charged ideologies that begins and ends in the same places.[15] Patricia Bonomi reconfirmed religion as a formative aspect of societal development.[16] Demonstrating that colonists were far more religious than admitted elsewhere, her detailed readings of primary documents unearth a plethora of evidence supporting the depth and extent of religious piety in the colonists. Bonomi clarifies how, as the colonial crisis deepened, the issues of "Divine Right," "unlimited submission," the Anglican bishop controversy, and the political activism of the clergy were key players in the unfolding drama. J. C. D. Clark clarified that the various religious groups that participated in the Revolution possessed different goals and experienced vastly different outcomes from the war than they perhaps intended.[17]

Nathan Hatch said that Heimert "jumps quickly from the Awakening to the Revolution" without a careful consideration of the Anglo-French wars.[18] Hatch, expanding the possibilities of argument facilitated by Bailyn's work on republican influences, described how "civil millennialism"—an amalgamation of millennial theology and politics, forming a belief that the world would end and God's kingdom would be established in America—exerted a profound influence on colonial society. This blending of religion and republicanism emerges as a promising explanatory theory able to incorporate a wider body of evidence and position the relative strengths of each antecedent in a proper relationship. Yet the religious landscape of the colonies was complex and provides notable objections to any simple theory.

Jon Butler's influential study, *Awash in a Sea of Faith*, began to reexamine the complexity of religious strains of thought in colonial America. His fine-grained analysis of various groups of people dispels any myth of monolithic Puritan origins of America, instead showing that a multiplicity of religious faiths competed for the minds of colonists along with Congregationalism.[19] Butler believes these other traditions brought their own seeds of influence, suggesting Heimert's view to be unnecessarily narrow in its favor of evangelicalism. Although he ulti-

mately calls the Revolution a "profoundly secular event," he devoted
thirteen pages of his book to the religious influence on the Revolutionary generation, a move that affirms Bonomi's scholarship.[20] Butler's
work also challenged the "greatness" of the Awakening period with
the effect of moderating historiographical views that foregrounded
the religiosity of the colonial generation. Seeking a balance between
Bonomi's and Butler's views, Charles Cohen stated that the Awakening was "not exactly an interpretive fiction," but that understanding
it as a "constellation" of localized occurrences within a "transatlantic
happening" allows a productive perspective.[21]

If there was a contest of ascendancy between the secular and religious hermeneutic lenses, the secular views appear to have emerged
on top after Butler's publications.[22] The influences of rationalism
and republicanism have great explanatory power, and tend to over-
shadow religious influences on the Americanization process. Yet none
of the aforementioned scholarly paradigms were mutually exclusive
in explanatory power and none claimed to be. Several studies have
since appeared that question the neglect of religion as a factor. Calling for a reintegration of religious themes, Harry Stout pointed out
how Progressive-era historians downplayed religion as an influence
on American cultural development, suggesting that such views had
guided later scholarship:

> In the formative phase of American history writing, there was no
> integration of religious history into American history, no sense that it
> constituted a "main theme" in the profession's priorities. Other ideo-
> logical and environmental forces were used to explain the main course
> of American history.[23]

Although Stout articulately expressed this situation, he was not the
first scholar to observe it. Earlier, Perry Miller had noted that "an historian not versed in the discriminations of theology" may have difficulty interpreting formative documents from the colonial period.[24]
Yet no formal contest had been announced, and certainly the perspectives provided by each view were well grounded in scholarship
and somehow can form a coherent picture. Stout explained that criticisms of Heimert's evangelical paradigm are valid only when looking
for "direct intellectual links" between shifting religious theologies and
political rebellion.[25] In his view, the links between religious thought

and political ideology were perhaps more McLuhanesque than direct, locating them in underlying modes of persuasion that conveyed the content of political ideology.[26]

More recently the work of Mark Noll has fleshed out many of the connections between republican thought and the developing theologies of colonials. Noll further integrates what appeared to be disparate theories of influence, showing how an increasingly intertwined and ambiguous vocabulary allowed political ideals to be expressed in theology and vice versa. Though he does not presume any direction of influence between rationalism, republicanism, and religion, his account effectively portrays how the interaction empowered Revolutionary polemics in an increasingly blended society.[27]

In addition to the underlying *modes of persuasion* that forged links between the revival and the Revolution, one must not quickly discard the *content* of religious discourse. Miller, Heimert, and others had elucidated some important elements that need to be considered along with other explanatory factors. Religious discourse contained the forms of thought that blended with emerging political ideology of the Revolutionary period. As historian Arthur Berthold explained:

> The period was not only one of transplanting of ideas but also of the building of a new culture. In this activity, ideas had an importance which it is hard to realize in an age where economic determinism has become almost a household word and an explanation for nearly everything. The colonial mind, on the other hand, was almost entirely governed by ideas, and these ideas were, for the most part, religious. This is true not only of Puritan New England and Quaker Pennsylvania, but also largely of the South.[28]

These "implied doctrines" are what cry out for further analysis and will provide the focal point of this study. Along with modes of persuasion, these implied doctrines (axioms) emerged out of popular religion to fashion the conceptual system of the colonists, which then supplied a receptive mind for the influences of colonial political thought as it allowed republican ideas to proliferate among people who could readily comprehend its vocabulary. As our study unfolds, we will identify these doctrines and trace their meandering trail of development throughout the mid-eighteenth century.

## Shifting Communication Patterns

Given the reliance of historians on printed records, one must ask if those records accurately represent a cross section of the population. Clearly, those records would favor the literate and the well educated, especially with respect to published materials that comprise the backbone of the public sphere of the period. Along with the printed public sphere, an oral sphere materialized in colonial America that also exerted an intellectual force on its population, a sphere that hides behind and within the published texts of the period. One scholar has argued that this *oral* public discourse (a new mode of persuasion and civic discourse) influenced colonial Americans to a greater degree than *printed* materials and with a deeper impact than previously supposed.[29] The orature of the period, which largely consisted of sermons (frozen into print), still retains its oral flavor, and embedded therein are the ideas and arguments that formed the substance of much public discourse.

Equally important to the creation of the oral public sphere was the question of who would be allowed to use it! The itinerant ministers of the Great Awakening introduced a style of public communication, and not without controversy, that ultimately reshaped the rules about who had the privilege of a civic voice.[30] Stout's research into this phenomena has shown that the mass address of voluntary audiences, a practice invented and popularized during the Great Awakening, initiated a conversation between religious leaders and the people, a conversation *irrespective of social hierarchy and traditional contexts*. Nonsanctioned leaders could now reach the public through print and oral venues as they exploited new modes of persuasion to promote ideas. Respected ministers legitimized itinerancy and outdoor meetings in America as they created religious networks and paved a preaching circuit that ultimately served more secular voices. As an added benefit, the foundation of the oral sphere was infused with "inspired" discourse from ministers whose connection with the divine lent that sphere an epistemological credibility that printed discourse (except for the Bible) could never match. By the time of the Revolution, political orators such as Patrick Henry and James Otis were equipped with a well-respected method of disseminating their propaganda orally. People would attend outdoor meetings and ascribe to them a high level of authority, perhaps including an embedded suggestion of divine inspiration, just as they had ascribed to many itinerant ministers of the revival years.

During the same period, oratory itself was undergoing a transformation as scholars and practitioners finally recognized the low estate of rhetorical praxis and took steps to reinvigorate it. In 1741 David Hume complained, "Many do not think themselves sufficiently compensated, for the losing of their dinners, by all the eloquence of our most celebrated speakers."[31] A decade later Thomas Sheridan echoed his view: "A man shall rise up in a public assembly, and, without the least mark of shame, deliver a discourse to many hundred auditors, in such disagreeable tones and unharmonious cadences, as to disgust every ear."[32] In response to the situation, George Campbell explored the role of emotions in the persuasive process in his influential book *The Philosophy of Rhetoric*, and Thomas Sheridan led a group of writers known as the elocutionists in publishing rhetoric manuals that emphasized the role of natural delivery.[33] Their research was beginning to explore an emotion-laden natural style of oratory that began to displace the listless sermons and political speeches in colonial America and Great Britain. This natural style of oral delivery quickly becomes the benchmark for oratory in any venue due to its clear superiority of rhetorical efficacy.

The development of the oral and written public spheres enabled colonists to begin thinking about "collective identity." Fashioned from the discourse of religious leaders, an "imagined community" of American colonists began to form during the Great Awakening. This community originated in the cities of the eastern seaboard and extended westward with the proliferation of publishing and ministerial itinerancy. In addition to loquacious newspaper accounts of the revivals, new publications such as Thomas Prince's *Christian History* allowed religious audiences to learn of the commonalities in one another's lives, successes, and struggles. It was a community where people might never know the other members, yet still behave as if its members were as near as their neighbors.[34] This developing, religiously flavored community was nurtured by voices in both oral and printed spheres.

## EVIDENCE IMPLICATING GEORGE WHITEFIELD

In light of a seminal role for religious ideas in the development of colonial thought, and given the contested role of the revivals—one way or

another—to shifts in thinking that certainly contributed to Revolutionary impulses, one can easily identify key individuals who likely exerted
an intellectual impact on colonial society. Theoretically, such leaders
would have had one foot in religion and the other in politics, exploiting both oral and print media—leaders who developed, popularized,
and forcefully propagated the "implied doctrines" that shaped colonial
thought, leaders who introduced and promoted *a rhetoric of identity formation and unification,* or something like it. The rhetoric of the period was
fossilized into printed versions of oral discourse that today's rhetorical
critics may still analyze. Through the rhetorical analysis of key texts
of the colonial period, the rhetorical action of implied doctrines that
impelled change can be lifted from obscurity for inspection and analysis. But among the thousands of extant texts, where might the search
for a rhetoric of identity begin?

Heimert and Miller identified the Anglican itinerant minister
George Whitefield as the catalyst of the Awakening, claiming that
the revival followed his first American tour (1740).[35] Most scholarship
acknowledges that Whitefield combined the sporadic local revivals
into a consistent and generalized Awakening, impelling it to the fore of
colonial society.[36] Stout established Whitefield's importance in popu-
larizing oral public discourse by providing a pragmatic model for this
new mode of communication.[37] Historian Frank Lambert illuminated
Whitefield's innovative work in the use of print, how he demonstrated
its power as a mass medium to promote his enterprise on an intercolonial (indeed international) scale, contributing to the formation of this
imagined community of colonists interested in the Awakening.[38] And
although each of these scholars has subordinated political themes to
other focal points in his or her research, all consistently implicated
Whitefield in spheres of political action.

But we would be mistaken should we assume Whitefield was the
sole inspiration behind the Awakening, its rhetoric, and its ensuing
conceptual system. Jonathan Edwards played his own part in shaping Protestant thought through publications teaching and defending
revival theology. Others, such as Charles Chauncy, challenged the
revival and helped reign in its emotional excesses, ultimately forcing
many revivalists back to the mainstream of society. But while Edwards
stood as the intellectual genius and official spokesperson of the revival
theology, and Chauncy weeded out heresy, George Whitefield was
the person who did the rhetorical work of disseminating and promot-

ing its conceptual system. Whitefield only added one key element to the message that Edwards had been preaching to his congregation in Northampton, Massachusetts, since 1735, and he agreed more often with Chauncy than disagreed. Perhaps his primary contribution was to take the revival message, encapsulate it in a simplified vocabulary, spread it far and wide, and argue persuasively for colonists to accept it. Moreover, Whitefield was followed by and assisted in disseminating this rhetoric by a plethora of mimetic itinerants who spread revivalism with its Protestant-implied doctrines to the more sparsely populated agricultural areas that extended from civilized regions to the frontier.[39] These rhetorical tasks arrest the attention of rhetorical scholars. Whitefield's itinerancy and his rhetorical skills emerged as the factors that differentiated him from his contemporaries. More than any other individual, Whitefield had the rhetorical skills and energy to spread this rhetoric of identity formation across the British American colonies, making him a key figure for inquiries into American origins.

Whitefield also played a larger role in colonial politics than understood by most admiring religious biographers, who exclusively tout his preaching successes. As will be shown, from 1745 until his death, Whitefield inserted his voice into political issues, especially where political ideologies were implicated in religious praxis. Consequently, individuals like Whitefield, who promoted innovative changes in religion and shifts in modes of public discourse that structured the emerging colonial American culture, provided a rhetoric through which discursively represented antecedents of colonial identity and religious contributions to the American Revolution might be profitably examined.

A rhetorical perspective seeks to understand the rhetorical process of ideological development, focusing on the substance, strategies, and choreography of the circulating discourse that impelled transformations. Consequently, the contribution rhetorical criticism offers is rooted in the analysis of key colonial texts, seeking to better understand those texts, seeking to connect with the minds that produced them, and attempting to recreate, by inference, a preferred relationship between their producers and their audiences. Since Whitefield was essentially an orator, an informed analysis of his discourse justifies a close-up view of his enterprise from the inside looking out, from Whitefield's eyes to the America that he loved. Through the rhetorical analysis of Whitefield's sermons and political propaganda, we can get into the minds of colonial Americans as Whitefield understood

them, index their core beliefs, and then illuminate how these beliefs
reflexively informed their theology and politics. Ed Black eloquently
articulated the profound ramifications of ideological rhetoric: "In all
rhetorical discourse, we can find incitements not simply to believe
something, but to be something. We are solicited by the discourse to
fulfill its blandishments with our very selves."[40]

"Rhetoriography"—the application of rhetorical methods to the
study of historical objects—comprises a multifaceted and encompassing methodological approach to the study of rhetoric, addressing both the rhetorical messages and the historical scope constraining
and impinging upon a text and its dialogic interaction with its audience.[41] Thus, the rhetorical critic is able to partially resolve the tension
between text and context along with its implications for agency.[42] A
rhetoriography tells the story of a rhetor with acute attention toward
the events and relationships that shaped that individual's rhetorical
sense and abilities. Second, through various methods of close textual
analysis, rhetoriography queries the text about the rhetor, audience,
relationships between them, and the text's influence—both intended
and actual. Third, sensitive to the complex notion of a rhetorical situation, a rhetoriography incorporates perspectives of history and structural forces that impinge on the circulation of rhetorical discourse.

The present inquiry is not an archival study seeking to uncover
and catalog new information about historical figures and events.
Rather, it takes a close look, through a rhetorical lens, at persuasive
individuals and analyzes well-worn texts, as well as more obscure
ones, to illuminate their persuasive intent and strategies and uncover
something meaningful about the author and intended audiences. As
the notion of "agency" has been hotly debated in rhetorical circles
in recent decades (denounced among historians as the "great man"
theory), many scholars have rejected the possibility that an individual
can have a pronounced influence on a society. In this debate, as in all
issues, moderation may be the key to furthering our knowledge. The
present study espouses the notion of "limited agency" founded upon
structuration theory—that dialogic interactions between community
members produce culture, that beliefs change over time, and that specific thinkers or influential individuals can introduce or promote catalytic ideas that seem to take on a life of their own. To view this study as
employing the great-man theory is to misunderstand rhetorical criticism as well as the study's intent. Rather, the study looks for and exam-

ines the *rhetoric* of an influential individual in order to understand the interactions between that rhetoric and the American colonists.

As any discourse constitutes a performance of culture between the members that dialogically enact it, Whitefield's performances were anchored to his view of reality in the discursive space that his rhetoric created. The coherence of social action is guided from an unwritten cultural code and is evidenced in an "index" of conceptual distinctions that provide structure to performances of culture. By mapping these distinctions, one can unearth a blueprint of thought. A theory of "indexical order" was forwarded by Michael Silverstein, a linguist from the University of Chicago, who defines it as the "necessary concept that shows us how to relate the micro-social to the macro-social frames of analyses of any sociolinguistic phenomenon."[43] By mapping the indexical order of dialogic interaction, the analyst can create a window into the thought and culture of those producing and receiving the discourse. Silverstein claims that all discourse is structured by "deictic parameters—a matrix of relational positionings toward represented states of affairs—such as epistemic, ontic, and phenomenal."[44] Examples of deictic parameters would include the concepts of "this-that," "past-present-future," "I-you," "us-them," and "good-evil." These deictic parameters are the fundamental units of analysis that represent states-of-affairs in the dialogic process. The mapping of such deictic parameters reveals the implied doctrines of thought as the participants of discourse articulate a version of reality called into being from out of the cultural repository. These deictic parameters (I will refer to them as "reality distinctions" hereafter) structure the essence of an individual's conceptual system, functioning as a framework upon which all the specifics of a situation are organized. Thus, a Whitefield sermon, a Samuel Adams editorial, a Thomas Paine pamphlet, or any other kind of discourse, may be queried to index the conceptual system of the author and perceived audience.

To represent systematically what kind of audience Whitefield enticed his audience to be, the analytic portions of this study shall isolate the implied doctrines lodged in terms, metaphors, and reality distinctions that provide structure for discourse both implicitly and explicitly. These distinctions are primal as they materially and nontropically represent a reality; they underlie and give force to the phrases, terms, and metaphors that were the vehicles by which thought was reflected and transported to others. These reality distinctions construct the "implied doctrines" (societal *endoxa*) that made colonial rhetoric, in all its forms, intelligible and forceful. T. H. Breen and Timothy Hall have suggested that consequents of these implied doctrines revolve around choices about "the nature of boundaries, social and spatial, about the fluidity of social relations, about the problematic character of foundational values, and finally, about the possibility of a recognizably 'liberal' or modern 'self.'"[45] Linguistic reality distinctions prefigure such issues, making their intelligibility possible and suggesting directions for choices in these four arenas of social interaction.

Yet, the implied doctrines of a particular conceptual system do far more work than simply providing an index of beliefs. With some conceptual development, they can form the essence of what Aristotle labeled the special *topoi* (topics). Also known as "first-stage rhetorical topics," they are defined by Walter Jost and Michael Hyde as "insights that are kept incomplete and whose very deficiency enables inquirers to deploy their understanding within a new situation."[46] These "insights" operate like formulaic axioms inviting specific content from any particular situations. Their incomplete nature invites a conversation with new situations that will subsequently offer innovative conclusions or solutions that extend the situation in a logical direction (much as a mathematical formula containing an *unknown variable* will provide a different, but predictable, solution for each concrete element that replaces the variable). The inventional nature of these first-stage rhetorical topics provides avenues to new knowledge and truths as they allow ideas from one sphere to permeate into others. Hence, as the study unfolds, it will also identify and closely explore any implied doctrines that evolved into first-stage rhetorical topics to empower arguments of Whitefield and other colonial polemicists.

Whitefield's rhetoric drew upon what Gordon Wood labels "popular Christianity," an unorthodox conceptual system that many uneducated or apostate colonists held prior to the Awakening.[47] His sermons were discursive acts that built upon these preexisting metaphysical and socioreligious beliefs through the dialogic process to create a conceptual system amenable to his intention of increasing piety and his latent extensional purpose of transforming American society. As the Awakening-era conceptual system evolved into that of the next generation, it provided the unwritten, but powerfully constraining, cultural code by which all colonial discourse may be indexed.

Hence, to answer our central question, "How did colonial Americans develop into an interpretive community that allowed republicanism and notions of independence to occur, let alone proliferate?" this book offers the following thesis: George Whitefield produced and circulated a "rhetoric of community," distilled from Edwardsean Calvinism, that successfully promoted a common conceptual system among the variegated colonial cultures, establishing a "we-ness," a sense of personal and collective identity, initially within a community of revived parishioners and their families and ultimately within the wider society as religious requirements were loosened and then dropped. Additionally, Whitefield remained involved in the evolution of this collective identity in response to specific challenges in the decades following 1740, steering it toward a more formal "British identity" (a situation that T. H. Breen believes has not "been persuasively resolved by English historians).[48] Whitefield's ministry also greatly contributed to the blending of theology with republican ideologies of the Revolutionary period. It is not that a *majority* of colonists subsequently rushed to join churches during and after the revival and became direct community members (although Patricia Bonomi makes a strong argument for such a scenario).[49] Yet, those who did join churches found religious consubstantiality and began articulating a conceptual system that prescribed a place for all members of their society. And since religion plays such a critical role in articulating the foundational beliefs of a society, especially in colonial America, this rhetoric of community exerted a degree of influence even on those who were not "awakened." The story that follows will endeavor to demonstrate how this rhetoric helped formulate a uniquely American community in 1740, and chart the progress of its evolving identity as this religious community expanded and redefined itself, prescribing beliefs in response to various opportunities and threats over the next three decades.

This study does not attempt to describe a simple cause-and-effect relationship; rather, it looks at how a specific rhetoric operated within a society and examines the role a particular individual played in the social process. By virtue of being the "Oracle, Pattern and Patron" for influential itinerant ministers, in addition to his activity in key times and places, Whitefield's contributions, considered in relation to all the other relevant components of societal formation, ignited and fueled the unification process to overcome cultural inertia and nudge America toward fundamental change.[50] Implied doctrines that evolved along

Whitefieldian lines—beliefs that certainly existed but had not proliferated prior to 1740—can be uncovered in the Revolutionary propaganda, doctrines that demonstrate paradigmatic similarities between
the two rhetorics. As Bonomi explained:

> The institutional disruptions and church separations of the Great Awak-
> ening thus provided a kind of "practice model" which enabled the pro-
> vincials to "rehearse"—though unwittingly—a number of the situations,
> and the arguments appropriate to them, that would reappear with the
> political crisis of the 1760s and 1770s.[51]

Her description here of first-stage rhetorical topics being developed,
practiced, and then reemployed describes the portions of rhetorical
action that we will explore in greater detail.

Additionally, the study will analyze discourse from the leading
propagandists of the Revolutionary period, compare the conceptual
system ostensibly revealed therein with the one promoted in the Awakening through Whitefield's evolving rhetoric of community, and see
how each rhetoric was directed at similar audiences: religious rhetoric to create the audience, and Revolutionary rhetoric to motivate it.
As we will see, notions articulated in the Revolutionary propaganda
reflect conceptual changes in two different ways: either argumentation
departs from an identity anxiety (economic or political concerns about
being "in" or "out" of the British "family") or the writers construct
arguments upon unmistakable first principles of Protestantism, spew-
ing religiously charged barbs clearly intended to arouse a zeal founded
in religious beliefs. Consequently, by analyzing Whitefield's rhetoric,
illuminating its identity and community-building function through
embedded implied doctrines, and then showing how the resultant religious community grew and evolved, we can elucidate the rhetorical
process that contributed to political unification. Our conceptions of
George Whitefield, the Great Awakening, early American political origins, rhetorical agency, and the process of fundamental social change
all have much to gain from investigating the rhetorical messages that
shaped the United States of America.

Several questions immediately emerge to guide our exploration of
American origins, which this study will attempt to address: What kinds
of communities existed when Whitefield arrived? How did the Ameri-

can scene contribute to or reflect a "rhetorical situation"? Where did this orator originate who was able to arrest the interest of a continent and influence it through his rhetoric? What are the implied doctrines or first principles of the Awakening conceptual system to which he converted colonists? How are these doctrines embedded in linguistic and discursive elements to form his rhetoric of community? How was Whitefield received? How often did others employ his implied doctrines, indicating that they had adopted this conceptual system? How did particular religious communities conflate into a moderate and ecumenical political community that espoused the Whig ideology? What other issues contributed to this evolution, and to what degree did Whitefield participate? Are religious modes of persuasion to be found in the Revolutionary propaganda? And finally, to what degree does Revolutionary propaganda appear to explicitly address audiences with a respect for religious beliefs, evidencing a sector of the colonial society that espoused this conceptual system?

Adding to our knowledge of how "constitutive rhetoric" operates in societal formation,[52] we will find that Awakening theology supplied a *preconstitutive* rhetoric that reached into the core of its audiences, asked them to change their identity, and transformed those who did change so that the genuine constitutive rhetoric of the Revolutionary period would be intelligible. And even those who did not directly adopt Awakening theology were swept along by this belief system, ascribing to its definitions of "us and them," "right and wrong," "good and evil." In this way the rhetoric of community was primal, addressing fundamental questions of knowledge and identity, ultimately furnishing a solution to engaging life, which was, in Tocqueville's words, "clear, precise, intelligible to the mass of mankind and lasting."[53]

Perhaps what made Whitefield effective as a rhetorical agent was his fresh, invigorated oratorical style set against a context of homiletic ineptitude, not to mention the general neglect of oratorical arts that Hume and Sheridan decried.[54] As the story unfolds, we will examine Whitefield's life to determine what factors comprised his formation as an orator, then analyze the message he brought to colonists in 1740 and thereafter. From that point we will refocus attention on particular constraints that began to lead colonists down the road to revolution, finally ending with an assessment of influential polemic texts from the Revolutionary period that demonstrate the nature of the colonial audience as well as a conceptual system that evolved from religious influences. Within the larger story this study will also provide an overdue accounting of Whitefield's natural delivery, a detailed accounting of his rhetorical strategies, and an analysis of the substance of his rhetorical practice—a substance that consistently inserted itself in political debates whenever freedom of religious practice was threatened. The Whitefield story supports a theory of social change founded in an identity-shaping message potently disseminated and adjusted in response to constantly shifting conditions. The quest to understand American origins can be advanced by closely studying the rhetoric and community-building efforts of George Whitefield.

## CHAPTER 2

## WHITEFIELD: FINDING HIS TALENTS, FORMING HIS IDENTITY

George Whitefield's childhood resembles that of any fatherless youth experiencing self-doubt, searching for a vocation, and attempting to find his niche. For Whitefield, born a commoner in England, discovering his talents was simple; deciding where those gifts should lead him was a struggle. The rise from a commoner to an influential international figure did not often occur in the early eighteenth century, and Whitefield would have to figure out the method for himself. But through chance, luck, providence, and diligence, Whitefield prepared himself to lead an international religious revival that would have consequences far beyond anything he ever imagined. If ever there was one, Whitefield was a born orator, and through study and practice he sharpened his natural gifts to fashion an oratorical practice comparable to top orators throughout history. Add to this practice a message that could profoundly transform his audiences in nearly every place he preached, combined with assiduous energy to disseminate that message, and the reasons for his personal success become apparent.

As a youth desperately searching for identity and meaning, Whitefield reported conflicting urges toward both good and evil. He composed his autobiography around the struggle between these dual impulses until it climaxed with his conversion experience. Composing his early drafts from a diary he kept during his time in college and offering no reasons to question his essential accuracy, Whitefield's *Journals* provide a portrait of Whitefield and his life *as he wished to be known*. The work reflects a self-understanding from his perspective at age twenty-six, after he had already become a celebrity, self-interpreting the events of his youth in light of a greater destiny that he was then realizing. Yet in so doing, the *Journals* ultimately do not mislead the reader, because as Whitefield matured, he indeed conformed to the character he portrayed.

Within the *Journals* Whitefield embellished accounts of his youthful depravity; his stories are probably overstated to make his conversion seem more dramatic. Whitefield sensationalized his early life, comparing his birth in an inn to that of Jesus, as he illustrated the dual impulses that characterized his childhood. Even so, as a window into whatever rhetorical education he may have experienced, the *Journals'* historical accuracy can be relied upon, as Whitefield's goal was to create a certain persona rather than to reveal or conceal facets of his life that contributed to his rhetorical formation. Thus, for our purposes, the *Journals* can be read confidently as a compendium of rhetoriographical facts.

Whitefield was born December 16, 1714, in Gloucester. His father died shortly thereafter, so his single mother, Elizabeth, raised him. Whitefield described little of his early life other than his propensity for "impudent" and "brutish" behavior. From a young age he reported conflicting duplicitous personality traits, betraying the impulses that would eventually develop into an identity crisis. On the one hand Whitefield declared, "It would be endless to recount the sins . . . of my younger days," but on the other he said that in his playtime he would pretend to be a minister.[1] Likewise, he recorded pilfering coins from his mother's apron while she slept, but then he would give some of them to the poor; he would also steal books with religious themes.

Perhaps the most ironic twist of fate relating to his natural oratorical ability was a childhood bout with measles.[2] The resultant muscle degeneration caused a squint in his left eye and a cross-eyed condition that is obvious in every portrait. The ramifications of his cross-eyed squint would later prove to be profound. Eighteenth-century British commoners held a superstition that associated exotropia with divine blessing—people believed such persons had a direct connection with God.[3] Whitefield's squint was so well known that it earned him the derisive nickname of Dr. Squintum in the play *The Minor*, written by the British comic Samuel Foote. But that squint also helped to frame his message and give it an impact that a "normal" preacher could hardly match. With pupils aimed in different directions, his eyes may have given each listener the impression that Whitefield was staring directly at him or her. His physical body, supplying proof of a divine connection, combined with an inescapable gaze that continually kept one eye aimed at "you," produced a result that could be profound.[4] For the irreligious member of the audience, that gaze, supplemented by an implicit accusation that one may be damned, could have marked effects upon the imagination.

Whitefield's natural talent for oratory and performance was evident in his childhood when he already felt a tension between spiritual or secular employment—between the service of heaven or the theater. Whitefield regularly brought his abilities to the stage as a child actor in the local Gloucester theater community. But perhaps betraying his true calling, Whitefield noted, "I was always fond of being a clergyman, used frequently to imitate the ministers reading prayers." His biographer wrote, "So effective were his abilities that they came to the attention of the pastor of Southgate Independent Church, Thomas Cole, who found that the young lad was repeating his pulpit stories almost exactly as he had told them."[5] Whitefield described a public exhibition of his talent at age twelve in his local parish: "Having a good elocution and memory, I was remarked for making speeches before the corporation at their annual visitation." Clearly, to employ him on such occasions demonstrates that his mentors perceived both talent and poise that would not disappoint the audience.

Since antiquity, teachers of rhetoric have insisted that students learn best by patterning their practice after another. Quintilian said, "[I]t cannot be doubted that a great portion of art consists in imitation."[6] Thus, from his youth Whitefield observed and imitated competent models, both on the stage and in the pulpit, providing a head start in his introduction to rhetoric.

Whitefield's preoccupation with drama bordered "on obsession," a claim supported by Whitefield's total disavowal of drama later in life as a jilted lover spurns his or her beloved.[7] As a young man living in the city, undoubtedly with time on his hands, Whitefield spent much of his money either attending plays or purchasing scripts, and he often skipped school to practice: "During the time of my being at school, I was very fond of reading plays, and have kept from school for days together to prepare myself for acting them." Whitefield referred to his dramatic rehearsal five times in the first ten pages of his journal, giving private performances to his sister, ultimately admitting, "[M]uch of my time I spent in reading plays." Whitefield did not abandon drama until he matriculated at Oxford.

During one's youth not only are the mind and body eager to learn, but the time required for mastery is available as the responsibilities that dominate adulthood are yet to come. A youth also has few bad habits to unlearn, and with capable models to imitate, competence can emerge quickly. In addition, acting manuals were readily available, and Whitefield had a drama tutor. To further develop his budding skill in oratorical delivery, Whitefield studied physical actions, gestures, and expressions that communicated passions and emotions the dramatist wished to convey to the audience. Later in life, his sermons garnered the attention of the professional drama community in London, who simultaneously appreciated his talent while hating the financial competition. Interestingly, Whitefield never explicitly attributes his oratorical skills to drama, yet neither does he attribute his skills to a supernatural anointing, as clearly biased religious biographers have done. Perhaps, considering acting a sinful activity, he was not willing to acknowledge its role in developing his preaching skills. But wishing to enlighten posterity on the origin of his talent, Whitefield may have felt the benefit derived from drama was too valuable for him to pass over.

Resigning himself to the commoner's life, Whitefield dropped out of grammar school at age fifteen to work in his mother's inn. But seemingly aware of his unique talent, he communicated to his sister his desire to attend Oxford: "God intends something for me which we know not of." George's mother, seeking a religious career for him, also apparently felt the same and would not be content to see her son a commoner. Perhaps dictated by fate, an old friend stopped by their home one day and informed his mother how a lower-class person could attend Oxford University as a "servitor," cooking and cleaning for the "gentlemen commoners."[8] Elizabeth immediately turned to George and asked if he was willing to become a minister and train at Oxford. He replied, "With all my heart!" and she subsequently secured a place for him through the help of friends. Although he had never been a dedicated student, he immediately reentered school and completed his studies.

Yet in his personal life Whitefield describes his adolescent years as beset with conflicting inner desires that drew him either toward depravity or piety. His dilemma is resolved step-by-step, through his renunciation of drama, his self-denial, and his conversion experience. His journal describes a youth searching for identity, and the resolution of that search ultimately fueled his message upon the start of his ministry—a message that steered others toward a similar identity.

His identity search is revealed in his teen years by his imitation of his peers. At age sixteen, Whitefield recorded making a "great proficiency in the school of the Devil," surrounding himself with "debauched, abandoned, atheistical youths," endeavoring to look and think more like them, "I affected to look rakish, and was in a fair way of being as infamous as the worst of them." Yet Whitefield was never completely comfortable with the wild life as he struggled with his internal conflict—one impulse nourishing his "secret and darling sin" pitted against another impulse calling him to the ministry. Whitefield indicates that the nature of this sin was sexual, though he never explicitly names it, asking "why God had given me passions, and not permitted me to gratify them?" His conscience eventually steered him back toward his clerical destiny, and he distanced himself from the "principles and practices" of his "debauched" friends.

After rejecting his secular peer group, he retreated within himself and his religion, believing that the extreme perfomance of religious duty was what he needed to master his sinful impulses and establish a suitable identity:

> I began now to be more and more watchful over my thoughts, words and actions. I kept the following Lent, fasting Wednesday and Friday thirty-six hours together. My evenings . . . were generally spent in acts of devotion, reading . . . practical books and I constantly went to public worship twice a day.

Anglican piety in pre-Methodist England consisted of assent to an inherited religious orthodoxy rather than any personal sense of religious connection. Thus, Whitefield endeavored to make himself worthy of his calling in the only way he knew how, dedicating himself to every aspect of religious duty available to him. Yet this performance of duty did not resolve his inner tension or settle his sense of identity. It just served to heighten the incongruity between his impulses and calling.

In the midst of his struggle between sin and piety, Whitefield continued to complete his grammar education. Offering clues regarding the character and content of his studies that promoted his oratorical abilities, he thanked his schoolmaster "for the great pains he took with me and his other scholars, in teaching us to speak and write correctly." He also learned Latin and Greek. Thus, in addition to his structured training in drama, Whitefield received a linguistic foundation for learning the Western tradition of rhetoric and was given initial training in oratory at an early age. After completing grammar school, he entered the venerable Pembroke College of Oxford University to study to be an Anglican priest.

At Oxford, Whitefield again wrestled within himself; he renounced drama and playing cards and then entered a period of personal crisis brought on by his continued sense of hypocricy—a crisis that would eventually force him to leave school. He had to know for certain that he was indeed a genuine Christian. Still a boy searching for himself, pinched between a call to ministry and the passions of youth, he merely changed his mode of rebellion from the "young rake" in grammar school to the "odd-fellow."[9] He resented his studies and adopted the persona of a loner. Disgusted with the lifestyle of "excess" and "riot" of his roommates, he turned to an even stricter performance of religious duty: "I began to pray and sing psalms thrice every day, besides morning and evening and to fast every Friday and to receive the Sacrament at a parish church near our college." He was no longer the corrupt youth of his teen years but had reacted against that persona with excessive performance of religious duty, so much, in fact, that it provided an excuse for him to neglect his studies. Yet Whitefield felt that "hypocrisy crept into every action." The battle between conflicting impulses continued, but it retreated from the visible sphere and raged within his heart.

## WHITEFIELD'S CONVERSION

Soon after his matriculation, Whitefield became aware of the Oxford Holy Club, a small society of students led by Charles and John Wesley dedicated to promoting piety and virtue. Sensing that perhaps they had solved their own identity struggles, he "longed to be acquainted with some of them." Twelve months went by before this acquaintance would happen, and in the meantime he began to idolize these embryonic "methodists," receiving sacraments at the same church and emulating their pious, spartan lifestyle.[10]

The crisis over his identity peaked in his second year at Oxford as he still sensed the ineffectiveness of religious duty in resolving the incongruity between his call to the ministry and his sinful desires. He expressed his internal conflict through an increasing neglect of his appearance and personal health. Whitefield wrote, "As once I affected to look more rakish, I now strove to appear more grave than I really was." Whitefield further immersed himself in religious duty, becoming

more the odd-fellow, attempting to look the part of a zealous devotee
in his search for a resolution to his identity:

> I soon found what a slave I had been to my sensual appetite, and now
> resolved to get the mastery over it by the help of Jesus Christ. Accord-
> ingly, by degrees, I began to leave off eating fruits and such like, and gave
> the money I usually spent in that way to the poor. Afterward, I always
> chose the worst sort of food. . . . My apparel was mean. I thought it
> unbecoming a penitent to have his hair powdered. I wore woollen [sic]
> gloves, a patched gown and dirty shoes. . . . I resolutely persisted in these
> voluntary acts of self denial, because I found them great promoters of
> the spiritual life. . . . For many months, I went on in this state.

Amidst increasing bouts of illness his personal crisis deepened,
affecting his studies and gaining the notice of his tutors. Finally, Whitefield's wish to become acquainted with the Methodists was answered
when Charles Wesley came to visit him and pointed the way to a conversion experience by recommending that he read several books, specifically *The Life of God in the Soul of Man*.[11] Written by Henry Scougal,
a Scotch Puritan, the book's influence upon Whitefield manifests a
connection between Whitefield's Anglican pedigree and a clear Puritan influence in his theology and preaching. One can presume that
same Puritan influence was manifest in Wesley and other members of
the Holy Club, suggesting that seeds of ecumenicity resided within as
they focused on common and essential elements of Christianity. Upon
reading the book, Whitefield wrote:

> Though I had fasted, watched and prayed, and received the Sacrament
> so long, yet I never knew what true religion was. . . . At my first reading it
> I wondered what the author meant by saying, "That some falsely placed
> religion in going to church, doing hurt to no one, being constant in the
> duties of the closet." . . . "Alas!" thought I, "If this be not true religion,
> what is?" God soon showed me; for in reading a few lines further, that
> "true religion was union of the soul with God and Christ formed within
> us," a ray of Divine light was instantaneously darted in upon my soul
> and from that moment, but not till then, did I know that I must be a new
> creature.

For Whitefield, becoming a new creature would require a conversion experience, an event not necessarily eschewed by Anglicans, but

neglected and much more closely associated with Puritan practices in England. Now aware that conversion was the key to true religion, Whitefield began his introspective quest. Returning home to Gloucester for six months to recover from the illness brought on by the stress of his inner struggle, Whitefield experienced a transformation described in his Journal as a sequence of temptation, persecution, physical affliction, spiritual oppression, mourning, and finally his conversion. At the conclusion of the process Whitefield declared, "Now did the Spirit of God take possession of my soul, and, as I humbly hope, seal me unto the day of redemption." Whitefield had been granted conversion to his own satisfaction. His lifelong identity tension was nearly resolved. He now believed and felt himself to be on the inside what he strove to appear on the outside. His external performance of religious duty was now motivated by an inward purity of the Spirit as his conversion experience disarmed hypocrisy. For Whitefield this was a rite of passage into manhood as well, and he displayed maturity beyond his years from that point forward.

After his conversion and the recovery of his health, but before returning to Oxford, Whitefield began devoting much of his time to studying the Bible and Christian theology with the aid of commentary volumes. He visited old friends and encouraged them, with some success, to seek conversion. By the time he returned to Oxford, he was ready to approach his classical studies with a new vigor and purpose. Whitefield wrote of his transformed perspective:

> From the time I knew what was true and undefiled Christianity, I entertained high thoughts of the importance of the ministerial office and was not solicitous what place should be prepared for me, but how I should be prepared for a place.

To prepare, Whitefield continued his study of doctrine, seriously considered the biblical qualifications for ministry, and examined his motives for wanting a ministerial position. As suggested in the above quote, Whitefield's conversion apparently extended to his study habits as well. While he was admittedly not an exemplary student up to this time, his turn toward preparation here argues that he dedicated more time to study than ever before. And his familiarity with the classics and his effective and efficient use of rhetorical principles (demonstrated below) indicate that his new attitude toward study provided tangible benefits. Whitefield's conversion and claim about being "prepared" challenges scholarship that downplays his education and attributes his rhetorical skills to innate ability.

Literally a new man, from this point on Whitefield would place the conversion experience at the center of his theology and preaching. His spiritual struggle would provide him with a perspective to evaluate the spiritual condition of other ministers, churches, and parishioners. He became a regular, energetic member of the Holy Club. Here he formed relationships with the Wesleys that would continue to the end of his life (albeit not without conflict). Whitefield's own sense of identity and an accompanying sense of destiny were solidified by the combination of his conversion and his participation in a religious society where members strengthened one another in piety.

In addition to Whitefield's desire to see everyone he interacted with seek conversion, he also desired for all believers to participate in a religious society, modeled after the Holy Club. Whitefield understood firsthand how a small, intimate religious community could encourage its members and that the filial affection permeating the relationships could assist genuine and long-term change. From these two values, the need for conversion and the need for religious fellowship, Whitefield established the foundational elements of his future enterprise. He was compelled to insist upon conversion and a subsequent participation in church and religious societies in order to promote regeneration into becoming a new creature, because these two experiences resolved the identity tension through which he had struggled and, he knew, others had struggled as well. His developing message would constitute a "rhetoric of community" that invited one with an unsettled identity into a Christian community through the conversion experience. Converts became "new" people, their "new" natures shaped and fashioned within the confines of a close community of like-minded believers, being identified with one another and distinguishing themselves from people who merely practiced an outward performance of their religion. Whitefield recognized the futility of the outward performance without the inward change that accompanied the conversion experience. Hence, the religious establishment and its "inherited orthodoxy" became a central target of his rhetoric in his efforts to reform a stale religious situation in England and America.

Through his *Journals*, Whitefield revealed his inner person to the interested reading public of England and America. Written after the fact, he carefully revealed himself as called by God to a great destiny of speaking out to the world. From its opening line, where Whitefield was "born in an inn," to his ordination, Whitefield suggested that a greater force orchestrated the events of his life and led him to the high-profile ministry he attained. Whitefield's story, as told by the *Journals*, was not a fiction but was interpreted in light of his vision for ministry and, among other things, was intended to promote the revivals and legitimate his enterprise.

## OXFORD'S RHETORICAL CURRICULUM

After returning to Oxford, Whitefield credited the development of his mind to his study of religious books. But in ways that he did not admit, his education provided necessary and useful tools that would propel his enterprise to its full measure. Oxford required him to complete a rigorous curriculum in rhetoric and dialectic as part of his education. Although the polemic nature of the Journals impelled him to give credit to spiritual activities for his oratorical development, the Journals also reveal his educational experience and confirm its benefits, providing examples of what students were studying at the time.

Presuming Oxford dutifully educated its students in the intended subjects, a more robust view of Whitefield's education emerges, a view that reveals where Whitefield learned the logic, rhetorical strategies, and artful figuration he consistently employed in his sermons. Along with other British educational institutions in the early eighteenth century, Oxford retained a system of scholastic disputations.[12] In the late seventeenth and early eighteenth centuries, several leaders at Oxford, known as the English Peripatetics, emphasized Aristotelian logic, embraced scholasticism, and temporarily downplayed budding scientific methods.[13] In short, the Enlightenment came late to Pembroke College where Oxford's ministers were prepared. Robert Sanderson's textbook, *Logicae Artis Compendium*, which promoted an Aristotelian system of logic, served Oxford from its publication in 1615 until being replaced by Henry Aldrich's *Artis Logicae Compendium* in 1691.[14] These and other similar works effectively kept Ramism (which relegated rhetoric to the study of style and delivery) from fully influencing education at Oxford as it had in some Continental institutions.[15]

Oxford provided a series of oral examinations based on mandatory lectures that Whitefield would have attended. Such lectures were "intended to impact the preponderance of the dialectical training" and "to encourage learning and polite letters." Whitefield was required to participate in public disputations as both the opponent and respondent under the direction of a senior sophister. Oxford assigned students to a mentor in both logic and rhetoric, endeavoring to make the bachelor's degree "more than a courtesy title." Among other classical books, Aristotle's *Poetics* and the *Rhetoric* were widely read throughout the century. Lectures attended in the first year engaged the works of Aristotle, Cicero, Quintilian, and Hermogenes—all rhetorical theorists. Students studied logic and moral philosophy and in their second year attended lectures on Homer, Demosthenes, Isocrates, and Euripides.[16] References to Greek and Roman authors color Whitefield's writings, reflecting his familiarity with classical texts.

While George Whitefield received ample opportunities to train and discipline his voice, becoming an orator involves more than just possessing talent and listening to lectures. It also involves a long-recognized element of skill in composition. In his *Journals*, Whitefield reports writing sermons as assignments. Many of his early sermons follow a pattern undoubtedly influenced by the writing style of his college themes.

Whitefield's vocal skills were further sharpened through declamation (the oral rehearsal of speeches to improve voice, diction, and speech patterns). In addition to the written exercises required of Pembroke undergraduates, students were expected to participate in "declamations of themes, both oral and written," presented in the hall to fellow students and family members, or at least to the "head of the house." The declamations were often corrected and resubmitted, usually in Latin, and intended to improve the student's understanding.[17] Whitefield himself reported his regular participation in the declamations. Recalling one instance before his conversion, he wrote, "I went into the hall. My name being called, I stood up, and told my tutor I could not make a theme. I think he fined me a second time." One author has argued that Whitefield's inability to "make a theme" was due to his poor study habits rather than to the troubled frame of mind that Whitefield reported in his *Journal*.[18] But it is more likely that Whitefield recalled and recounted the atypical event, and normally he was prepared and performed his themes adequately. Whitefield then mentions being encouraged and counseled by his tutor.

After renouncing drama, Whitefield continued the oral rehearsal by reading to the poor. Whitefield explained, "I was, from time to time, engaged to visit the sick and the prisoners, and to read to poor people, till I made it a custom, as most of us did, to spend an hour every day in doing acts of charity." Such public readings were not merely occasional, as he went on to say, "In a short time, therefore, I began to read to some poor people twice or thrice a week." His readings to the poor became more frequent as he approached his ordination. Regarding prisoners in Gloucester, where he returned just before taking Holy Orders, he wrote, "I constantly read to and prayed with them every day I was in town." Whitefield's first official act of ministry was to "read prayers to the poor prisoners," and he was explicitly aware of the benefit and preparation such readings were providing. After preaching his first sermon, he exclaimed, "Oh the unspeakable benefit of reading to the poor, and exercising our talents while students at the University!"

For Whitefield, these readings more than adequately replaced the vocal exercise he formerly gained from drama. Thus, his keen vocal skills were maintained by this continued practice. Whitefield exclusively credited declamation with the development of his unique preaching ability, and he encouraged other ministers to adopt its practice, specifically in the form of charity readings:

> Would the Heads and Tutors of our Universities but follow [Christ's] example, and, instead of discouraging their pupils from doing anything of this nature, send them to visit the sick and the prisoners, and to pray with, and read practical books of religion to the poor, they would find such exercises of more service to them, and to the Church of God, than all their private and public lectures put together.

Later, Whitefield praised his experience with declamation in preparing him for his first sermon, claiming that he spoke "with as much freedom as though I had been a preacher for some years."[19] Thus, Whitefield had been well prepared for his enterprise as far as his oratorical ability was concerned.

Whitefield cultivated his natural talent for oratory with an education steeped in the classics, and then he consciously exercised his oratorical skills through declamation. Recognizing his future as a preacher, undoubtedly Whitefield took his preparation seriously. Scholars who ascribe his penchant for eloquence and persuasive skills exclusively to an innate ability, *ethos*, acting skill, or market savvy, have overlooked Whitefield's achievement of fluency in the mechanics of eloquence and his grasp of the psychology of persuasion—all gained through a rhetorical education far more rigorous than modern colleges provide. The combination of talent, study, and practice constitutes the three essential ingredients of fine oratory that teachers of rhetoric have emphasized since the time of rhetoric's Greek origin. These ingredients were manifest in Whitefield: his rhetorical education began early; he had competent models to imitate; he received a complete education at Oxford; he developed his nonverbal delivery skills through obsessive participation in drama; he developed his voice through declamation; and even his eye deformity became an unexpected asset.

## WHITEFIELD'S IDENTITY

As Whitefield discovered and settled his identity through his conversion and the Holy Club, he developed a vision of who he was and who he would become. The elemental aspects of his unfolding enterprise were also set in motion at Oxford, though not yet fully developed. Supported by a new attitude birthed in his conversion experience, Whitefield completed his degree in the spring of 1736. He graduated and took Holy Orders as a deacon at age twenty-one. He was now a "letter learned" British cleric (though not yet a priest) who also boasted a personal conversion experience. A day after his ordination, Whitefield recalled that "[t]he next morning, waiting upon God in prayer to know what He would have me to do, these words, 'Speak out, Paul,' came with great power to my soul. Immediately my heart was enlarged. And Whitefield would soon speak out. Upon his graduation and ordination (a genuine rite of passage) he recognized a change in identity "from a servitor to a Bachelor of Arts—from a common drawer to a clergyman," and he also experienced a role change, becoming transformed into the "Man for God" in both the inward (personal), and outward (ecclesiastical) spheres.

Whitefield's previously adopted identities as the young rake and the odd-fellow demonstrated his propensity to change ways of being like garments, as any gifted actor is able to do. But as Whitefield found himself in his conversion, his new identity emerged as a "Man for God." He became convinced of his destiny as a revivalist and henceforth took concrete and direct steps to achieve that destiny. This new identity was never to be discarded; Whitefield increasingly strove to become the "Man for God" the rest of his life.[20]

Harry Stout suggested that Whitefield's dramatic abilities enabled him to play a role as a cleric to satisfy his ego, which had been displaced from the theater—a role that eventually overshadowed his persona. In Stout's view, Whitefield was himself when in the pulpit. The private Whitefield, if there ever was one, receded as his life progressed and his pulpit character increasingly dominated his being. By the end of Whitefield's life, Stout claimed, "The private man and the family man had long since ceased to exist. In the final scene there was only Whitefield in his pulpit."[21] Stout's bold interpretation of Whitefield's identity and pulpit motivations, while enlightening and accurate on one level, might mislead the reader who views character acting as a distinct activity not connected with "genuine" identity. Initially, Whitefield may have been an actor who made the pulpit his stage—an arrogant, youthful preacher whose polemic *Journals* portray a man called by God to evangelize the world. But for Whitefield, his activities in the pulpit transcended mere acting: he was playing a real role as the "Man for God" in a real world with real consequences. The minister did not disappear when the sermon was over; rather he often moved his ministry to the home of a host where Whitefield counseled new converts and people struggling with their standing before God late into the evening. Later in his life he would face mob violence and personal assaults.

George Whitefield cannot be seen as merely "acting" as a minister. Although he may have assembled himself into one, he was constructing a tangible and substantial part of his personality. The insightful Benjamin Franklin, perhaps Whitefield's closest friend, arguably would have recognized mere character acting and perhaps never would have maintained more than a polite familiarity with him.[22] Moreover, as Francis McConnell observed of Whitefield's relationship to the colonists, "People like the Americans of the eighteenth century cannot be mistaken in their judgment of a religious leader through a stretch of thirty years."[23]

Whitefield, as some might interpret Stout's insightful observation, did not merely discover a method to fame and fortune by bringing drama to the pulpit. Instead, Whitefield viewed drama as an oratorical tool, one for which he possessed a talent to be employed in the pursuit of his calling, to use when it would be beneficial. Any unwarranted extension of Stout's thesis, suggesting that Whitefield was merely a displaced actor who didn't care or know the difference between the pulpit and the stage, is challenged by Whitefield's conscious shaping of his public image through his *Journals* and his constant attention to media publicity—sober actions indeed. Moreover, Whitefield's sermons, even those taken in shorthand, evidence judicious dramatized scripting of biblical characters. Dramatism appears to be a selective tool, and while he may have included an element in every appearance, he was careful not to overemploy it and compromise its efficacy. Whitefield, as will be seen, relied largely upon commonplace arguments, figures of speech, and traditional rhetorical strategies for the force of his rhetoric. Even in the sermon "Abraham's Offering Up His Son Isaac," which is quoted by every writer who discusses Whitefield's dramatic ability, Whitefield severely limits the sections where he was "playing" the part of Abraham. Certainly a bit of scripting can be found in almost every sermon, but it lacks intellectual force for genuine persuasion and would surely warrant accusations of sophistry had it been his sole strategy. One might say that his extempore sermons were different than the written ones, but as stated earlier, even his sermons taken in shorthand display little drama, and if dramatism were his chief selling point, then one would expect to see much more of it in the printed versions he sold. Certainly his critics, Alexander Garden, Charles Chauncy, and Thomas Clap, would have condemned him had he used dramatizations to an extensive degree, deviating from standard homiletic practice. If Whitefield's pulpit acting, to whatever degree he used it, brought him personal satisfaction or fulfillment, any such benefit was secondary to his conscious intent to make the "whole world" his parish.[24]

## EMERGENCE OF A REVIVAL ENTERPRISE

After graduation, while still living at the university, Whitefield assumed duties of preaching to prisoners as well as collecting and distributing money to the poor. Content to stay at Oxford for a while, he continued in these duties throughout the summer of 1736. The Wesleys had already journeyed to Georgia, and the Holy Club was suffering from attrition as other members were ordained and sent out.

Through a connection with a close friend, Thomas Broughton, Whitefield was called from Oxford to temporarily fill a pulpit in the Tower of London during the absence of its regular minister. Assigning his Oxford duties to another recently ordained graduate, Whitefield traveled down to London. Upon his arrival people stepped out of their shops to gawk at such a young man in a gown and cassock walking London's streets with one person shouting out, "There's a boy parson." A large, curious congregation turned out to hear him preach later that week, and although they were initially dubious, his preaching arrested their attention.[25] Whitefield ministered at the Tower of London for about two months until the regular minister returned, and then he went back to Oxford to resume his prison duties. He still had not found his permanent niche in the British/Anglican world, but letters from the Wesley brothers, who were then ministering in Georgia, arrived to inspire Whitefield in his search. "Their accounts fired my soul, and made me even long to go abroad for God too," he wrote.

His next opportunity to preach regularly came in November 1736 when a minister in Dummer, in Hampshire, requested that Whitefield fill his pulpit while he attended to some other business. Whitefield accepted and took up ministry duties, but he continued to think obsessively about going to Georgia. At that time, Charles Wesley returned to London and contacted Whitefield to "procure labourers" for the work. Whitefield also received a letter from John Wesley, still in Georgia, informing him of the need for a minister. Wesley concluded with, "What if thou art the man, Mr. Whitefield?" Whitefield responded strongly, saying, "My heart leaped within me, and, as it were, echoed to the call."

Another minister took over Whitefield's Oxford position, and the church post in Dummer was then filled, freeing Whitefield to go to Georgia. Whitefield began to prepare for the journey, saying goodbye to his friends, but found he was gaining a following. He returned to Gloucester and was invited to preach, where, in his words, he "began to grow a little popular." In January 1737 he went to Bristol to say goodbye to relatives and attended the church. The minister asked him if he would provide the sermon and, having his notes with him, he complied. The next day Whitefield attended another lecture and again was asked if he would preach. His preaching startled the community. He commenced preaching every day and twice on Sundays to crowded churches and received a generous offer to stay in Bristol as a regular minister. Whitefield began to print his sermons at the request of people in Bristol and Bath, but he did not remain there long. Determined to go to Georgia, he left in the middle of February, returned to Gloucester, then Oxford, and finally he traveled to London to wait until the time for his trip.

Without explaining the circumstances, Whitefield records preaching in London regularly for three weeks, preaching more often and to larger crowds than before. He was requested to stand in for a minister in Gloucestershire for a short time, so he left London. After the return of the regular preacher, the congregation of Bristol invited him to come back in May 1737. His trip to Georgia being again delayed, he went to Bristol where the crowds increased. Perhaps at this point he began to recognize the efficacy of returning to preach in a venue after a short absence, giving the grapevine the opportunity to disseminate news of his abilities. Whitefield wrote, "Persons of all ranks, not only publicly attended my ministry, but gave me private invitations to their houses." Whitefield left Bristol to return to London in August 1737 just before the trip to Georgia.

At some point in these months before the trip, which Whitefield fails to distinguish in his *Journal* or *Memoirs*, his ministry transmuted from simply filling vacant pulpits to a revival enterprise. But he does supply a few clues illustrating the shift, mentioning almost in passing the first publications of his sermons and collecting money for Georgia's poor. Whitefield records being "prevailed upon" by importunate friends to print more of his sermons. Finally, back in London just before his departure, he "embraced the invitations" to preach and began ministering regularly to growing crowds without hesitation. Though Whitefield's writings downplay the response to him, crowds grew larger and increased in their fervor. Church and government officials observing Whitefield's unfolding enterprise may have been reminded of earlier tumultuous days and the power of crowds inspired by charismatic leaders. No doubt, it was the political intentions of such a crowd that instilled apprehension, not its religious expressions. Whitefield often had to schedule additional meetings to accommodate the throngs of people. He printed more of his sermons in August—sermons on conversion and religious societies, to which he attributed the revivals in London, Bristol, Gloucester, and Gloucestershire.

By September the London papers regularly followed Whitefield and his activities. During this time, he developed the essential strategies of his enterprise, preaching whenever he could, publishing sermons, and promoting his meetings in the newspapers. He soon "mastered the London press," keeping his name continually in the public eye.[26] Sales of sermons were brisk enough that several unscrupulous publishers printed and sold unauthorized editions.

Increasing numbers of ministers, angry with Whitefield for various reasons, closed their pulpits to him as opposition to his doctrines eventually coalesced. Inevitably, a London minister intending to silence Whitefield soon complained to the bishop. On the surface, such opposition was an initial reaction to Whitefield's arrogance and self-promotion, but at a deeper level perhaps his critics sensed the danger to social order through his ability to draw and manipulate throngs of people. Additionally, Whitefield was turning his rhetoric against the ministers of slumbering parishes, using them as a foil to highlight the conversion experience. Undoubtedly, his critics recognized the seeds of unrest in such rhetoric (at least implicitly), viewing religious theologies as expressions of political philosophies, as had been the case during the Cromwellian uprising in 1644 and the Glorious Revolution of 1688. The debate would remain in the religious sphere for now. Despite the opposition, Whitefield had sufficient friends to continue a rigorous ministry schedule that included nine sermons per week. At this point he defended his ministry and doctrine in an effort to retain pulpit privileges. As he matured, he used this opposition as a tool of promotion and publicity.

He continued preaching in London until January 1738, when he finally departed for Georgia. On his way out of town, Whitefield ran into John Wesley just returning to London. After facing opposition due to their harsh denunciation of slavery and insisting that foreign nationals conform to their Methodist practices, the Wesleys made few friends, became disillusioned, and left Georgia permanently. Now, John Wesley entreated Whitefield *not* to go to Georgia, but to stay in London. However, Whitefield only became more resolved to go as he now considered Georgians without a shepherd and believed it was his destiny to fill that position.

Whitefield departed on January 2, 1738, and arrived in Georgia in May after a voyage filled with delays due to inclement weather. His stay in Georgia, although not without some points of interest, was brief and largely uneventful (May 7 to September 4, 1738). As Methodism was not well received by the Georgian settlers, they were also suspicious of Whitefield upon his arrival, but he soon won them over. As the newly appointed Anglican minister to the Georgia colony, he planned to establish a parish in Savannah and eventually erect a meeting house, a plan that was met with approval by the people of Savannah. Whitefield spent most of his time visiting the neighboring villages and plantations, preaching regularly, and performing any other necessary ministerial duties for the small Georgian communities of only three to five families each. By his account the people of Georgia and South Carolina received him affectionately, and today Whitefield is counted as one of the colony's founders and leading early citizens.

Whitefield discovered that Georgia had numerous orphans who could become "useful members of the Colony" if only someone would take them in. At this time, the idea of founding an orphanage was settled in Whitefield's mind, though he does not emphasize the decision in his *Journals*. Throughout the summer, as he traveled in the locale, he was further convinced of the need for the orphanage project. Without explaining why, other than "God's will," Whitefield visited Charleston where Alexander Garden, the Anglican commissary, received him affectionately, then departed from Charleston for England (he left to be ordained as a Priest), intending to return and establish the orphanage that would become his life's project. Perhaps Garden's desire to found the orphanage was rooted in his own fatherless childhood, which provided a compassion for the children whose parents, unaccustomed to the difficulties of civilizing the wilderness, succumbed to Georgia's hot climate. The orphanage project also provided Whitefield a pathos-laden object worthy of charity, which he effectively wielded in his fundraising.

But Whitefield did not return to construct the orphanage for nearly two years. A desire to continue his revival enterprise, which had been on hold during his trip, was renewed on the return trip, probably due to the need to raise money for the orphanage construction. Further hardening his resolve to continue the revival upon his arrival in England, Whitefield and his shipmates suffered a particularly arduous journey back across the Atlantic; he attributed the difficulties to satanic opposition:

> If my friends ask me, why I arrived no sooner, I may truly answer, Satan hindered us. For I believe it is he who is permitted to do this; but this

> still gives me greater hopes, that a more effectual door than ever, will be
> opened in England for preaching the everlasting Gospel.

The wind stopped blowing and the ship drifted for many days while
the crew and passengers consumed the dwindling supplies of food and
water. After the rations, as well as their hope, had been depleted, they
finally spotted land and came to a port in Ireland. Whitefield, writing
in retrospect, literally believed the devil was attempting to kill him and
thus thwart the coming revival. Thus, he used the difficult journey
as evidence that supernatural forces were intervening in and around
his enterprise. Interpreting the events in this manner fits his pattern
of asserting that providential guidance accompanied each aspect of
his life. His critics were offended by his attribution in two ways. First,
most churchmen did not believe that God, or the devil, intervened in
the affairs of men in this manner. Enlightenment thinking was already
exerting its influence on theology, and supernatural acts were being
increasingly explained by science. Second, his claim that the devil
himself took notice and was inimical to his enterprise suggested that
whoever else might resist him was inspired by the devil. His critics
could not accept part of his message without finding themselves in a
dilemma. Because of such statements they either had to support or
denounce him. As Stuart Henry wrote, "Encountering him, one could
attack, flee, or surrender, but it was impossible to come into his presence and remain neutral about him."[27]

Writing as if the coming revival was unexpected and spontane-
ous, Whitefield described his arrival in England to raise money and
make arrangements for the orphanage. There he spent the next year,
filling vacant pulpits in Gloucester, Bristol, and London, improving his
already spellbinding preaching style, perfecting the business of revivals, and continuing his rise as the preaching sensation of England.
At this time, his commitment to itinerant preaching solidified as he
believed that "a sermon from a stranger may do more good than many
from those the people are constantly used to."

## SOLIDIFICATION AND REFINEMENT

During his six-month stay in England, in between his first and second
American tours, Whitefield became a purposive, dedicated young man
with a vision, in his words, to "preach the Gospel . . . in every Province

in America belonging to the English."[28] To accomplish this monumental task, he developed an efficient enterprise complete with a public relations team that made advance arrangements and publicized his meetings. By November 1739, near the end of his English tour, he formulated his ultimate vision of having the "whole world" as his parish. He dreamed of initiating a transdenominational, international movement composed of an ecumenical community of like-minded believers within the British Empire, founded upon the conversion experience, whose religious practice emerged from an inward change of heart. Whitefield's ecumenical impulses, as will be shown, supplied an obvious component to colonial unification. While it may be a stretch to say he was successful in this endeavor, the impulse does suggest that he preached a consistent message in all locales. And to a certain degree, popular audiences perhaps did view him as their "pastor" and felt a level of intercolonial connection due to his ministry.

Whitefield's first step in reifying that dream would be to establish a national "parish" in England, where he found much opposition among the English clergy. Notwithstanding clerical resistance, the people in England eagerly came out to his events. Whitefield wrote, "Preached nine times this week and expounded near eighteen times with great power and enlargement. I am every moment employed from morning till midnight. There is no end of people coming and sending to me."[29] As he traveled around southern England, Whitefield collected money for the orphanage and began to perfect the strategies he would use in his revivals: fine-tuning his preaching style, integrating the use of print, and strategically returning to an area a few weeks after an initial appearance.

Impressive as it was, Whitefield's preaching was still developing, and he would shortly employ two more innovations that would propel his enterprise to its full rhetorical potency: extemporaneous sermons and outdoor preaching. Up to this point in his ministry, as was customary for British ministers, Whitefield still took a manuscript to the pulpit with him. But two months after returning from America, on February 2, 1739, he tried preaching extempore. In typical fashion, Whitefield recorded little about this significant shift, only mentioning in passing that "[t]his is the first time I have preached without notes . . . but I find myself now, as it were, constrained to do it." Whitefield attributes this shift toward extempore preaching to God to divert criticism from him, claiming that he would hinder God's work if he did not. A day later Whitefield said, "I find I gain greater light and knowledge by preaching extempore, so that I fear I should quench the Spirit, did I not go on to speak as He gives me utterance."[30] Extempore sermons gave his preaching a natural quality that further enhanced his already strong ethos. Unchained from his manuscripts, Whitefield could more effectively dramatize his sermons, moving, gesturing, punctuating, and underscoring his words with bodily action. Yet his style remained without contrivance, backed by the careful scripting of his various sermonic themes, which he could recall and deliver as the occasion demanded.[321]The natural style of his preaching emerged from his belief that he was telling people truths that God had called him to broadcast. Without a manuscript, he had the freedom to adapt his sermons to the peculiarities of each audience as his relationship with them unfolded in the performance. Whitefield could now genuinely interact with the people who were accustomed to "listening" to a sermon, not participating in one. Armed with his theatrical abilities, carefully composed ideas, and the freedom to interact with his auditors, Whitefield orated in a way Britons had rarely experienced.

The next innovation took him out of the church buildings with their limited space and moved his revivals outdoors where the force of his powerful voice and his public relations abilities could reach even more people. Whitefield's shift to preaching outdoors came in response to organized opposition from established Anglican clergy, who had closed their pulpits to him. As his vision expanded, opposition increased. In the summer of 1739, the bishop of Gloucester admonished Whitefield to preach only in the parish to which he had been assigned. Whitefield refused his request, replying, "But, my lord, if you and the rest of the Bishops cast us out, our great and common Master will take us up."[32]

Whitefield's conflict with the Anglican leadership peaked when he was invited to preach at St. Margaret's Parish where, unbeknownst to him, several supporters," who had just locked the regular minister into his pew, led Whitefield to the pulpit. Someone purporting to be a church officer gave Whitefield permission to preach. But the minister did not stay locked up forever. News of the malicious incident caused numerous ministers of churches to close their doors to Whitefield as they accused him of masterminding the scheme. Whitefield denied any knowledge of a scheme, but the closing of pulpits gave him the needed pretext to begin preaching outdoors in earnest.

On February 17, 1739, encouraged by Howell Harris, a Welsh evangelist with whom he had been corresponding, Whitefield tried outdoor preaching. He preached in a field at Kingswood to an audience of two hundred and afterward exclaimed, "Blessed be God that I have now broken the ice!"[33] The numbers at his outdoor sermons rose steadily, reaching ten thousand within nine days. Whitefield immediately recognized that people who would not come to a church to hear his message would go to a park. Although he was not the first to preach outdoors, Whitefield's talents and the excitement surrounding his ministry drew throngs of people to his meetings. His ability to draw a crowd, combined with his voluminous voice and a willingness to travel, provided the opportunity to reach people face-to-face on a mass scale—a mass-media innovation that equaled the advent of radio in the twentieth century in terms of its ability to reach mass audiences.

In addition to affording Whitefield greater access to people, leaving the confines of established churches emphasized the ecumenical nature of his enterprise. To him there was but one church—his parish—in which all members were part of a family. His ecumenicity sent a strong message to the colonists of America. Dissenters who would not grace the interior of Anglican churches would come to a field or park and hear Whitefield with no qualms. He had moved his message to neutral ground, bypassing any bias people had toward the Church of England and overcoming people's misgivings of entering a "sacred" place while in a "state of sin." He took his message to them.

Whitefield claimed that God was confirming these innovations in his enterprise by his improved health after preaching, by the success of his message, and by God's judgment on his critics. A few days after beginning extempore preaching, he wrote that he was so ill that he was almost unable to speak, but upon entering a pulpit he claimed, "God gave me courage to begin, and before I had done, I waxed warm and strong in the Spirit." Whitefield attributed this upturn in his immediate health to God's miraculous touch and interpreted it as divine approval of his extempore preaching. Responding to his critics, who resented both his extempore preaching and outdoor sermons, he later wrote, "See ye not, ye opposers, how you prevail nothing? Why do you not believe that it would not be thus unless God was with me?" Conversely, God's blessing on Whitefield meant judgment against his vociferous critics. Upon hearing that one of his "great opposers" was given only a few days to live by physicians, Whitefield took the opportunity to say, "Alas poor man! . . . We all prayed most heartily for him, knowing how shortly he must give an account of what he had most unjustly said and written against me." Within one month of beginning outdoor, extempore preaching, Whitefield was attracting crowds of over twenty-thousand people.

From February to April 1739, Whitefield itinerated across southern England, perfecting his new techniques, preaching at various locations to immense audiences, and successfully raising funds for the orphanage. As the tour progressed, he developed two specific strategies to reach England's masses, the first of which has been labeled "print and preach."[34] Whitefield's publications were already being circulated by this time, and he was also keeping his name in the news with the help of media-savvy colleagues like William Seward. The publicity generated by Seward fueled Whitefield's popularity, drawing the large crowds that were beginning to throng to his revival meetings. Secondly, Whitefield employed a "preach and return" strategy.[35] After preaching in one location, Whitefield would leave and preach elsewhere, returning when he sensed another visit would be worthwhile.

An agricultural metaphor helped Whitefield, and other ministers of that era, to understand the nature of evangelization. They believed that the ground (human hearts) must be "plowed and broken up" before the "seed" could be productively planted. Norman Pettit explains that this preparation of the heart had been an essential stage in the *ordo salutis* since Puritans began grappling with the actual mechanisms of the process.[36] While in the Calvinist system there was nothing one could do to gain salvation, one could prepare the heart for grace and facilitate the process. Then, after a time of "germination," and "cultivation," the minister could return and claim a harvest. The prepared heart would receive grace as the elect saint crossed over into sainthood. Whitefield and others used "terror" sermons to do the plowing and then preached on conversion for the "planting." Upon returning to an area where Whitefield had already performed these tasks, he would preach "cultivation" sermons on the need for religious societies, or he would preach "lifestyle sermons" that condemned certain deeds or practices and encouraged others. Here the new saints received needed teachings and connections with other believers critical to a healthy Christian journey. Whitefield's "preach and return" approach helped to prepare hearts, and then he would return and help to incorporate new believers into the established churches. Consequently, his itinerating would not follow a straight line through an area, but would form a series of epicycles, before moving on to another region. This incremental approach was grounded upon the process of conversion described in John Bunyan's popular and influential book *Pilgrim's Progress*, wherein the preconvert faced a period of difficulty before "entering the narrow gate" into full conversion.

An "enterprise," as Frank Lambert has labeled it, is by far the most accurate term to characterize Whitefield's revival ministry. He took care to establish a public image, promoted his meetings, satisfied the demands for his message, and generated revenue for his orphanage as well as his travel expenses. Whitefield made extensive efforts to prepare his attire for preaching events, understanding the critical role of his appearance in the formation of his public image.[37] Beset by criticisms that he was fanatical or radical, he always appeared in public in his cassock and wig to reinforce his commitment to the Anglican Church. At one point he even sat for a portrait—with a somber expression on his face—to counter perceptions that he was the "radical enthusiast" portrayed in satirical London editorials and cartoons.

The British Empire was itself in the midst of the rise of a capitalistic consumer revolution in the mid-1700s. Showing Whitefield's familiarity with the English business world, Lambert describes Whitefield's training in the hotel business, explains his immersion in the world of publishing, and reveals his use of mercantile metaphors that promoted the "new birth in the language of goods." For six months, in 1739, Whitefield matured as a businessman, promoter, and preacher. His return to America would bring a tested and smooth enterprise to the task of reaching everyone in the British colonies.

## WHITEFIELD THE ORATOR

The philosopher David Hume reportedly said that Whitefield "was worth going twenty miles to hear."[38] Precisely what was it about his preaching that drew people to hear him? Certainly any short drama routines he incorporated into his sermons were a novelty. Since no electronic record of Whitefield's eloquence could have been produced, and firsthand witnesses who could have imitated him (in a type of oral tradition) are also deceased, the only option for re-creating his manner of delivery is through the extant writings of friends and antagonists. Delivery, as an object of study, does not willingly lend itself to written description; the subtle nuances of voice inflection and gesture are exceedingly difficult to describe with words in a meaningful way. Nevertheless, many have put their impressions of Whitefield's presence and delivery into words, and these impressions form the only "recording" of Whitefield available.

John Gillies described Whitefield's appearance in some detail: "His person was graceful and well proportioned; his stature rather above the middle size. His complexion was very fair. His eyes were dark blue in color, and small, but sprightly. . . . His features were in general good and regular. His countenance was manly." Most portraits of Whitefield show a corpulent older man, but Gillies insisted that "in his youth he was very slender, and moved his body with great agility to action, suitable to his discourse," providing an energetic, dynamic oratorical manner. In addition to Whitefield's fastidious appearance, his "deportment was decent and easy," observed Gillies, "without the least stiffness of formality; and his engaging, polite manner, made his company universally agreeable." Thus, in dress and polite manner he charmed his audiences.

The texture of his enchanting voice may be forever lost, but several people attempted to capture it in words. Gillies provided the most extensive evaluation of his vocal skills, which other contemporaries affirm:

> He had a strong and musical voice, and a wonderful command of it. His pronunciation was not only proper, but manly and graceful. Nor was he ever at a loss for the most natural and strong expressions. Yet these in him were but lower qualities. The grand sources of his eloquence were, an exceeding lively imagination, which made people think they saw what he described; an action still more lively, if possible, by which, while every accent of his voice spoke to the ear, every feature of his face, every motion of his hands and body, spoke to the eye; so that the most dissipated and thoughtless found their attention involuntarily fixed, and the dullest and most ignorant could not but understand.

Whitefield's unaffected speaking style stands as a thread of continuity, in various descriptions from friends to enemies—"artifice" being a term never used by any of his critics. Gillies asserted that he failed to offer any appearance of falsehood in his discourse, seemingly genuine in both his thundering denunciations and ubiquitous pathos, recalling his voice as "exceeding strong; yet . . . softened by an uncommon degree of sweetness," and that his demeanor "was utterly devoid of all appearance of affectation."[39]

Eugene White recorded that when faced with an "insufficient emotional response, Whitefield would stamp up and down complaining: 'Where's your contrition! Where's your tears! Nobody weeps! No meltings amongst you! Come, my friends, I will weep with you and for you.'"[40] And Whitefield himself regularly wept while preaching. For him the consequences of the audience's response to his message were paramount and deserved his unrestrained emotional investment: "Would weeping, would tears prevail on you, I could wish my head were waters, and my eyes fountains of tears, that I might weep out every argument, and melt you into love."[41] His audiences, for the most part, believed him and responded with self-concern. Every biography of Whitefield records the white furrows cut by tears in the coal-stained cheeks of miners in England as they listened to him preach after a day in the mines. The pathos with which he could clothe his words was observed by the actor David Garrick, famous for introducing a natural style of drama to the British stage: "Whitefield could make his audiences weep or tremble merely by varying his pronunciation of the word Mesopotamia."[42] On another occasion Garrick said (or quipped), "I would give a hundred guineas if I could only say 'O' like Mr. Whitefield."[43] In an oratorical age of flat and stale preaching, Whitefield provided a contrast that few people could resist. Whether or not Garrick was humorously exaggerating Whitefield's vocal ability is open for question, but certainly Whitefield did possess an ability that invited the comments.

Not all of Whitefield's contemporaries were so flattering, finding flaws in his homiletic skill to counter the strengths: Henry Angelo, a prominent London citizen, contrasted Whitefield's "energy, feeling, and pathos" with other instances of "extravagant ravings, and pious rhodomontade." Angelo also quoted the playwright Samuel Foote as saying "like the cow, after giving a good pailful of milk, he was apt to kick it down again."[44] Even the sympathetic Gillies saw room for improvement: "Had his natural talents for oratory been . . . somewhat more improved by the refinements of art and the embellishments of erudition, it is possible they would soon have advanced him to distinguished wealth and renown."[45]

However, expressing a more balanced view of Whitefield's ability, Alan Heimert asserted that Whitefield's antagonists, construing him as "a fulminating and flailing declaimer," were overzealous in their representations and that "less partial observers suggest that there was in fact nothing extravagant in Whitefield's manner."[46] These sober reflections by Gillies and Heimert suggest that strategy and substance, as we will see in the analytical portions of this study, lent a significant weight to Whitefield's rhetoric.

Largely overlooking his rhetorical strategies, Whitefield's critics consistently focused on his delivery skills, painting him as a sophist. In fact, one should not be surprised that an oratorical age influenced by Petrus Ramus would frown upon the canon of delivery. In particular, the Puritans understood rhetoric as "a garment to cloath [*sic*] our reason" in the words of Alexander Richardson, a Puritan who defended Ramism.[47] Such a view, according to John Charles Adams, provides "a habit of interpreting speech" that undoubtedly goaded many to turn against Whitefield.[48]

By the time Whitefield left England on August 16, 1739, and journeyed to America for the second time, colonial newspapers had reported his London popularity across the Atlantic and created a strong curiosity in Americans to hear him. In fact, the news of his enterprise was just hitting the American press as Whitefield arrived in Philadelphia, providing an ideal environment and perfect timing for his debut. The next fifteen months would see him in every colony and alter the face of the continent as the Great Awakening followed in his wake. His tour would shake the slumbering American settlers out of their repose of religious desertion, challenging their transitional identities and calling them (for those who would accept the call) into a body of converts through his rhetoric of conversion and religious societies.

CHAPTER 3

AMERICAN IDENTITY

The America that George Whitefield found on his arrival was uniquely situated to receive a rhetoric of community, although neither he nor the American settlers understood just how closely that rhetoric could address their situation. Beyond the fact that Great Britain granted the charters and protected all the American colonies in what is now the United States, the diverse groups of colonists living in America possessed little in the sense of a shared identity (except for the English colonists), and the immediate horizon did not offer much that could extend an English identity to groups such as the German settlers of Pennsylvania. In fact, according to Breen, English communities were making it clear that those with other national backgrounds were not necessarily welcome in the English fold.[1] The colonies along the Eastern seaboard were separate political units with dissimilar charters and populated with both English and non-English settlers from Europe. While many settlers understood themselves as English, many did not, and even those who did faced tensions that would confront their identity. Everyone who lived in the colonies was affected by what it meant to be an American regardless of one's national origin. Common challenges tended to dissolve European ways and previous self-understandings, and in their place these challenges offered "American" ways and ultimately impelled settlers to understand themselves in a distinctly American manner. But before 1740, this American way of understanding oneself (as we know it today) was not fully defined, nor could its immature nature provide a foundation for intercolonial unity.

AMERICANNESS

Both Continental immigrants and those who originated from England were forced to examine their self-conception upon arrival, creating a continuous tension that would regularly remind them that they were

foreigners. Michael Warner explained that English settlers were trying
to negotiate tensions between being English and something else—
living far from England and the concerns of London's citizens, yet
trying to retain critical elements that constituted their English self-
understandings. For example, Benjamin Franklin vacillated between
being a Londoner who wore a powdered wig and being American
with the long unruly hair in his most popular images—the image he
adopted beginning with his diplomatic visits to France. Warner characterized colonial culture not as "a framework of shared meaning but
multiple contexts of discourse in shifting relations." In these multiple
contexts, Warner asserted that early American writers did not exhibit
any sense of national identity:

> Many [colonists] lived in local worlds of less moment, relatively indiffer-
> ent to markets, wars, printing, and other venues of the English Atlantic
> . . . [and] as soon as we stop looking for Americanness [sic] we see that
> none is aptly described as American. Most have conflicted transitional
> identities.[2]

The usual sources of identity were undermined: National and agrarian traditions were at odds with a strange land; communities and
farms were separated by wilderness; prosperity and shifting contexts
provided new experiences for many immigrants; and religious institutions were threatened by the apostasy of new generations. But in the
midst of these challenges to identity, economic prosperity indicated
to the colonists that they really were somebody and they now had the
"goods" to prove it. Providing answers to identity questions, the Awakening rhetoric became a catalytic element for the self-understanding
of these settlers who had found a prosperous and good life and now
desired to assign it a meaning.

In addition to the tension caused by being foreign, the reasons
no distinctly American identity had yet formed emerge quickly upon
examining the historical record with a lens of identity formation. On
the one hand, America lacked any distinct story; there was no single
encompassing event or shared experience that would set an American
apart. On the other hand, obstacles to shared identity emerged from
six interrelated sources: a diversity of ethnic and national heritage, the
agrarian economy, physical isolation, an ever-shifting social environment, financial prosperity, and diverse religious affiliations. Each of

these aspects of life in America conspired to resist European identities, and, in addition to a zeal for education in America, ultimately aided Whitefield in the dissemination and acceptance of his message. The first stirrings of revival, which began in 1728 and flared on and off until 1736, provide striking evidence that America was a place where colonists' personal and group identity, as well as their reasons for "being," were yet unresolved and open to influence.

The national diversity of colonists stood as an initial aspect of so-called Americanness that impeded the formation of an American identity. Charles Cohen reminds us that the "operative P-word is pluralism, not Puritanism."[3] Beginning with the settlement of New England, British immigrants constituted a majority of the American settlers. However, by the beginning of the eighteenth century, the number of English transplants in America declined because of better economic conditions in Great Britain. In their place poured French, German, Swiss, Irish, Welsh, Jewish, Scottish, and Scandinavian immigrants (among these were also Africans forced into slavery) in increasing numbers. Patrick Griffin has described the process of identity formation among Scots-Irish that settled in Pennsylvania, pointing out that isolation, disorder, and other problems of frontier life threatened societal stability in the void of a settled identity.[4] New arrivals and native-born colonists doubled the population between 1740 and 1770. In colonies with a strong majority of English settlers, a pseudo-English identity was the natural outcome and indeed increasingly developed as the Revolution approached, as Breen has ably demonstrated.[5] But in colonies with a blended population, ascribing an English identity was more problematic.

Each of the national groups that were settling in America constituted what public relations professionals of our day would call a separate "public," with the colonial population as a whole comprised of multiple publics. Naturally, new immigrants tended to find land and homes through their connections with relatives and countrymen and settle where these were already living. In some of these regions English served as the tongue of the economy but was not necessarily used for routine communication between settlers. Religious services were typically held in native languages such as German or Dutch throughout Pennsylvania, New Jersey, and New York. Many new immigrants did not even speak English, and some never had a reason to learn. America offered an intricate combination of ethnic and religious groups, each struggling for survival while working to find its place in a wider society politically identified as English.

Not only did colonists live and work with "foreigners," but foreigners also became part of one's family. The international flavor of the colonies remained a leading feature of Americans well into the late eighteenth century, a people of whom J. Hector St. John de Crèvecoeur wrote:

> He is either an European or the descendant of an European; hence that strange mixture of blood which you will find in no other country. I could point out to you a family whose grandfather was an Englishman, whose wife was Dutch, whose son married a French woman, and whose present four sons have now four wives of different nations.[6]

American-born children, torn between dual heritages, continued to fuel the sense of unsettled identity through the normal search for one's niche that all youth must undergo.

Interestingly, Whitefield was best received by audiences in the Middle colonies where the settlers were the most diverse. While New England initially welcomed Whitefield, here he found his sharpest theological critics as well. The Middle colonies provided little opposition as Whitefield found many friends among dissenters and other Protestant groups who left continental Europe for religious reasons.[7] As an Anglican who affirmed the legitimacy of their denomination, Whitefield was able to find interested ears as he adapted his messages to their situation. The South was settled by the British and retained a strong British identity but provided a destination for many immigrants as well. Here Whitefield encountered the usual opposition from the Anglican leadership over doctrinal issues, but the wider population eventually welcomed him and his message.

Another feature of the Americanness that kept colonists diverse was their closeness to the land. Besides farming, even those in the population and trading centers made their livings in industries such as fishing, mining, timber, or agriculture, supplying British factories with raw materials. Regional crops helped to maintain diversity in agricultural practices. Thrust into a foreign world, the colonists' European ways did not necessarily serve them well. In order to survive, colonists needed to invent and implement new means and strategies for engaging the rugged environment, while continually in the shadow of conflict with

Native American groups. As the land was deforested, surveyed, and populated with accompanying roads and communities, it developed its distinct flavor complete with its own stories, pulling colonists away from any familiar traditions of England the Continent.

The colonists' connection to the land aided Whitefield's efforts to promote a rhetoric of community beyond merely impeding collective colonial identity. The mysterious, dangerous, strange land in which these agrarian colonists lived strengthened and encouraged belief in the supernatural, providing interested ears for one who preached a tangible religious experience. Farmers are traditionally somewhat religious (or superstitious), and they were especially such in colonial America. In David Hall's words, the colonists were "infused with ancient attitudes and practices."[8] The colonial communities held established beliefs about causes for weather patterns, threats to crops, and other adversaries of their lifestyle that were rooted in their sense of place. Mortality rates among children were high, keeping death familiar and close. Even dying in one's prime was not uncommon. When Jonathan Edwards mused on the longevity of members of his flock at the end of his famous sermon, the thought easily sobered his congregation to the closeness of death:

> And it would be a wonder, if some that are now present should not be in hell in a very short time, even before this year is out. And it would be no wonder if some persons, that now sit here, in some seats of this meeting-house, in health, quiet and secure, should be there before tomorrow morning.[9]

Writing to his brother-in-law, Samuel Adams wished him and his family "health and happiness," but then pessimistically reflected that "common experience convinces me that there is very little Dependence upon either in this Life."[10] Thus, a minister's warnings about damnation or pestilence and the fleeting nature of life were neither idle nor distant threats to a superstitious people for whom death came often and inclement weather or pests could, and did, destroy life-sustaining crops.

Americanness also inflicted colonists with a daily burden upon their lives that can be bluntly characterized as physical isolation. The distance and difficulty of travel between communities combined with poor public communication in the early eighteenth century created formidable obstacles to intercolonial unification. Any community bonds that might have encouraged a collective identity were impeded by the colonists' isolation, which in surprising ways intermeshed nicely with Whitefield's enterprise. Living on scattered farms provided few opportunities for people to become acquainted with one another other than Sabbath meetings. Trips into the town or to church would be the only events where one might have contact with anyone but the nearest neighbors—a situation especially true for women and children.

Yet this physical isolation prepared colonists for Whitefield in two distinct ways: by making their lives somewhat mundane through the scarcity of close neighbors or diversion and by normalizing travel in order to hear a minister. By providing opportunities for distraction in their toilsome lives, Whitefield was able to attract huge audiences wherever he stopped. Nathan Cole described the sense of anticipation and subsequent frenzy upon hearing of Whitefield's imminent arrival as he and his wife frantically rode twelve miles to hear the sermon.[11] Religious historians describing Whitefield's reception often use Cole's story as an exemplar. If Whitefield was able to announce a meeting a few days or hours beforehand, farmers from as far as twenty miles away would attend the event. He did not have to plan numerous events in towns just a few miles apart, but could count on audiences traveling these distances to one location.

But in areas where people were just too isolated to hear about Whitefield's meetings, or in areas where he did not visit regularly, he still exerted an influence through newspapers and printed sermons. A group of believers in Virginia led by Samuel Morris read Whitefield's sermons at each meeting because they didn't have a regular minister. Morris's group began to grow in number, as he centered the group's worship on the Whitefield sermons, until it was forced to build a meeting house, eventually becoming the first Presbyterian congregation in the colony.[12]

The constantly changing nature of colonial life further prevented the social stability necessary for colonists to develop an identity consistent from generation to generation. Life was in constant flux as new lands were being opened for settlement and new occupants were arriving regularly from Europe. As the frontiers quickly pushed west, settlers established new communities; these rudimentary communities speedily grew into towns, and many towns eventually became cities.[13]

America and its cities were subjected to the influence of steady and staggering population growth. In 1700 there were just 250,000 nonnative Americans, but by 1740 the number increased to over 900,000 and would top two million by 1770. Change was so rapid that European visitors were filled with "astonishment and approval" to see thriving established cities, such as Boston or Charleston, providing the luxuries of Europe when they expected "tall trees, fierce animals, and red savages."[14]

The rapid growth fueled by fruitful families as well as steady immigration ensured the frontier's steady westward creep. Sons coming of age found it necessary to carve new farms out of the wilderness as the limited family land, sufficient for their ancestors, couldn't be viably subdivided among the increasing number of descendants. Moreover, English policies restricting the construction of factories ensured that city economies limited the opportunities they could create for new citizens. While Boston, Philadelphia, and New York each had less than 20,000 residents, by contrast London experienced a robust growth, housing 300,000 in 1700 and reaching 700,000 by 1750. But in America, people were always on the move, seeking new opportunities or cheap land.

While some facets of American colonial life merely impeded the formation of identity, other facets served to either highlight Englishness or exacerbate the lack of identity. One such facet was the colonists' economic prosperity. Several scholars, among them Breen and Lambert, identify the rapidly budding consumer marketplace as contributing to that prosperity as people began purchasing consumer goods within a booming economy, making excessive consumption possible.[15] The transatlantic world was absorbing an invasion of commercial goods and its accompanying consumerism. A demand for American crops and raw materials across the ocean combined with increasing transatlantic trade fueled the growing economy. Per capita expenditures steadily increased from 1720 to the 1750s, providing a strong market for goods as well as publications. The marketplace development gave rise to a middle class throughout the British Empire that provided opportunities for intercolonial connections, while the expanding economy brought wealth to both farmers and merchants. Economic prosperity indicated to the colonists that they were moving up in the world. Colonial merchants and other businessmen boasted wealth that could place them in elite circles back in England, justifying their belief that they were as British as anyone in London. The non-English settlers prospered as well, affording their own acceptance into middle-

and upper-class colonial circles. The advertising industry came into
its own after 1720 with sophisticated ads populating the newspapers
selling goods of every type. Products "just in from Europe" attracted
buyers who flocked to obtain the latest fashions, wares, and other items
that their peers in England were consuming. Inasmuch as a person's
identity is establish through the goods one possesses, this proliferating
consumer culture provided fertile ground for identity formation.

The colonists' prosperity increased to a point where it began to
cause social problems—problems that called into question or exacerbated identity development. David Lovejoy pointed out that the causes
of the Awakening revivals "have stumped historians for years," and
many historians concur that some type of social or psychological crisis
precipitated it. Perry Miller labeled the American situation a "chronic
state of affairs."[16] Namely, the crisis has been described as a decline of
religious zeal due to urbane living, or tensions between prosperity and
the evils of worldliness, or the reconfiguration of social boundaries.[17]
But among all these factors, Breen also concludes that as the colonial
crisis of the 1760s approached, dual standards of citizenship (British
and Colonial) questioned the validity of the English citizenship of any
of these settlers.[18] The British identity they had been able to nurture
was directly challenged as Parliament and the King rejected colonial
pleas for equal treatment.

The prosperous, conflicted, shifting, mercantile economy aided
Whitefield by more than just stirring up the identity issues; it provided many practical benefits as well. All the major cities were located
near water, making travel convenient. Whitefield took further advantage of the increasingly prosperous economy in America by selling
editions of his *Journals*, peddling copies of his sermons, and soliciting donations for the orphanage. Whitefield's solicitations for charity
gave colonists an outlet for their wealth that eased their consciences
regarding urbanity and luxury. His message also explained, for those
who accepted it, who they were and why they had prospered. Their
wealth, in Whitefield's view, was a gift from God to help promote the
Awakening message. As will be shown below, Whitefield contributed to
this developing trust among colonists by helping to establish additional
common ground through religion. Moreover, he was immersed in this
rising consumer culture as much as any other capitalist. According to
Lambert, the consumer economy specifically contributed to Whitefield's enterprise by supplying a means to market Whitefield's revivals

through direct advertising, press releases, newspaper stories, and every other means of mass communication that availed him. Lambert concluded that Whitefield was a "merchant for the Lord."[19] Among the consumer goods Whitefield offered for sale were his sermon pamphlets and bound collections. As has already been shown, religious materials were among the publishing industry's best sellers throughout the pre-Revolutionary period. In this way, the changing economy and culture enabled his enterprise, and indeed it is difficult to imagine similar success without these advantages. The evolving economic climate of America stood as an obstacle that Whitefield had to overcome, and the rapid travel of his itinerating provided the means to do it. Within a brief fifteen months, with the aid of modern public relations tactics, he thoroughly spread a rhetoric of community to each colony, visiting many locales more than once. Thus, Whitefield's tour simultaneously offered the colonial world his invitation to a religiously based identity, and subsequent preaching tours would spread his augmentations of that identity with equal rapidity.

Not every aspect of colonial life, as thus far has been sketched, impeded identity or provided obstacles to nationalization. A "zeal for education" grew into a facet of Americanness that immensely contributed toward acceptance of the rhetoric of community and enabled the long-term prosperity of Whitefield's enterprise. The church valued the ability to read Scripture and took leadership in educating the American colonists, creating an ideal marketing opportunity for Whitefield, who was aggressively publishing his sermons and *Journals*. The New England Congregationalists, believing that reading the Bible promised a way to salvation, expected those who could afford it to educate their children. Though New England led the country in establishing educational institutions, other communities were also concerned about education and endeavored to supply it through the establishment of public schools. Where schools could not be established, such as in the rural areas of the South, ministers, missionaries, and itinerant schoolmasters often filled the gap, "providing the rudiments of learning for a considerable portion of the population."[20] Consequently, literacy rates were surprisingly high in the colonies, approaching 90 percent among the religious and those immersed in the mercantile economy, groups who found Whitefield's message appealing.[21] As one colonist observed, "Scarce any are to be found among us, even in the obscurest parts, who are not able to read and write with some tolerable propriety."[22]

Literacy certainly accelerated the rise of print media as colonists provided an eager market, of which Whitefield took full advantage to establish his American parish. In the seventeenth century, information was a scarce commodity in the colonies because of the high cost of printing. Books and newspapers were for the wealthy. Only the large population centers had newspaper publishers. But all this began to change as advances in printing technology in the early eighteenth century brought the price of subscriptions down to a more affordable level. In 1700 there were no newspapers in the colonies, but by 1740 there were eleven.[23] A central reason for this proliferation of papers was the construction of a paper mill in 1730 by Daniel Henchman, which drastically cut costs for colonial printers who previously bought expensive imported British paper. So critical was the cost of paper to publishers that Benjamin Franklin invested in a paper mill to stabilize his own supply. The price of newspaper subscriptions in the years before Whitefield's 1740 tour dropped from approximately one-fourth of a laborer's annual salary in 1710 to about one-half the price of a loaf of bread for a single issue in 1735—roughly the equivalent of today's papers.[24] Additionally, newspapers became available to those who could not afford them as coffeehouses and taverns provided public access. Also keep in mind that colonists probably did not flippantly discard newspapers and other periodicals, as we do today, but they were passed along to others or saved for visitors to read. These short editions were likely read from cover to cover, and the news passed on orally to acquaintances who may not have had access to the paper. Thus, the rise of a public sphere, constituted through the medium of print, was emerging upon Whitefield's arrival.

An "imagined community" of colonial American readers began to evolve in the eighteenth century, providing, through the press, a depiction of the lives and ideas of other colonists who had previously been inaccessible due to distances between population centers. The colonial newspapers established between 1700 and 1740 began to develop a community of readers, and as the century progressed, the number of printers began to increase, extending the depth and breadth of the reading community. Hence, the colonies, which heretofore had remained largely isolated and concerned with local business, began to turn their attention outward as this new public sphere evolved. The imagined community of colonial Americans also thrived on the increasing availability of other reading sources. The number of publishers specializing in books, magazines, broadsides, and pamphlets multiplied in the early part of the eighteenth century, doubling from ten to twenty in Boston alone.

The rise of a reading community provided an ideal opportunity for Whitefield to promote his revival enterprise. From the outset of his 1740 tour, Whitefield exploited printing as a strategy to reach his audiences, literally inundating the American colonists with waves of materials. Whitefield found his London publications already being reprinted and sold in Philadelphia upon his arrival, much to his advantage. Newspapers and magazines often tripled or quadrupled the availability of Whitefield's ideas through partial reprints or serialization, creating an appetite for his revival meetings. Thus, emerging reading communities were aware of who Whitefield was and what they might expect upon his arrival.

Had Whitefield's appearances not been publicized or the public appetite not been whetted by the newspapers, attendance at his meetings might have been lean. Had paper remained expensive, he could not have published his *Journals* and sermons and sold them at a price the common person could afford. For Whitefield, printing and preaching evolved into a circular mechanism in which each facet reinforced the other. Reading about him created the desire to hear him, while hearing his sermons encouraged the sale of their printed versions. Through the course of his career, Whitefield provided a full array of printed works to meet the demands of the reading public through his journals, sermons, news accounts, paid advertisements, a magazine, and published position statements (i.e., his publication of letters explaining his stand on certain issues or replies to his critics).

William Seward and other Whitefield publicists supplied advance publicity everywhere Whitefield went. To promote public interest, Seward fed newspaper editors with accounts of the revival meetings and itineraries of his travel. Whitefield and Seward also purchased newspaper space and offered narrative accounts of the revival meetings as an early version of "infomercials." Whitefield remained a regular "item" in American papers throughout his 1740 tour.

As intercolonial awareness manifested itself through the newly constituted public sphere, the revivals and George Whitefield competed with European political news for space on the front pages. Converts in Boston or Charleston could now identify with Jonathan Edwards' congregation in Northampton, and vice versa, as they read in the press and other publications about each other's existence and common struggles. In fact, Thomas Prince, a Boston publisher, began printing news of the revival's outbreaks at various locations in his *Christian History*, a magazine dedicated to disseminating news of the revivals in America and Great Britain.[26] Thus, the rise of the print industry became essential to nurturing and sustaining the emerging community of converts created by the Awakening revivals.

## IDENTITY AND THE STATE OF RELIGION

By the mid-1720s the American colonists were increasingly prepared to receive a "heartfelt" version of Christianity. The common features of three local pre-Awakening revivals led by Theodorus Frelinghuysen, Gilbert Tennent, and Jonathan Edwards reveal facets of American identity questions and the ways in which a religious conceptual system addressed them. While decline of piety provided the contrast needed to distinguish the coming movement, the revivals evidenced the willingness of colonists to align themselves with and understand themselves in terms of an intercolonial Christian community.

Religious uniformity within a diversity of Reformed Protestant sects became a leading feature of Americanness. Yet as religious institutions faced the challenges of ministering to a diverse and changing society, they found decreasing success in the wake of scandalous ministers, ill-advised doctrinal adaptations, mediocre preaching, and the steady stream of immigrants entering each region who did not necessarily bring piety along with them. By most accounts the church was failing in its goals of promoting piety and providing a meaningful religious experience for colonists. Revivals that had occurred prior to 1740 stood out in contrast to the norm of religiously apathetic communities. Patricia Bonomi has labeled the state of religion in the colonies "forlorn" as established state religions felt a decline of power in part due to the rise of dissenting groups.[27]

On a personal level, individual ministers were also alarmed at the state of religion within their local parishes. William Shurtleff, a venerable New England minister, described the religious scene immediately before Whitefield's arrival:

> An affecting Spectacle I confess! What no serious Christian could behold
> in the Time of it, without a heavy Heart, and scarce without a weeping

Eye. . . . When there was no more than a monthly Lecture even a large
Parish, what a small Handful should we find attending upon it? . . . Even
whilst the Word of GOD was dispensed, how many Eyes, if they were
not slumbering, would be wandering and gazing? [28]

Too often the preaching available in the British Empire was simply
pitiable. A village atheist, according to Jon Butler, unimpressed with
local sermonizing, dismissed it as "sharp shitting in a frosty morning."[29]
The "unconverted," "letter-learned" ministers guilty of such preaching stood as the embodiment of slumbering religion, and indeed, there
were notable examples of ministers who filled their spare time with
debauchery.[30] The widespread neglect of religion eventually bore fruit
characterized by a generalized impious lifestyle that earned New England a deserved, cynical epithet: "New English Sodom."[31]

William Sweet insisted, "Times were ripe for some new emphasis
in religion as well as a new type of religious leadership to meet the
peculiar situation which the American colonies presented." Sweet's
metaphor (ripe) creates the image of a mature grain field waiting for
somebody to come along and gather it. Sweet explained that Whitefield had no need to plant, that he merely needed to put in his sickle
and claim the harvest.[32] But this agricultural metaphor obscures reasons that people were receptive to a new kind of religious experience.
It was not because anybody prepared the soil or planted; rather, an
identity deficit was inviting a redefinition.

Consider the evidence against an agricultural metaphor: Edwards
stayed in the Connecticut valley while Frelinghuysen and Tennent
stayed in the Raritan valley of New Jersey. The Pre-Awakening revivals remained local in character and only touched a small percentage of
the colonists and cannot be fully credited with preparing the way for
Whitefield. Inhabitants of the major cities, though they heard about
the revivals, had not experienced them. Moreover, each revival had
cooled for at least two years before Whitefield's arrival. Even if these
revivals were helpful by preparing the soil for Whitefield in limited
locales (as no doubt they did to a degree), the revivals in the other colonies were initiated and nurtured by Whitefield himself. In fact, recent
scholarship has defined the role of early revivals in the Awakening as
more symbolic than substantive, even suggesting that the extent and
breadth of the later religious awakening was limited.[33] If indeed the
pre-Awakening revivals were symbolic, they reveal that communities

were seeking to resolve social tensions and understand themselves in relation to their world. Indeed, nobody could have prepared the soil for the earlier revivalists, yet they still found success. If colonists were ripe, it was due to the conditions that created the identity deficit in the first place. What the earlier revivals indicate is that Americans at large were open to a resolution for their identity deficit, a situation illuminated by the common features of each revival.

The most notable of the pre-Awakening revivals began in the Connecticut Valley under Jonathan Edwards. Upon succeeding his grandfather, Solomon Stoddard (who experienced six revivals during his pastorate of the Northampton Church), Edwards was greatly distressed by the licentiousness of the town's youth and began to meet with them to show his pastoral concern. They responded favorably, and by 1733 Edwards reported that most were regularly attending public worship. The spread of Arminian notions ("universal redemption" and the belief that human efforts were sufficient to secure salvation) also troubled Edwards. He responded in 1734 with an emphasis on justification by faith, to which his congregation reacted favorably and intensely. The ensuing revival spread to neighboring towns and congregations as Edwards visited other congregations through 1736. The revival ended suddenly in 1737, almost three years before Whitefield's arrival in New England. The revivals led by Frelinghuysen and Tennent followed a similar trajectory.

Common elements among early revivals evidence the identity issues and social crisis in America. The growing crevice between class, status, age, and theological positions reveals that younger people increasingly disowned European authority structures and irrelevant versions of personal identity based in European heritages. Each revival was initiated by youthful ministers, Edwards being the eldest at age thirty-one, and each found success among the youth from which new converts were more easily drawn because their conceptions of identity were not as crystallized as in the older generation. Opposition arose from older established clergy and respectable members of the community who had likely settled for some form of a transitional identity. The rational, impersonal character of traditional religious practice precipitated each revival. In its place, the revival ministers offered a personal, emotional approach to Christianity that challenged the legitimacy of established churches. Even in Puritan communities, where identity was perhaps best established, there existed a tension between an English Puritan identity and the questions that someone awaiting his or her conversion experience might ask. Prior to conversion, the pre-Puritan might ask if he or she were genuinely a community member. Cohen explained that the conversion experience "precipitates" an identity crises and then serves to resolve it.[34]

While religious diversity and neglected belief systems logically would have divided colonists further had beliefs been deeply held, they, in fact, supplied the potential for unification and the development of a unified identity. As Whitefield arrived and began his tour, the colonies were confronted with a particular and dynamic message tailored to expose spiritual inconsistencies and address identity concerns. Without a deep commitment to a particular theology, colonists were free to adapt their loosely held preexisting religious beliefs to something more functional. Whitefield was not forcing colonists to abandon their inherited denominational beliefs; he was inviting them to take religion seriously. In contrast to the stale orthodoxy the established church was serving its parishioners, Whitefield offered a fresh version, complete with a strong emotional element that the colonists could smell and taste. If for no other reason, people came out to hear Whitefield because his meetings stood in sharp contrast to dead orthodoxy.

The revivals indicate that American colonists were receptive to the guiding hand of a sincere minister who had their best interests at heart. Just as Charles Wesley led George Whitefield to received conversion, now ministers such as Frelinghuysen, Tennent, and Edwards were leading Americans to conversion experiences en masse, satisfying the colonial search for religious meaning and personal identity. For such a movement to become intercolonial in scope, someone was needed who was willing and had sufficient rhetorical skill to bring the revival message to the rest of the continent.

## THE NEW BIRTH AND PROTESTANT PRACTICE

As already noted, religious diversity was a salient feature of colonial life. While a historical emphasis has traditionally been placed on the Congregationalists, and not without reason, there existed a multiplicity of other religious groups that had immigrated to America from all over Europe. Many of these were newer groups birthed out of the Reformation who were seeking relief from the hegemony of state churches across the Atlantic. As this section attempts to sketch outlines of the theological climate in the colonies with regard to conversion, it will focus on the essential tenets of Reformation theology shared by these denominations. Specifically, the notions of the conversion and community were central to most Christian denominations with differences orbiting around how conversion was achieved rather than its necessity. Although there were several theological schools of thought that guided the Reformed denominations, perhaps the most dominant was the theology of John Calvin.

According to Mark Noll, Calvinism supplied an influential school of religious thought, not just for the Puritans, but throughout colonial America.[35] Calvinism's defining characteristic, as many understood its belief system, was a commitment to a first principle of "predestination," an ideographic term with multiple meanings. Generally speaking, this aspect of Calvin's theology held that God is the sole agent in the *ordo salutis* (way of salvation), elects the saints, appoints the time of their conversion, and holds their salvation secure. For churches, such as the Puritans, the *ordo salutis* typically required substantial time and in some communities occurred as a portion of the rite of passage into adulthood.[36] Charles Cohen summarized the Puritan conversion process, explaining how "the stirrings of sorrow over sin intensify into hatred of it, which occasions the despair of perceiving one's incapacity to achieve salvation. As an awareness of faith emerges, despondency passes into joy, peace of conscience, and love of God."[37] Cohen's description corresponds strongly with what Whitefield described in his own life. Human agency was irrelevant in both election and the salvation process itself—a pessimistic thought for one desiring conversion. Although each of the major colonial denominations constructed its own nuances of Reformation theology, the notion of predestination as an expression of God's sovereignty was perhaps its most well-understood doctrine.

While colonial Calvinism was founded upon two hundred years of Reformed practice, it was not the only influential religious paradigm in the colonial world. First, conversion experiences stood in contrast to Anglican practices (and others) where conversion was a more ambiguous event. Prior to his conversion, Whitefield was taught that one's Christianity was established by the rejection of sin, devotion to religious activities, and partaking of the sacraments. In essence he was a Christian and Anglican because it was his family's religion; he embraced it and participated to the fullest extent that he could. There was no conversion experience outside the decision to involve oneself in the church. Second, the rising influence of Arminianism rejected the pessimistic predestination of Calvinism. Its central difference was that God's grace was available to all who would believe, that predestination merely indicated that God knew beforehand who the believers would be. In this system, human agency codetermines conversion by necessitating a response of faith to God's offer of salvation. In Calvinism, faith to believe was God's gift to the believer; in Arminianism, faith was a gift from the believer to God. Hence, while both theological systems could promote the practice of conversion, it was achieved by different means. As this study of Whitefield's rhetoric proceeds, a finer-grained look at the Puritan version of conversion will be useful since, even though he was an Anglican, his conversion (as well as the Wesleys') demonstrated a strong Puritan influence and shaped the experience toward which he persuasively exhorted his audiences.

While theologians like William Perkins, Thomas Hooker, and John Cotton debated and explained and published their views on the dogmas of Calvinism,[38] ministers perhaps had the more exasperating task. Working with people in their parishes, they were forced to grapple with the impracticalities of working out such a system in their churches. What is the point in preaching the gospel if the preaching really doesn't matter in terms of calling people to conversion? For the preacher, whose ministrations were held to be God's primary means of communicating and effecting grace onto the elect, the rigors of Calvinism were counterproductive. Pettit summed up their problem: "As spiritual preachers, 'physicians of the soul,' and builders of faith, how could they urge on all men the biblical question, 'What must I do to be saved?' without violating this rigid discipline derived from reformed dogmatics?"[39] Even if one felt conviction for sin and desired conversion, the actualization of salvation was still the prerogative of God. The dilemma manifested itself in colonial America in the form of declining church memberships as second- and third-generation colonists inherited the society from its founders.

The Puritan response was what they termed "preparation of the heart" for salvation. Pettit provides a comprehensive account of the various ways and means that Continental and American churches grappled with preparation and the conflicts between practice and dogma in *The Heart Prepared*. Although one could not prompt, goad, or hasten God in the process, preparation was viewed as a prerequisite to and a necessary part of the salvation process. Hence, Puritan ministers availed themselves to assisting their parishioners in preparation to receive grace, yet without any assurance that it would come. Preparation of the heart became pervasive in Puritan practice, ostensibly allowing a degree of human agency to sneak into the *ordo salutis*. Yet conversion itself ultimately remained a passive activity with the prepared sinner anxiously awaiting God's action.

The next question for Puritan theologians then revolved around the efficacy of preparation. "Was there an inherent logic between preparation and predestination, or were they mutually exclusive?"[40] Their concern was the gray area prior to conversion where God might be at work, but where human agency seemed to make a difference. As might be expected, controversy occasionally erupted over the tension between changing practices that incorporated preparation and theologians who desired to maintain pure predestinarian doctrine. But as Pettit pointed out, "The more they directed their preaching toward the experience and practice of religion, the less concern they showed for the rigors of theory.[41] Thus, one can discover subtle shifts in the sermonic record evidencing practical attempts to address the ambiguities of predestination, preparation, and conversion. For our purpose here the point is that rigid Calvinism faced challenges from within and from pragmatic ministers who desired to see more people converted.

From the impetus of Edwards, a revival theology was evolving out of strict Calvinism. It was the heart, not the intellect or the conscience, that was Edwards' focus and indeed had been the focus of Puritanism since its inception nearly two centuries earlier. Edwards (and many others) felt and practiced a connection between preparation and conversion, encouraging the preparation of the heart among half-way parishioners to aid in their journey to the elect. But after leading parishioners through preparation, Edwards could say little more. Describing the rhetorical action of "Sinners in the Hands of an Angry God," Ernest Bormann pointed out that after skillfully constructing a view of the state of being for sinners, on the brink of hell with nothing but God's grace withholding destruction, Edwards could not fully take advantage of his audience's emotional openness. Bormann wrote, "Clearly, the speaker's heart is not in it at the end. When the time came to speak of hope and outline the plan for salvation, Edwards' artistry stumbled and he could not reach the rhetorical peak that he had scaled minutes before."[42]

Despite Edwards' unwillingness to expound on hope, his preaching style opened the eyes of many of his ministerial contemporaries as he intertwined the doctrinal and application sections of his sermons. Prior Puritan sermonic practices kept these two phases of a sermon separate with knowledge first and then application, light necessarily preceding heat. In contrast, Edwards intertwined reason and emotion to blur the traditional divide between knowledge and application, blending "light and heat," allowing significant overlap as his sermons unfolded, and establishing a new rhetorical paradigm—a "consciousness-creating communication" style, in Bormann's words, that revivalists would follow and extend.[43]

As Pettit expressed, ministers employed the exercise of preparation to allow for a role of agency in the preconvert. Edwards extended the agency of the preconvert in his ministry without crossing the predestinarian line. Inspired by John Locke, that an epistemology of sensations can be a reasonable way of knowing "truth," Edwards asserted that the emotions (feeling God) provided a legitimate way to "know" God.[44] As Edwards depicted the terror of damnation, he relied on the audience's own imagination to instill emotive reactions (fear, anxiety, guilt) that provided tangible evidence for the one who felt it. Likewise, the "sweetness" of salvation counted as the evidence for the consummated conversion experience (as Edwards described in his own life). But the notion of conversion was difficult to adequately capture in words. Its experiential, emotional character resisted attempts to portray it, prompting critics who lacked the experience to question its validity.

Edwards distinctly described and articulated the personal character of conversion in his publication *Treatise Concerning Religious Affections* (1746), which marks perhaps the best attempt, in the opinion of his contemporaries, to explain and describe it.[45] Edwards used various terms throughout his writing to characterize conversion, including "conversion," "a new nature," "a state of acceptance," "justification," "redemption," and "holiness of heart."[46] Yet Edwards also lamented the difficulties of conveying the concept to others accurately:

And indeed it appears very plainly in some of them, that before their
conversion they had very *imperfect ideas* what conversion was. It is all new
and strange. . . . It is most evident, as they themselves acknowledge, that
the expressions used to describe conversion, and the graces of God's
holy Spirit—such as a *spiritual sight of Christ, faith in Christ, poverty of spirit,
trust in God, &c.*—did not convey those distinct ideas to their minds which
they were intended to signify. Perhaps to some of them it was but little
more than the names of *colours* are to convey the ideas to one that is blind
from birth.[47]

Of several ministers who were stretching beyond the dogmatic
fence, John Corrigan wrote, "They stressed the importance of the fac-
ulties in regeneration and they often portrayed God as an adopting
father. But they were most concerned with the aftermath of conversion, with the bonding of the converted individual to the community
of the regenerate. Conversion remained for them, as it did for other
New Englanders, somewhat mysterious."[48] The abstract character of
the message, as they taught it, required continued contact to cultivate
comprehension. Thus, the revivals in the pre-Awakening decade were
confined to locales where a minister consistently cultivated preparation, had taught about the conversion experience, and parishioners
enjoyed the benefit of repeated explanations.

Edwards' rigorous theology eventually settled into a friendlier version of Calvinism that prized a warm heart, valued reason as a way
to know God (an Enlightenment influence), and required adherence
to God's moral law. The revivalists of the Awakening period rebelled
against the notion that observing the outward duties of religion was
sufficient to be a genuine Christian. Instead, they insisted upon a
definable conversion experience from every believer and sought subsequent piety motivated by a genuine internal change of heart rather
than external constraints such as strict obedience to legalistic codes. As
the Puritans had understood for two centuries, the conversion experience reached into a person's very core, altering his or her fundamental
identity, and in this way it transcended denominational boundaries
to emphasize common elements of Christian denominations. This
combination of sentiments, reason, and moral accountability gave
the revival theology a staying power lacked by the traditional Puritan
theological system.[49]

## Conversion According to Whitefield

Whitefield's conversion, described earlier, conformed to a classic Puritan pattern (as revealed in his catalytic reliance on Henry Scougal's writings) of emotional turmoil followed by relief. While Edwards may have extended the believer's agency with a more thorough preparation, Whitefield took a step further by implying that the prepared heart had a choice, and this choice afforded partial agency to the believer. By suggesting that preconverts held a degree of agency, Whitefield's practice departed from the rigorous predestination that saturated Puritan, Presbyterian, Baptist, and other central religious groups.

To avoid any charges of a drift into Arminianism, Whitefield overtly defended Calvinism, constantly citing the Thirty-Nine Articles of the Church of England as his bedrock of theology. But Whitefield introduced a subtle grammatical shift in his message that suggested a resolution to a tension in prior conversion theology. Ernest Bormann has highlighted this critical feature of Whitefield's preaching:

> Whitefield often spoke in such a way that his listeners could easily assume that, by an act of faith on their part, they would be saved. Such phrases as "come poor, lost, undone sinner, come just as you are to Christ…" easily suggest that the listener can make a decision and receive the "new birth."[50]

In fact, nearly every extant sermon of Whitefield's includes a section addressed to sinners exhorting them to some action: "Fly to him then by faith; say unto him, as the poor leper did, 'Lord, if thou wilt,' thou canst make me willing." This example from *Marriage of Cana* shows Whitefield's addition of human agency to work with God's toward conversion. The sinner must "fly" in response to God's call. Whitefield grammatically makes the listener, not God, the noun of the sentence instead of the object. The verb in these exhortations is enacted by his audience. Whitefield tells the audience to do something, and in this doing, they make their choice and seize agency for their own salvation.

Moreover, Whitefield characterized the conversion experience, not with abstract theological language, but with a concise metaphor: The "new birth," a term that thoroughly permeated the Awakening vocabulary within months, provided a compact, comprehensible, and memorable rendering of revival theology. New birth was a term sufficiently vague to encompass many meanings, yet sufficiently precise so as to convey both the travail and joy of the experience.[51] But most importantly, the "new birth" operated in Whitefieldian discourse as a noun, as a thing to be obtained. His sermons could awaken mimetic desire in listeners, unleashing the natural human impulse to "have what others have" as he exhorted "sinners" to obtain the new birth, which the "saints" already possessed.

His grammatical shift heavily emphasized the concept of "choice" for his listeners. He set a choice before his audience and encouraged them to a decision and subsequent action. In choosing the new birth, his audiences were choosing a central aspect of personal identity. Up to this point, it had been a Calvinist God's choice whether or not one was converted. The people had no choice in the matter, prepare as they might. The religious aspect of their identity was chosen for them despite their hopes. And as Whitefield's itinerating and colonial saturation of his message progressed, he created central religious issues of the necessity of conversion and personal choice in the *ordo salutis*. As will be argued later, introducing choices to religion facilitated the acceptance of republican ideologies. As Noll stated, "Republican instincts prized human self-sufficiency more highly than dependence upon God."[52] If one had a choice in matters as weighty as salvation, where could personal choice be denied?

In addition to providing an essential component of identity, the new birth also encouraged individuals to have a personal relationship with God, to pray extemporaneously, to even converse with God. The convert boasting a new birth no longer needed a priest or minister to mediate his or her relationship with God. Catholicism had provided priestly mediators, and after the Church of England broke away, Anglican priests continued to mediate the relationship between God and a community. The new birth and the models of thought that it produced were to have profound ramifications for the development of colonial culture. As Francis Fukuyama concluded, "In the long run, the individual's ability to have a direct relationship with God had extremely subversive consequences for all social relationships, because it gave individuals a moral ground to rebel against even the most broadly established traditions and social conventions."[53] As Heimert argued, the new birth came to embody the "pursuit of happiness," a republican theme that would play an expanded role in coming decades.[54]

By introducing and promoting the term "new birth," Whitefield demonstrated his practical application of rhetorical principles by instructing his audience members, which enabled them to make an informed decision about his message. Harvey Yunis, a philologist, pointed out that Athenian orators, such as Pericles and Demosthenes, reached the pinnacle of ethical public service by explaining ideas and policy to Athenians and persuading them based on enlightened understanding.[55] The Athenian audience did not constitute a crowd that was "stupid and ineducable," but they were a reasonable people, who, with proper teaching, were able to make wise choices. Likewise, Whitefield, who studied the classics at Oxford and apparently grasped this aspect of rhetoric, understood revival theology and was able to explain it to uneducated people whom he respected and valued. In addition, Whitefield had a reputation of being divinely anointed, causing people to take him seriously.

Whitefield condensed a theology of the conversion experience into this metaphor of the new birth; the term was clear, precise, intelligible, and could be easily grasped and assimilated by his popular audiences. Consequently, the term facilitated the rapid advancement of the revival. Whitefield employed terms and ideas that likewise simplified previously difficult notions. He promoted terms like "regeneration" and "common privilege," as well as the means to tell who was converted and who was not. Whitefield did not require multiple exposures to his audience for them to understand and recall his message. He effectively communicated his ideas and the message of the new birth in the few sermons he would deliver in a locale before moving to the next.

But Whitefield supplied a far more dynamic and powerful tool than simply a vocabulary and grammar that facilitated the acceptance or republican political ideals. The implied doctrines of the Awakening conceptual system established a set of first-stage rhetorical topics that were applied to later questions as colonial America matured. As we will see, Whitefield promoted several inventional rhetorical topics that paved the way for the advancement of republican thought in the colonies and that were co-opted by Revolutionary writers as they formulated arguments to support their judgments of escalating British oppression in the American colonies. If the new birth stood as a central revival doctrine, the implied doctrine from which it was drawn held the greater significance, suggesting that there was a community, which one could choose to enter and of which the rest remained outside. The ensuing reality distinction of "us-them," with its consequent distinctions of "in-out," "good-evil," and "liberty-slavery," then became a compelling feature that found expression in spheres other than the religious by operating as inventional rhetorical topics, neatly bifurcating the "possibilities of being" into limited and discreet categories whether applied to religious theology, social problems, or political questions.[56]

## A RHETORICAL EXIGENCE

It was into a prosperous, relatively stable American environment, whose divisions were many but increasingly superficial as European ways dissolved into American ones, that George Whitefield introduced himself with his initial focus on the spiritual condition of people. In 1740 many colonists were hungry for meaningful religion and receptive to the identity Whitefield's rhetoric would help supply. By bringing the revival to all the colonies, Whitefield supplied a common encounter, for those who accepted it, that provided an initial, uniquely American collective experience. Whitefield did not invent a new perspective for self-understanding in the new birth; what he did was take an existing perspective, simplify it, codify it, and spread it throughout the colonies. Through published sermons, news articles, broadsides, polemic journals, infomercials, instigating theological controversy, and preaching everywhere he could, Whitefield's message and enterprise was the first intercolonial event that all colonists could share, an event that fashioned a momento of emerging American culture. By 1741 settlers from Maine to Georgia (unless one was isolated on the fringe of civilization) were aware of Whitefield and the essentials of his message.

In November 1739 George Whitefield, now twenty-four, arrived in Philadelphia to begin a fifteen-month tour. Whitefield's challenge was to reach as many colonists as possible and then sufficiently hold their attention to let his message sink in. In addition to printing his sermons and *Journals*, he aggressively took his message directly to the people by providing ample opportunities for them to hear him in person. In the 1740 tour Whitefield recorded preaching over 350 times while traveling two thousand miles on horseback and three thousand miles by boat, visiting over seventy-five cities and towns. In his spare time he gave several hundred "exhortations" to smaller groups. He was constantly on the move, never staying put for more than a week.

Under the impact of this tour, Americans were exposed to his rhetoric of community, and a substantial number participated in a religious revival, if not led by Whitefield then by one of his emulators who soon followed.[57] As Whitefield addressed each local group of colonists, he attempted to lead them to the new birth as Charles Wesley had done for him. His message was consistent in every colony and city that he visited. For the first time in American history, a particular rhetoric spread throughout every colony, inviting everyone who heard it to adopt a new identity and join the imagined community of believers who embraced the new birth.

Just as he had in London, Whitefield found success in America at capturing and maintaining his auditors' attention. Benjamin Franklin recorded one of the most detailed portrayals of Whitefield's engaging style. The following excerpt, written in late 1739, assessed Whitefield's vocal skills and inquired into the possibility that the unusually large crowds of London could actually hear him. He first described the strength of his voice and then described its sound:

> He had a loud and clear voice, and articulated his words and sentences so perfectly, that he might be heard and understood at a great distance, especially as his auditories, however numerous, observ'd the most exact silence. He preach'd one evening from the top of the Court-house steps, which are in the middle of Market-street, and on the west side of Second-street, which crosses it at right angles. Both streets were fill'd with his hearers to a considerable distance. Being among the hindmost in Market-street, I had the curiosity to learn how far he could be heard, by retiring backwards down the street towards the river; and I found his voice distinct till I came near Front-street, when some noise in that street obscur'd it. Imagining then a semi-circle, of which my distance should be the radius, and that it were fill'd with auditors, to each of whom I allow'd two square feet, I computed that he might well be heard by more than thirty thousand. This reconcil'd me to the newspaper accounts of his having preach'd to twenty-five thousand people in the fields, and to the ancient histories of generals haranguing whole armies, of which I had sometimes doubted. . . . By hearing him often, I came to distinguish easily between sermons newly compos'd, and those which he had often preach'd in the course of his travels. His delivery of the latter was so improv'd by frequent repetitions that every accent, every emphasis, every modulation of voice, was so perfectly well turn'd and well plac'd, that, without being interested in the subject, one could not help being pleas'd

with the discourse; a pleasure of much the same kind with that receiv'd
from an excellent piece of musick. This is an advantage itinerant preachers have over those who are stationary, as the latter can not well improve
their delivery of a sermon by so many rehearsals.[58]

Franklin captures something of the extraordinary eloquence of Whitefield and provides carefully considered reasons for it. Whitefield dutifully articulated his words and spoke with great volume; he thoughtfully
(based in his rhetorical education) crafted his phrases, improving them
over time; he was finely attuned to the sound of his words—their
rhythm and accents—displaying a concern for every aspect of the discourse. Consequently, audiences were quiet because of their interest
in his message and their enjoyment of its sound. According to one
account, his voice had sufficient vocal volume to carry to the other side
of the Delaware River two miles below the city.[59]

## CHAPTER 4

## AMERICA AWAKENED

George Whitefield traveled directly to Philadelphia upon his arrival in America with an agenda and a message. He intended to initiate an American revival to add an American extension of his "parish" and raise money to build the orphanage. In his eight-day visit to the city (November 3–11, 1739) Whitefield reports to have attended three church services and to have preached at least eleven times in various places to crowds of up to eight thousand people.[1] Whitefield describes his participation in services and meetings with Anglicans, Quakers, Presbyterians, and Baptists; he had numerous meetings with local ministers to discuss theology and even dined with the governor. Undoubtedly, members of all these religious groups comprised his audiences. Whitefield's acceptance by such a diverse company and their permission to minister to their own parishioners attests to a genuine ecumenical spirit.

Perhaps Whitefield's encompassing view of Christianity that downplayed sectarianism and emphasized a community of believers promoted colonial unity as much as the other aspects of his ministry. Whitefield bifurcated his audiences: those who were converted and those who were not. In one sermon Whitefield clearly states this view: "It is very remarkable, there are but two sorts of people mentioned in Scripture: it does not say the Baptists and Independents, nor the Methodists and Presbyterians, no Jesus Christ divides the whole world into but two classes, sheep and goats."[2] Upon choosing the new birth, a person entered the ecumenical community of believers, a notion that Whitefield promoted throughout his lifetime and that he was one of the first to widely encourage. All his biographers were careful to point out this aspect, typically evidencing it with the following dramatic vingnette that apparently Whitefield used often:

Father Abraham, whom have you in heaven? Any Episcopalians? No!
Any Presbyterians? No! Have you any Independents or Seceders? No!
Have you any Methodists? No! No! No! Whom have you there? We don't
know those names here! All who are here are Christians.[3]

American audiences that had previously understood themselves as
diverse and somewhat distinct from one another were challenged by
such a message that held a powerful logic. That logic was especially
potent once a person was convinced of the need for conversion and
made the choice to attain it. Of which community was one a member
then? Whitefield had an obvious answer for this fundamental question.
Making a choice for conversion served as a rite of passage into this new
community that transcended nationality and denominational heritage
and, in America, built upon the commonalities of colonial life.

While in Philadelphia, Whitefield first met Benjamin Franklin as
he needed a publisher to promulgate his "print and preach" strategy in
the colonies. Their relationship likely began out of business necessity
but eventually grew into a genuine friendship.[4] Given Franklin's zeal
for colonial unity throughout the American political crisis, he clearly
had grounds to respect Whitefield's ecumenism. The two men powerfully symbolize the melding of republicanism and religion as each
tended to stay in his respective sphere of influence while maintaining
continuing business partnerships and a deepening friendship. Their
ideologies were compatible, with sufficient common ground upon
which their differences were negated.

Although Franklin capably described Whitefield's eloquence, he
commented little on the content of his sermons—an essential task
for determining what degree of influence he had on the people. To
support an argument that Whitefield indeed introduced a "rhetoric
of community," it will be necessary to identify such a rhetoric in his
discourse, showing elements and strategies that called people to be
something different from what they currently were, illuminating the
implied doctrines of a conceptual system to which Whitefield hoped
to convert his audiences.

Whitefield was convinced that good works such as "going to
church, doing hurt to no one, being constant in the duties of the closet
[i.e., prayer], and now and then reaching out . . . hands to give alms"
did not constitute true religion but merely an "outward Christ."[5]
He wrote of his disappointment with the Quakers shortly after he

arrived in Philadelphia, wishing "that they would talk of . . . an inward Christ," concluding that to neglect the heart promoted mere religious duty.[6] As Whitefield understood it, the outward Christ—evidenced by good deeds and piety—could be concocted by anyone, as Whitefield himself had attempted before his conversion. The possibility of being religious without being converted immediately justified the promotion of the new birth among even pious church members, not to mention the irreligious.

## THE NEW BIRTH AND REGENERATION

Whitefield's earliest publication, *The Nature and Necessity of Our New Birth in Christ Jesus*, first published in London in 1737, was being reprinted and sold in America before his arrival.[7] It was released under the title *On Regeneration*, the version analyzed here, by Benjamin Franklin, who sold out a two-volume set of Whitefield's sermons in January 1740 just weeks after Whitefield visited town. *On Regeneration* was the lead sermon in the publication, and it was released in pamphlet form in Boston later in the year. The sermon introduced and explained the new birth from Whitefield's perspective, defined it, and distinguished between those who had experienced it and those who had not. Here, Whitefield featured a tangible distinction between saints and sinners along with an explicit appeal for his listeners to choose the new birth as a rite of passage from sinner to saint, as substantiated through physical and emotional sensations. Whitefield contends for the scriptural origination of the new birth and then advances several "reasonable" arguments that support it from experience and common sense. The sermon also employs the term "regeneration" to suggest a continuum of Christian maturation. This regenerative growth confirmed a believer as a "genuine" Christian by providing concrete and measurable evidence.

Whitefield begins by pointing to an unacceptable inconsistency: that the new birth and regeneration should be at the center of Christianity, but little evidence of it can be found among the "generality of professors."[8] The inconsistency invites deeper inquiry, and from it he concludes that not all Christians have experienced a genuine conversion. Consequently, Whitefield implies that an unholy religion exists, populated by this generality of believers, and it stands in dialectical opposition to "our holy religion," populated by "sincere Christians, of every denomination." This is a fundamental distinction, one that exhibits Whitefield's division of people into deictic categories of "us" and "them." In its various forms the distinction appears in his discourse as us-them, saved-damned, saints-sinner, regenerate-unregenerate, sincere-insincere, and almost-altogether Christians.

Noting that "all sincere Christians" agree, he labels the new birth as a "hinge on which the salvation for each of us turns." He continues by explaining that many "who call themselves Christians" neglect this "fundamental" doctrine. Not only do they neglect it, he says, they do not even understand it. By addressing "those who call themselves Christians," Whitefield attacks his nonpresent *critics* instead of his immediate audience, letting his audience become a passive observer of his debate with an imaginary foil, even though he was well aware of sympathetic perspectives within his immediate audience.

Calling the new birth a hinge reveals it as an experiential doorway between the unconverted world at large and those who embrace genuine Christianity, echoing the biblical teachings that Christ is a "door" or a "gate." The new birth takes one through that door as the rite of passage from "them" to "us" and consequently, from death to life. Whitefield assesses and evaluates the actions of those who deny the new birth, calling their denial a "fatal mistake" because it prevents members of a church from entering the genuine Christian community. The sermon will attempt to cure this mistake. Following his introductory remarks Whitefield formally previews the sermon. His argument, which ultimately intends to persuade his hearers to embrace the new birth, unfolds in four phases, closing with his call to action.

Whitefield's first point defines the new birth and explains how one can know whether or not it has been experienced. He highlights two aspects of the sermon's scripture text (2 Cor 5:17), "in Christ" and "new creature," granting that many people may be said to be "in Christ" but that does not mean they are new creatures. Whitefield antithetically declares, "Comparatively but few of those that are 'born of water,' are 'born of the Spirit' . . . many are baptized with water, which were never baptized with the Holy Ghost." Whitefield complains that the rite of water baptism can be experienced without a change of heart or preparation necessary for conversion. True conversion, Whitefield insists, is best evidenced by the "baptism of the Holy Ghost," which was demonstrated by a regenerated lifestyle.

As a consequent of the us-them distinction, Whitefield posits a second dissimilarity: "in Christ," or as he implies, "not in Christ." One who is "not in Christ" can perform a "bare outward profession," but that person is not a member of God's kingdom (or family). Genuine membership in this community is evidenced by an "inward change" and a "cohabitation of the Holy Spirit." To clarify his meaning, Whitefield uses a metaphor of a "vine." Just as branches receive nourishment and life from the vine, the true Christian receives "spiritual virtue" from Christ as a benefit of being grafted "in" to the body of Christ, receiving all that is needed for life from God.

After completing this explanation, he defines precisely what he means by a new creature. This section acts as a measuring stick by which audience members can judge whether or not they have passed through the "door" via the new birth. Whitefield says that being a new creature is not a "physical change," and neither is one "reduced to our primitive nothings," but, as he claims, one is "altered as to the qualities and tempers of our minds, that we must entirely forget what manner of persons we once were." Thus, for Whitefield, *a transformation of the mind* evidences the conversion experience. Three different metaphors (all biblical allusions) then describe such a transformation: the refinement of gold, the cleaning and polishing of glass, and being healed of disease. The transformation from old to new occurs as part of a purification process. People who experience the new birth, in Whitefield's words, "are so purged, purified and cleansed from their natural dross, filth and leprosy, by the blessed influences of the Holy Spirit, that they may be properly said to be made anew." The Holy Spirit is the agent who effects the purification, not the person. This is a key difference between Arminianism and Whitefield's pseudo-Calvinism. Arminian theology taught that human effort was efficacious for personal purification from sin after conversion, but the revivalists relied solely upon divine assistance for purification.

Whitefield admits that this transformation "cannot easily be explained" or that it is "hard to be understood," so he employs the terms "mystically" or "invisible workings" to describe them. Whitefield teaches that the new birth should not be rejected simply because it has a mysterious nature—such an argument by negation provides no evidence.

Whitefield then moves to his third point, which is supported by four arguments of the type that his "Enlightened" critics would require: one from the "written Word of God" and three based on natural reason. He adopts his critics' own point of view and their own standards for judging doctrine to demonstrate the reasonableness of the new birth. Proceeding with the first argument supporting the new birth, Whitefield muses "one would think it sufficient to affirm . . . that God himself, in his holy word, has told us so." He explains the meaning of selected scriptural passages regarding the doctrine of original sin: "being derived from carnal parents, and consequently receiving the seeds of all manner of sin and corruption from them." Hence, Whitefield's claim is founded entirely upon a biblical assertion—evidence persuasive only to those who revere the Bible.

But Whitefield is aware of the limitations of his first argument, so he moves to his three rational arguments directed at those who require natural reason for proof. He contrasts the purity of God with the impurity of man and the incongruity of the two dwelling together. "Can he, in whose sight the heavens are not clean, delight to dwell with uncleanness itself?" Whitefield presumes that man must be purified or regenerated before dwelling with God. Mixing natural reason with biblical assertion, he avers a Calvinist belief that people are "conceived and born in sin," having "no good thing dwelling" within, being "carnal, sold under sin." Whitefield continues, "Can any one conceive how a filthy, corrupted, polluted wretch can dwell with an infinitely pure and holy God . . . ?" In other words, incongruent things cannot coexist, a clear use of reasoned logic by Whitefield.

The third argument does not begin with any biblical assertion at all. Whitefield states, "Unless we have dispositions wrought in us suitable to the objects that are to entertain us, we can take no manner of complacency or satisfaction in them." If one is not purified, there can be no appreciation or enjoyment of an inheritance that is pure. He uses analogies of the inability of the blind to enjoy a beautiful picture or the deaf to enjoy music, and then he says, "Can a tasteless palate relish the richest dainties, or a filthy swine be pleased with the finest garden of flowers? No." Thus, a person, in Whitefield's view, must have a new nature—a spiritual nature—to enjoy the delights of heaven.

Whitefield quickly moves to his last argument in support of regeneration after conversion, his strongest point. His belief that one's essential nature is changed upon his or her new birth extends what it means to be "in Christ." He establishes his argument upon both common sense and theological orthodoxy:

But then, if the benefits of our dear Redeemer's death were to extend no farther than barely to procure forgiveness of our sins, we should have as little reason to rejoice in it, as a poor condemned criminal that is ready to perish by some fatal disease, would have in receiving a pardon from his judge.

His poignant image of a diseased prisoner portrays the effects of sin and suggests that one needs his or her vitality restored as well as a pardon for the reprieve to be of value, and that certainly a rational God would pardon sin and assist the believer in the purification process.

Next, Whitefield advances to the prescriptive portion of the sermon. For those familiar with the contending theological positions, it was necessary for Whitefield to defend his theology—to demonstrate that he was not ignorant of the criticisms, had considered them, and held his theology from an informed perspective. Although some modern scholars of persuasion might consider "inoculation theory" a modern innovation, here Whitefield is "inoculating" his audience against the teachings of revival critics, which he knew from experience in England were soon to follow his tour.[9] Alexander Garden's critiques had not yet been published, but Whitefield anticipates his objections to the letter.

Continuing, Whitefield addresses both "us" and "them," the regenerate and the unregenerate, providing only two categories of ontological being with which an audience member might identify. If Whitefield only *implied* the distinction between "us" and "them" before, he makes it explicit now, challenging the notion that an "inherited orthodoxy" is sufficient for becoming a genuine Christian. The lack of inward change becomes evidence that one is not regenerated and thus still in need of the new birth.

Whitefield argues that ethical behavior is insufficient, that even a reformation to good behavior still allows the heart to harbor a "hidden lust" or "some vicious habit." He concludes his remarks to "them" with a carefully crafted passage:

It will profit thee but little to do many things, if yet some one thing thou lackest. In short, thou must not only be an almost, but altogether a new creature, or in vain thou boasteth that thou art a Christian.

As seen here, Whitefield typically structured and embellished the climactic portion of each sermon with rhetorical figures.[10] In fact, he
artfully enlarges his use of such figuration as a sermon proceeds, beginning with sparsely figurated language, increasing its use near the end,
but never so much as to betray his art. He antithetically sets "many
things" a person does against the "one thing" left undone—achieving
the new birth. He also antithetically holds up the "almost" and the
"altogether" Christian to distinguish between those who are regenerated and those who are not. The notions of "almost" and "altogether"
imply that a single issue—the new birth—separated genuine from disingenuous Christians. Whitefield announces the new birth to be an
"infallible rule" (employing the Enlightenment vocabulary) by which
any person might judge his or her life. He lists a set of characteristics
or actions that signify the new birth, implying that if one lacks these
characteristics, then he or she is one of the "almost" Christians yet in
need of grace:

> Let each of us therefore seriously put this question to our hearts: Have
> we received the Holy Ghost since we believed? . . . Do we constantly and
> conscientiously use all the means of grace required thereto? Do we fast,
> watch and pray? Do we, not lazily seek, but laboriously strive to enter in
> at the strait gate? In short, do we renounce our own righteousness, take
> up our crosses and follow Christ?

In a passage spiced with antithesis and alliteration, Whitefield's questions strike directly at the "almost Christians" and seek to create tension
within people who cannot answer yes to all of them—a difficult task
for even the pious! Whitefield confronts his listeners with the issue and
urges them to become one of "us" and to enter "in." Should the audience member answer "no" to these questions, Whitefield pronounces
them "strangers, nay enemies to the cross of Christ," and that their
"lives of worldly-mindedness, and sensual pleasure" will cause other
genuine seekers to "think, that Christianity is but an empty name, a
bare formal profession." Hence, not only does he establish the distinction between "us" and "them," he evaluates each side of the distinction and judges "them" to be damned and "us" to be saved—a sober
ramification of being in or out.

Regardless of the labels Whitefield uses, his meaning is clear. And
though his audience members may have accepted his representation

of their spiritual state, especially if they could not reply "yes" to his questions, the established clergy were highly offended at the suggestion that they were not genuine Christians—not to mention that Whitefield calls them "enemies." As Whitefield stated earlier in the sermon, to be one of "them" and belong to the "out group" constituted a fatal error. It does not take a prophet to foresee the coming conflict.

From this point in the sermon, Whitefield invites the audience to embrace his perspective, to seek the new birth, to become one of "us" and belong to the "in group." Here he offers an action that those motivated by his arguments and emotion could choose to perform to facilitate their conversion. Here, as Black portrayed effective rhetoric, Whitefield exhorts his audience "not simply to believe something, but to *be* something."[11] Whitefield warns of the ridicule that may accompany embracing his perspective and identifying with the revivalists but assures his audience that God's peace will accompany them. He closes the sermon with an antithetical section, eloquently composed, rhythmically punctuated with *membras* and commas, employing rhetorical figures of *asyndeton* and *climax*, and contrasting the destiny of the "unconverted, unrenewed sinner" with those who are "regenerate and born again." His final lines illuminate the transformation process initiated upon reception of the new birth:

> Methinks, every one that has but the least concern for the salvation of his precious and immortal soul, having such promises, such an hope, such an eternity of happiness set before him, should never cease watching, praying, and striving, till he find a real, inward, saving change wrought in his heart, and thereby doth know of a truth, that he dwells in Christ, and Christ in him; that he is a new creature, therefore a child of God; that he is already an inheritor, and will ere long be an actual possessor of the kingdom of heaven.

True religious conversion is an identity-establishing process that transmutes the very core of the believer from that day forward. The new birth was not metaphorical for Whitefield and his converts, but it established and reinforced an in-out ontological distinction in terms of family membership and the right to a generous inheritance. These implied doctrines of us-them and in-out provided unmistakable structure to his entire message.

Whitefield taught that the new birth occurred at a specific point in time and space, but his description of regeneration indicated a *process* of purification. He intertwined the notions of new birth and regeneration to a degree, using metaphors that signify cleansing, purification, polishing, cleaning, and total renovation. The new birth occurred instantaneously, while regeneration required a temporal progression of gradual change for its completion. In other words, membership was established legally and instantly, but it took time for one to behave and feel like a member. As Bunyan portrayed in *Pilgrim's Progress*, regeneration was a lifelong process requiring much toil and suffering.

The implied understanding of a growth process made the doctrine of the new birth repulsive for the established clergy, holding strong implications for their status in the religious community, as well as the social community. By accepting Whitefield's new birth, a person became a "babe in Christ" (as the apostle Paul describes), calling into question the right and qualification of a newly converted minister to oversee a parish. Other revival ministers, such as Edwards, Frelinghuysen, Tennent, Wesley, and Davenport had grasped the import of conversion, experienced it, and taught it, entering their respective ministries as "mature" Christians. Thus, they were immune from any suggestion that they were unqualified. (In fact, a number of American ministers did subsequently embrace the new birth, and their clerical authority was never questioned.) Those ministers who denied the doctrine of the conversion experience would soon face direct challenges to their authority to minister, first from Whitefield and then more forcefully from Gilbert Tennent. Additionally, in Massachusetts where the church and state were intertwined in "glorious New England tradition," labeling political leaders as outsiders to God's kingdom directly undermined their authority to govern. The offended ministers would lead the attack against Whitefield, so any resentment on the part of civil leaders remained concealed.

Philadelphia's response to Whitefield mirrored the response in London with escalating crowds coming out to hear him. Any cultural or religious differences seemed to be set aside at his meetings as substantial portions of the local population came to hear his message. Just as Charles Wesley led Whitefield to conversion, Whitefield was leading colonists to conversions. He recorded some of his impressions of Philadelphians' response to his message:

> Most wept at the preaching of faith. . . . Even in London, I never observed
> so profound a silence. . . . At present they seem most gladly to receive the
> Word. . . . Many to my knowledge, have been quickened and awakened
> to see that religion does not consist in outward things.[12]

Benjamin Franklin was amazed at "how much they admir'd and
respected him, in spite of his common abuse of them, by assuring
them that they were naturally half beasts and half devils."[13] The
effects of Whitefield's preaching did not wear off after his departure.
Even six months later Franklin attested to a change in behavior of
Philadelphia's citizens:

> It was wonderful to see the change soon made in the manners of our
> inhabitants. From being thoughtless or indifferent about religion, it
> seem'd as if all the world were growing religious, so that one could not
> walk thro' the town in an evening without hearing psalms sung in differ-
> ent families of every street.[14]

Whitefield's message had been received and chosen by enough citizens
to change the city, even as viewed through discriminating eyes.

Although other ministers concurrently came to similar conclusions
regarding the effectiveness of inherited orthodoxy, Whitefield was the
person who popularized the term "new birth" and gave it a wide circulation. No other minister clarified the nature of the new birth like
Whitefield. By circulating a compact, potent phrase that accurately
communicated a theological reality, *any* minister could explain the
conversion experience in the language of the common people and be
much more likely to convert them in one or two hearings. Whitefield's
contribution of the terms "new birth" and "regeneration" was decid-
edly rhetorical, breaking down the barrier of theological ignorance
while it sidestepped logical objections through the power of metaphor.
Moreover, the vocabulary itself encouraged listeners to understand
identity as a member of a religious community or family. Nationality
and denominational heritage faded in importance to conversion and
membership in the ecumenical Christian community.

For Whitefield and his Christian followers, the notions of new birth
and regeneration were not figurative, but literal, and these terms held
a meaning that modern societies may not fully appreciate. His idea
of regeneration connected powerfully with farmers who were familiar

with the process in their orchards, gardens, and fields. Additionally, in the eighteenth century, the travail of birth normally occurred at home with a midwife, who provided guidance and encouragement, and where the entire family would participate in the experience one way or another. Perhaps the notion of a spiritual midwife is not far removed from the actual role of the itinerant ministers who exhorted and encouraged their auditors during revival meetings. A sarcastic account in the *Anglican Weekly Miscellany* reveals the symbolic midwifery present in Whitefield's preaching: "Hark! He talks of a Sensible New Birth—then belike he is in Labour, and the good Women around him are come to his assistance. He dilates himself, cries out [and] is at last delivered."[15] This was certainly a joke not missed by his audiences, and it outlined his sermonic style accurately. Perhaps there is more to the midwife humor than merely trying to discredit Whitefield. Many of Whitefield's converts were women, enough that cartoonists and playwrights could lampoon his relationship with them. Charles Chauncy pointed out that young women were especially attendant to Whitefield's ministering, and in America as in England the Methodist movement was well supported by women.

Was Whitefield employing a feminine manner of expression that attracted women to his ministry? Sarah Edwards recalled, "You have already heard of his deep-toned, yet clear melodious voice. It is perfect music. . . . He speaks from a heart all aglow with love and pours out a torrent of eloquence which is almost irresistible."[16] Whitefield often cried during his preaching, and his tears would produce an empathetic response in his listeners who would begin crying as well. His biographer Gillies was perhaps too careful to point out that Whitefield's manner of speaking was "manly."[17] Was Gillies trying to counter a perception of effeminacy in Whitefield's preaching that fueled the satire in the *Anglican Weekly Miscellany*? His ubiquitous crying was not a manly thing to do. Whitefield was raised without a father, he did not get along with his older brother, and he spent many hours in the company of his sister. As the youngest of his siblings, he grew up in a home of women. He married a woman ten years his elder. After 1748, his employer was a woman. Perhaps noting these facts is overspeculating, but maybe Whitefield used "women's language" to bridge the gap between male and female so that his message would be more easily heard by women in his audience? If so, his enterprise was an exception to "muted group theory," where men exclude and trivialize women with their logic-driven communication style that ignores feelings, feminine experiences, and ways of interacting.[18]

With profound ramification in later decades, Whitefield and the Methodists legitimated a leadership role for women in the religious societies established for new converts. Michael Casey partially attributes the rule changes to Whitefield, explaining that "[b]y undercutting the authority of the church, Whitefield let the genie out of the bottle—now anyone, who felt called by God, could preach even if any and all churches disagreed."[19] Catherine Breckus indicates that, against the odds, the preponderance of female preachers began in earnest in 1740, a history that was all but erased from church records by later evangelicals.[20] Sarah Crosby was one of many women who forcefully preached in the Methodist movement, downplaying sexuality and emphasizing a maternal role for Methodist women.[21] By exemplifying a speaking style that used the careful argumentation of the men's realm but also included a feminine side filled with emotion and passion, Whitefield's crossover into a feminine speaking style may have encouraged women to cross over to the typical male style. In the next century, Angelina Grimké employed the "resources of argument" in an "agonistic art" as a leader in the antislavery movement.[22] Is it too much to suggest that women's leadership in the abolitionist movement was foreshadowed by the Methodists' development of women in leadership roles?

## THE SPIRIT AND COMMON PRIVILEGES

After leaving Philadelphia, Whitefield arduously traveled through New Jersey by horseback and then south through Maryland, Virginia, and the Carolinas, preaching wherever he could find an audience. Since the Charleston Anglican pulpit was closed to him in Alexander Garden's absence, Whitefield preached three sermons to "most of the town" in one of the "dissenting meeting-houses." Whitefield recorded that the "polite" congregation showed "little concern" and seemed to mock him.[23] The following day he preached again to a more receptive audience where "many were melted into tears" with a "visible concern on their faces." As he left town, Whitefield mused that the Charlestonians were "formal professors, all polite and foolish," and he hoped they would respond to the "good work" he had begun.[24]

Judging by Garden's angry response upon his return home and
the content of his publications, Whitefield likely preached his sermon,
*The Indwelling of the Spirit, the Common Privilege of All Believers*. Garden had
apparently obtained a copy of the sermon, as it was Whitefield's most
popular American publication. Therein, Whitefield berated unconverted ministers, completely undermined their authority, and called
into question their motives and qualifications to judge the revival or
even to hold their ministerial offices. It is no wonder Garden was livid.

*Indwelling* extended the ramifications of the new identity Whitefield promoted in *On Regeneration* and encouraged the formation of a
consubstantial Christian community. It was the responsibility of the
Spirit to conform the mind and heart of each person to Christian
principles, so that he or she would fit into the community. Though
Whitefield's main tasks in the sermon were to confront the slumbering or unconverted clergy and to provide the rationale for a Christian
community, a blending of religious and legal/political spheres through
an interchangeable vocabulary of religious and republican terms may
be the more interesting feature, a feature that slips past the attention of
the reader focused solely on the theological debate.

Whitefield selected a Scripture text for exposition that embodies
the theme of his sermon (John 7:37-39) and opens by accusing his
critics of denying the spiritual nature of Christianity and intellectual-
izing the Christian message. Whitefield presumes his audience to have
some notion of the current theological debate over enthusiasm as he
fails to preface the conflict with any introductory material. His critics, in his view, held a "supposition" (he implicitly contrasts with a
"truth") that the miraculous work of the Holy Spirit was not intended
for modern Christians. His thesis is clear, direct, and has profound
implications: "The Holy Spirit is the common privilege and portion
of all believers in all ages; and that we as well as the first Christians,
must receive the Holy Ghost, before we can be truly called the children
of God." Whitefield defines the Spirit in a way his detractors might
have accepted: "By the Spirit, is evidently to be understood the Holy
Ghost, the third person in the ever-blessed Trinity, consubstantial and
co-eternal with the Father and the Son, proceeding from, yet equal
to them both." He then cites three biblical passages where the three
are seemingly equated. He expects assent from all Christians, believing this to be a self-evident issue. And indeed, he is departing from

common ground with his critics. Garden himself referred to the Holy Spirit as "the *third* person of the ever blessed *trinity*."[25]

Following his definition, Whitefield seeks to establish that "all believers" are entitled to receive this Spirit. By asserting that the indwelling is a "common privilege," Whitefield draws upon the political tradition of the English people. The rights of Englishmen were an integral feature of their political system, providing the heritage of individual rights that modern Americans understand so well. Certain rights were "common" to all the people, and references to such rights can be seen throughout the writings of influential Whig political theorists such as John Locke. Vestiges of Locke's ideas populate Whitefield's writings, as his use of the term "common privilege" indicates.[26] Using this vocabulary, Whitefield co-opts implicit republican beliefs to explain religious realities.

Whitefield takes care to distinguish himself from ministers who expected to work miracles as the apostles did by the power of the Spirit, evidencing that he was not guilty of the radical enthusiasm with which he was charged. Instead he takes a moderate approach. For Whitefield, the real work of the Spirit was internal and not external. Again Whitefield is identifying with Garden's position, eschewing the zealous enthusiasm of others. Emotional reactions of revival auditors are their personal responses to the work of the Spirit. For Whitefield's audiences, the emotional response normally involved weeping, a practice that blurred gender boundaries as he legitimated this feminine form of expression. His moderation places his critics at the conservative end of the theological continuum, implying that they err as greatly as do the radical enthusiasts. After arguing that the ability to perform miracles without God's saving grace is futile, Whitefield reinforces his shared beliefs with Garden and others, saying, "We join issue with our adversaries," and from this point of departure he formulates his complaint against them.

Whitefield charges his critics with believing the first part of the Scripture text in question (John 7:37-39), but not the second part. Whitefield gives the impression that he is performing his interpretive task reasonably, taking the words at face value, and implying that his critics espouse unorthodox views or perform hermeneutical gymnastics to justify their position. Whitefield argues, "Again, our Lord, just before his bitter passion . . . when his heart was most enlarged and he

would undoubtedly demand the most excellent gift for his disciples,"
referring to the Spirit. He appeals to an expectation of consistency,
that circumstances of great magnitude demand a response of great
magnitude, or in this case, a great gift.

Having supported his second point, Whitefield responds to charges
of enthusiasm. It is clear that his definition of enthusiasm differs
qualitatively from that of his critics, who distrusted emotional expressions. Charles Chauncy, who eventually led opposition to the revivals,
explained their position:

> The word, enthusiasm, from its etymology, carries in it a good meaning,
> as signifying inspiration from God. . . . But the word is more commonly
> used in a bad sense, as intending an imaginary, not a real inspiration:
> according to which sense, the Enthusiast is one, who has conceit of him-
> self as a person favoured with the extraordinary presence of the Deity.
> He mistakes the workings of his own passions for divine communica-
> tions, and fancies himself immediately inspired by the Spirit of God,
> when all the while, he is under no other influence than that of an over-
> heated imagination.[27]

With their authority under attack, antirevival ministers radically characterized "enthusiasm" and thus weakened the strength of Whitefield's charge through *ad hominem* attacks. Whitefield, also jettisoning
the extremism of others, attempted to rehabilitate the term. (He later
gave up this rehabilitation and used the term himself to describe radicals.) He identifies with the apostles who were also "cast out as evil,"
thus associating his critics with those who persecuted the apostles.

Whitefield replaced the notion of "enthusiasm" with the moderate idea of the "indwelling of the Spirit," an easier doctrine to
defend, which attributes the "enthusiastic" responses to God, who is
mysterious and incomprehensible. While his definition did not immediately catch on, it did likely deflect criticisms upon his return in 1745.
The sermon emerges as a confrontation of definitions over the term
"enthusiasm." Whitefield reclaimed the term and attached the more
moderate connotation, while his detractors were using it in an exaggerated, pejorative sense. But the two sides held incommensurable
perspectives from which their definitions emerged, grounded in practice, not theology. After establishing their common ground, Whitefield clarifies their differences:

Indeed, I will not say, all our letter-learned preachers deny this doctrine in express words; but however, they do in effect; for they talk professedly against inward feelings, and say, we may have God's Spirit without feeling it, which is in reality to deny the thing itself. And had I a mind to hinder the progress of the gospel, and to establish the kingdom of darkness, I would go about, telling people, they might have the Spirit of God, and yet not feel it.

In other words, Whitefield is calling them hypocrites for not maintaining a consistency between Anglican doctrines and their preaching and thus heightening a state of cognitive dissonance (he always named the Anglicans in his theological disputation, never another denomination). Moreover, he defines them as dupes who serve the "kingdom of darkness" instead of Christ, reinforcing his implied doctrine of "in-out" and insisting that they are "out."

Explaining the necessity of "the indwelling," Whitefield gradually heads toward a prescription. He asks the rhetorical question, "But, my dear brethren, what have you been doing?" Answering his own question with another, he continues, "How often have your hearts given your lips the lie? How often have you offered to God the sacrifice of fools, and had your prayers turned into sin, if you approve of, and use Anglican church-liturgy, and yet deny the Holy Spirit to be the portion of all believers?" By either creating or pointing out his audience's logical inconsistencies, he hopes to impel them to make a decision—one for which his arguments have paved a rational, reasonable road.

Having established his definitions to his own satisfaction, he continues the attack on the clergy with accusations containing his sharpest barbs yet: "But you are the schismatics, you are the bane of the church of England . . . feeding [the people] only with the dry husks of dead morality, and not bringing out to them the fatted calf; I mean, the doctrines of the operations of the blessed Spirit of God." His food metaphors, which antithetically compare the malnutrition of dispensational doctrine against the nutritious doctrine of the revivalists, may strike a resonant chord in a society that understood the meaning of famine. Whitefield presses the attack further, echoing the denunciation of the Jewish Pharisees by Jesus:

> Woe be unto such blind leaders of the blind! How can you escape the
> damnation of hell? . . . Jesus Christ, the great Shepherd and Bishop of
> souls, shall determine who are the false prophets; who are the wolves in
> sheep's clothing. Those who say, that we must now receive and feel the
> Holy Ghost, or those who exclaim against it, as the doctrine of devils.

He apologizes for the necessity of his criticisms, but insists, "If I could
bear to see people perish for lack of knowledge, and yet be silent
towards those who keep from them the key of true knowledge, the very
stones would cry out." His words in these sections demand performative emotion and energy; otherwise there would be a sin against form
that an orator such as Whitefield could never commit.

Whitefield next argues for the "reasonableness of this doctrine."
He begins by incorporating a series of terms designed to establish
the "reason" on which his view is founded. The rational terms "highest reason," "demonstration" (used two times), and "this self-evident
truth" all occur in one sentence wherein he defends the Calvinist doctrine of the depravity of man. He condemns the Arminian belief that
a germinal element of good resides in humanity, empowering people
to satisfy God's requirements. Instead, Whitefield scripturally justifies
the opposite view, placing the burden of proof on his detractors. Next,
Whitefield turns his passionate, bellicose rhetoric toward his audience
in a series of questions:

> Tell me then, O man, whosoever thou art, that deniest the doctrine of
> original sin, if thy conscience be not seared as with a hot iron! Tell me, if
> thou dost not find thyself, by nature, to be a mostly mixture of brute and
> devil? I know these terms will stir up the whole Pharisee in thy heart; but
> let not Satan hurry thee hence; stop a little, and let us reason together;
> dost thou not find, that by nature thou art prone to pride? Otherwise,
> wherefore art thou now offended?

Here Whitefield employs offended feelings of his audience against
them. Any anger that they may be feeling provides evidence that
Whitefield's claim regarding their pride is true. Next, Whitefield introduces another metaphor: "keeping animals out of the house," an anal-
ogy that constitutes another of his "reasonable" arguments.

And if creatures, with only our degree of goodness, cannot bear even the thought of dwelling with beasts or devils, to whose nature we are so nearly allied, how do we imagine God, who is infinite goodness, and purity itself, can dwell with us, while we are partakers of both their natures? We might as well think to reconcile heaven and hell.

Hence, the unregenerate person is not fit to enter heaven and requires purification through the process of regeneration from "original sin" before communion with God is possible. His "dwelling with beasts" metaphor fits the colonists' everyday experience and is another example of how Whitefield used ordinary illustrations to connect with people.

Winding up the sermon, Whitefield says, "If I have wounded you, be not afraid; behold, I now bring a remedy for all your wounds." Here Whitefield attempts to create tension and subsequently relieve it. Perhaps many came to hear out of curiosity. But Whitefield strove to create an interest in the discourse by first attacking the status quo clergy and then turning his discourse against the audience itself, offending them, then trying to convince them that their offended feelings stood as tangible evidence to support his case. He finally provides a resolution for any anxiety they may have felt.

That anxiety, as Whitefield reveals, was evidenced by the emotional response manifest in particular audience members: "Do not some of you think, though I mean well, yet I have carried the point a little too far? . . . Is not this driving people into despair?" It is to these emotionally moved persons that his prescriptions are directed. Of course his remedy is the new birth, which Whitefield explains and depicts as a choice between life and death. Whitefield grammatically offers agency to the audience for salvation, saying, "Come then, my guilty brethren, come and believe on the Lord that bought you with his precious blood." He repeatedly uses the imperative "come," urging his audience to action. He then systematically refutes several objections an audience member might hold and eloquently exhorts his audience to receive the indwelling of the Spirit through the new birth. His call to sinners is not particularly manipulative, but invitational, as it relies upon the desire for piety and one's imagination for its impelling force. Most importantly, he is offering a choice to the "sinners" and urging them to act.

As in *On Regeneration,* Whitefield argued with textually represented critics (specifically identified as Anglican clergy) before an audience that was asked to choose between the two perspectives: should one support the established clergy, the "letter-learned" ministers whom Whitefield accused of being negligent in their duty, or support the revivalists who claim to offer a genuine form of Christianity? Whitefield refuted the notion that an outward performance of duty is adequate to earn salvation, and he placed blame for this misconception at the feet of the established ministers. In so doing he initiated the conflict between New Lights and Old Lights and would not back off of his position for another five years. Whitefield threw down the gauntlet, calling them "false prophets" and "wolves in sheep's clothing." Whitefield's challenge to their authority to govern the church was direct and unmistakable, and in colonies that blended religion and politics his position constituted a direct challenge to appointed and elected officials who identified with established denominations.[28] Once the meaning of his attack and the magnitude of the stakes became apparent, and after other ministers such as Gilbert Tennent began to echo Whitefield's charges, the established clergy rose up in united opposition against him.

## STIRRINGS OF OPPOSITION

After preaching in Charleston, Whitefield finally arrived in Georgia, obtained land for his orphanage about ten miles out of Savannah, and began construction of the facilities, which he named Bethesda. He soon left Savannah for Charleston to raise more money and continue his preaching tour. But before sailing out of Charleston, Whitefield met with the commissary, Garden, in his home where Garden challenged him. Whitefield wrote, "He charged me with enthusiasm and pride, for speaking against the generality of the clergy, and desired I would make my charge good. I told him, I thought I had already; though as yet I had scarce begun with them."[29] Garden threw Whitefield out of his house and warned him under the threat of suspension not to preach in his jurisdiction. Whitefield ignored the threat, rightly knowing that Garden had no authority to suspend him, and continued traveling and preaching as before. Garden then took his grievances to the people, publishing his criticisms and complaints just after Whitefield's tour ended.

Alexander Garden's opposition to Whitefield constituted the first phase of resistance to the revival. Garden's letter and two attached sermons provide an initial view into this conflict from the antirevival perspective. The conflict simmered on the back burner as Whitefield's tour continued, but eventually it developed into a theological rift over the legitimacy of the Awakening. Ironically, the resultant rift later pricked New England consciences and contributed to colonial unification in the years after the Awakening. Although Garden and Whitefield agreed upon much more than they disagreed, and although any outsider might have viewed their conflict as sectarian squabbling over trifling differences, their differences were critical since they defined a person's membership in God's kingdom. Garden differed with Whitefield on the instantaneous quality of the new birth and regeneration, and on the nature and work of the Holy Spirit.

Garden's vehement opposition to Whitefield seems out of proportion to the consequences of doctrinal squabbling. Perhaps what Garden insightfully sensed, beneath the surface of the religious debate, was that Whitefield's message threatened not just ecclesiastical order but political and social structures as well. Whitefield had "invented" his own position from Locke's first-stage rhetorical topics about the right of people to establish and change their own government, arguing that people had the right to choose how to worship. Garden may have intuitively recognized that this logic could undermine all hierarchies, whether ecclesiastical or secular. As Whitefield had disregarded Garden's censure, even though Garden was his elder and held a higher position within the Anglican Church, Whitefield's message could breed civil disobedience. But since Whitefield himself was not seditious and was not encouraging political rebellion, Garden's misgivings had to focus on doctrinal issues. For the time being the debate stayed on the theological level, and Garden became Whitefield's foil, representing the antirevival clergy. But as the next several years passed, Charles Chauncy, a well-educated and respected Boston Puritan, moved to the fore in the second phase of opposition to Whitefield, and Garden became silent. And as the revival ran its course, Chauncy was able to translate the doctrinal positions into political ones and directly charge Whitefield with political subversion.

## Onward to Boston

If Whitefield's reception in London encouraged him that his message would be widely accepted in England, then likewise Boston provided a comparable venue in America. If he could awaken Boston and New

England, then the revival would be greatly extended throughout the population of British colonies, as Whitefield had intended. Only Virginia, Maryland, and North Carolina, where, due to the sparse population and difficulty of travel, would Whitefield's influence wane on this first tour. Their time would come in the next decade. After itinerating through the spring and spending the summer in Georgia, Whitefield headed back to New England.

Whitefield's reception in New England and Boston was passionate, but here the controversy became the most heated. There was more for the established ministers to lose in Massachusetts' church/state society. By this time, Garden had published his criticisms of Whitefield, and evidently copies printed in Charleston were circulating among the Boston clergy. Bostonians had certainly been able to read Whitefield's accounts of his revivals in the other colonies, so when he arrived on September 19, 1740, four thousand people turned out at his first sermon, six thousand at a sermon the next morning, and eight thousand that afternoon. The following day, Sunday, fifteen thousand came to hear him preach. Whitefield wrote, "To see people ready to hear, makes me forget myself. . . . Most wept for a considerable time."[30] But what Whitefield and the revivalists viewed as a marvelous response to the preaching of God's Word, the established clergy espied as the formation of a mob with all its implications. Neither the established religious nor the civil leaders could draw such large crowds to hear a sermon or political speech.

On Monday, within a week of his arrival, tragedy occurred as Whitefield was preparing to preach at Rev. Mr. Checkley's meetinghouse. People continued entering the building, crowding into the seats and standing in the aisles until it was filled beyond its capacity. Someone made a seat by breaking a board. Upon hearing the sound, immediately people feared the gallery was collapsing and jumped from the gallery, rushing for doors and windows. Five people were killed (probably by asphyxiation) and many others were injured. Whitefield quickly announced that he would preach outside, and several thousand stood in the rain to hear him. Perhaps this tragedy provided a symbolic foretelling message for those who held reservations about the revivals and convinced them that Whitefield was dangerous. No longer were these meetings peaceful, but the people could get out of control. What if this enthusiasm was turned against the government leadership amidst Whitefield's censure of unconverted ministers? What if the crowds adopted a political stance and turned against civil leaders and the established order? The connection to such fears was rooted in the implicit recognition that Whitefield was indeed providing an alternative identity through his call to genuine Christianity, a call that was embraced by many. Two days later, any such suspicions were further exacerbated as Whitefield visited Harvard and offended its faculty by saying "discipline is at a low ebb. Bad books are become fashionable among the tutors and students. Tillotson and Clark are read, instead of Sheppard, Stoddard and such-like evangelical writers."[32] Harvard was the institution that trained all of Massachusetts' clergy and civil leaders. These and other such comments fueled upcoming criticism and provided the verification needed to make a case against the revival. Whitefield then left Boston to tour various towns around the New England coast.

After preaching for several weeks in the vicinity of Boston, Whitefield traveled west to Northampton, where he befriended Jonathan Edwards and reignited the revival Edwards oversaw a few years earlier. Traveling further south, Whitefield encouraged Gilbert Tennent to visit Boston and continue preaching to people there.[33] Tennent itinerated for much of 1741 before he settled back down at home in New Brunswick. James Davenport, inspired by Whitefield's and Tennent's successes, journeyed to New England to continue the revival the following year.

George Whitefield departed for England in January 1741 and set about tending to his English parish and spreading the revival to Wales and Scotland. His vision of having the whole world as his parish was becoming fully manifest with followers in the British Isles and now in America. Just as a country minister assigned to more than one parish would travel back and forth between towns, Whitefield itinerated between his self-created parishes within the British Empire. His was a ministry on a macroscale as compared to the microscale of other ministers assigned to several local parishes. In addition, he now had an official ministry post at the Bethesda orphanage, which required traveling to raise charitable contributions for support, supplying him with a legitimate reason to itinerate. The need to maintain parishes and support the orphanage generally motivated his decisions of when and where to travel.

In view of Whitefield's groundbreaking work, his extensive travels, his wide publication of ideas, and his encouragement of other itinerants, the Great Awakening can be strongly linked to his efforts. White-field brought the energy and leadership needed to spread the revival doctrines of the conversion experience to other colonies. Edwards and Tennent traveled little before 1740, remaining in or near their established parishes.[34] Moreover, there was no systematic plan to spread the revival to other locations, nor was there anyone for the task until Whitefield came to begin his preaching tour. The revival's intercolonial scope emerged during and after Whitefield's tour, after which, as Ahlstrom points out, "Whitefield, Tennent, and Edwards—Anglican, Presbyterian, and Congregationalist—felt themselves to be of one mind in their great undertaking."[35]

Alan Heimert explained, "The revival and the evangelical impulse pressed to the goal of a more beautiful social order—which meant, in the New World, a union of Americans, freed from the covenant relationships of the parochial past and united by the love which God's American children bore for one another."[36] In retrospect the final result of salvation, conversion, and regeneration, for both the revivalists and antirevivalists, differed little. The revivals ultimately served to strengthen the glorious New England religious tradition and extend it as they crept south into the Middle and Southern colonies in the following decades. Both revivalists and established clergy desired a similar product—a community of believers who maintained pious lives, peaceful relationships, and charitable behavior. Both camps ultimately benefited from the Awakening by increased church membership.

But the religious and political spheres were partially intertwined in colonial America, and comparisons between unqualified, impious, or insensitive ecclesiastical authority and insensitive or corrupt political appointees resonated with many American colonists. Whitefield's perspective on unconverted ministers, articulated as early as 1739, provided a pattern of thought that facilitated opposition to political authority that would emerge later in the century. His forceful and logical articulation of a stance toward corrupt clerical authority homogenized the thought of other revival ministers. Whitefield prescribed the adoption of a set of beliefs for those who held no strong opinions and supplied precise and fundamental argument formulas (first-stage rhetorical topics) that would later energize and inform Revolutionary polemics.

## WHITEFIELD'S RECEPTION IN AMERICA

Whitefield's rhetoric of community facilitated a return to piety and, for the first time, encouraged identification among members of the inter-colonial Christian community regardless of one's denominational heritage. But such change is practically meaningless if confined to Boston, Northampton, and Philadelphia. Was the Awakening truly "Great?" Jon Butler does not believe that the revival was nearly as extensive as was claimed. He critiques the historical account and argues that later evangelical writers, who wished to place an emphasis on events that did not warrant it, "invented" the Great Awakening.[37] However, Frank Lambert recently dedicated an entire book to challenging Butler's notion, demonstrating that the revivals were indeed extensive and recognized as such by their critics as well as those conducting and writing about them.[38] Patricia Bonomi also argued for a broad-based increase in church attendance in many communities in the decades after the revivals: "Churches were being built or enlarged everywhere, as one of the basic institutions of a stabilizing society took its place in the hierarchy of power."[39] A cautious view would reintegrate revival efficacy to a certain extent for which even Butler leaves space.

If one were to trust the written record, it would seem that widespread opinions regarding Whitefield in America by 1741 were equally divided. However, many of Whitefield's supporters and followers did not publish their views, creating a bias in favor of those who did publish. But even a review of publications from the mid-eighteenth century, by Whitefield's contemporaries as well as his critics, testifies to the popularity and controversy his enterprise engendered. They inform us that, whether one liked it or not, his reception was widespread and warm. Status quo leaders must have been asking themselves, where might this movement lead? as they considered the political fallout of what was shaping up to be a significant shift in colonial religion.

According to Gillies, "Wherever he went, prodigious numbers flocked to hear him. His audiences often consisted of four or five thousand; and in populous places . . . the concourse was so great that they have been computed to be from twenty to thirty thousand."[40] News of his arrival traveled fast in the colonies. Upon preaching to two thousand people in Neshaminy, Pennsylvania, in 1739, Whitefield wrote in his journal, "It is surprising how such bodies of people, so scattered abroad, can be gathered at so short a warning."[41] Crowds easily expanded to eight thousand in Philadelphia or New York and reached twenty thousand in Boston. Nathan Cole's account of his frenzied and hurried journey to hear a sermon eloquently attests to Whitefield's ability to draw a crowd on short notice. Such excitement in a society, which had little to amuse its citizens, further engendered interest in his meetings. Why would anyone miss Whitefield when he came to town in 1740? His meetings were the place to be!

One does not have to rely solely on Whitefield's own accounts or the opinions of his friends to evaluate his impact. Evidence for his reception into the hearts of the people can also be drawn from the writings and opinions of his critics. Charles Chauncy derisively wrote:

> Accordingly, about two years since, he was received as though he had been an *Angel of God; yea, a God come down in the likeness of Man.* He was strangely flocked after by all Sorts of Persons, and that much admired by the *Vulgar,* both *great* and *small.* . . . The grand subject of conversation was Mr. Whitefield, and the whole Business of the Town to run, from Place to Place, to hear him preach.[42]

Edward Wigglesworth, who called Whitefield's effect "more extensive and pernicious than any man could have imagined," penned another revealing statement: "Perhaps there is not now a single town in this province, and, probably not in Connecticut, in which there are not numbers of people whose minds are under strong prejudices against their ministers."[43] Whitefield's opponents would not have spent the money or dedicated the time to oppose him if his influence had been confined to mere corners of colonial society.

The pervasive publication and sale of his printed materials also attests to his widespread reception. By the end of his American tour, Whitefield's writings were circulating throughout the colonies. The bibliographic record lists 133 American publications in the 1740s, consisting of 64 sermon editions or collections, 31 journal editions, 34 publications wherein he defended his doctrine, and 4 works accounting for his ministry finances.[44] If only one thousand copies were printed per edition, these editions of Whitefield's writings constituted no fewer (probably more) than 133,000 individual works—one for approximately every five adult colonists![45] This does not include whatever was excerpted or reprinted in the newspapers—a common practice in the 1740s.

In regard to his rhetoric, Whitefield introduced elements and terms that simplified that which was mysterious and reified that which was intangible. The first element of Whitefield's rhetoric of community, the new birth, distilled the abstract notions of the conversion experience, previously expressed in an educated vocabulary foreign to the people, into a metaphor, rich with meaning that, in John Gillies' view, "the dullest and most ignorant could not but understand."[46] The term transformed the notion of conversion from an experience (indicated by the ending " ion," denoting an act or condition) into a noun (a thing to be possessed), in this case community membership with long-term consequences. This grammatical shift served to crystallize what had been an abstract conception—and change that reaches into a community's grammar is profound indeed! The term "new birth" also implied entering into a new metaphysical (or physical) reality. It was a rite of passage from the secular world (dominated by the devil through materialism, sin, and secular thought) into the kingdom of heaven—from a realm of evil into a realm of good. The new birth nonmetaphorically denoted the legal adoption into an ecumenical religious community that arguably supplied a foundation for a portion of the later American Whigs. Equally critical is that Whitefield presented Christianity as a choice. The offer of that choice placed emphasis on individuals, calling them to make decisions regardless of the effect on the greater society.[47]

A second element of the Awakening conceptual system is embodied in the term "regeneration," which implied an act or process of purification or the process of transforming one to thinking and acting piously. The term presumes the new birth and accounts for the behavioral transformation from evil to good that necessarily followed a genuine conversion. Regeneration provided the evidence for the new birth and warranted Whitefield's condemnation of any clergy who lived impious lives. After Whitefield's 1740 tour and the release of his sermon collection by Franklin, other ministers published sermons about regeneration, showing that the term was circulating widely among the colonial society.[48] Up to 1738, an average of one sermon every other year had been published with the term "regeneration" in the title, but after Whitefield's publication of *On Regeneration* in 1739, the publishing record shows a tenfold increase to five sermons per year until 1744, then a decrease back to a sermon every other year thereafter.

The third element of Whitefield's system was a simplified notion of the Holy Spirit as characterized by several terms. After acquiring the new birth, the Spirit "indwelt" the true believer, actually entering the body, initiating and effecting regeneration. The term "indwell" was understood in the mid-eighteenth century as "[t]he abiding of God or the Divine Spirit in the heart or soul."[49] Additionally, the noun "common privilege," a "right" that all believers possessed, provided a powerful strategy for winning people to the revival movement. This was perhaps the most potent term in Whitefield's verbal constellation regarding the Holy Spirit, drawing upon the notions of British natural law and natural rights, and seems to be peculiar to Whitefield's rhetoric. These terms called upon "common knowledge and accepted opinions," as Aristotle advised for effective persuasion, to blend political philosophy with religious belief, providing Whitefield's audience the necessary background to make an informed judgment on the role of the Spirit in the theological debate.[50] Based on their inherent conceptions of English natural law, his English audiences could quickly and easily side with Whitefield. Furthermore, after the term "common privilege" circulated with a religious meaning, it became a notion that translated back into the rhetoric of the Revolution with an increased force. The non-English settlers did not possess the political heritage of the British that allowed them to appreciate natural rights. But by adapting the concepts to religion, the terms and ideas they signified could then easily slide back to the political sphere with a substantially increased potency for non-English settlers.

Debate over the doctrines and practices of the revival circulated around the rite of passage and the means of possessing the Spirit, not about the reality of these notions. Garden, too, believed there was an "us" and "them" and "in" and "out." Where he differed with Whitefield was in believing that he was in and Whitefield was out. By not challenging the implied doctrines, but merely arguing about how one knows them, Garden reinforced the distinctions. Certainly the colonists were aware of the low estate of religion in the aftermath of thirty years of jeremiads (sermons warning of divine judgment) from preachers and the poor attendance of religious services. Whitefield's assertion that the status quo ministers were not really true believers and had caused the impious culture provided a logical explanation for the problem. For the people, it offered a rationale for well-documented ministerial hypocrisy and renewed the vision that a "true religion" existed, thus disarming cynical attitudes toward religion.

Identity, based in genuine Christianity, emerged as a fundamental issue as revival converts disassociated themselves with previous cultural connections and reestablished their identity with like-minded converts. Whitefield's rhetoric of community provided the arguments needed to partially deconstruct various identities and reconstruct them into a more unified one based on religious consubstantiality. As Fukuyama noted, "American culture is very different from European cultures, which are firmly wedded to 'blood and soil.'"[51] Whitefield's rhetoric of community transcended the "blood and soil," supporting the transitional identity with higher religious values. But, by accepting transcendent religious values, the colonists did not abandon their culture; they merely modified it. And these were modifications identical to those made by other religious and national groups that assimilated and were inclined to accept Whitefield's rhetoric. This identity-altering impetus was occurring at the precise time that consumerism was exerting its own influence on identity formation, providing two powerful constraints upon identity that worked pari passu within people groups that were in identity transition.

Once a community of awakened believers adopted this new aspect of identity, it provided implied doctrines that would operate as unquestioned "first principles" and would syllogistically steer subsequent thought not just in the religious sphere, but also in other spheres—*including politics*. Rhetorically speaking, the implied doctrines of the Awakening conceptual system became the first-stage rhetorical topics. Consequently, converts from many diverse groups would develop similar political attitudes to accompany their consubstantial identities guided by these new patterns of thought.

Physically, Whitefield brought people together. Living in their religious or ethnic communities and neighborhoods, the colonists did not often have a cause that would call them all to one physical location to consider some issue. While representatives often met for colonial governmental business, the citizens did not. Whitefield changed that pattern and established a venue where people in the community came on equal footing to consider his message.[52] The importance of breaking down the physical barriers between people must not be overlooked. People tend to trust those with whom they spend time and share beliefs. Whitefield's events provided an initial experience where people of diverse national and religious origins had the opportunity of common worship, encouraging the development of other intercolonial public venues. And it was the egalitarian nature of these venues that threatened the status quo colonial political leadership. Their authority did not legally extend to these public meetings (or especially into the public sphere of print) if meetings remained religious in their nature. They could neither prevent nor control the content of the revival meetings. Here was a behemoth rising up in society that was beginning to break out of civil and rational constraints. Already several people had died at a meeting, and with regularity people were driven by passion into "unreasonable" behavior.

In addition to promoting a sense of community based on physical proximity, the new relationships among colonists also helped fuel the explosion of commercialism throughout the latter half of the eighteenth century. As Fukuyama explained, "A people's ability to maintain a shared 'language of good and evil' is critical to the creation of trust, social capital, and all other positive economic benefits."[53] Trust, between individuals and associations, ensures that economic (as well as other) partnerships can develop and thus paves the way for large-scale organizational cooperation. Jennifer Mercieca has pointed out that recent theories addressing the evolution of American nationalism all posit trust as an essential factor, stating, "[T]here could have been no nation without trust."[54] Fukuyama also wrote, "When membership in a church extracts a high price in terms of emotional commitment and changes in lifestyle, it creates a strong sense of moral community among its members."[55] Whitefield's role in this process was to draw people into these religious organizations and instill in them a common vocabulary, sense of morality, and a conceptual system that assisted in their development of trust.

As a result of this rhetoric of community, the class distinction between ministers and parishioners dissolved—especially as Whitefield argued that counterfeit ministers were guiltier than apostate parishioners of promoting vice. Whitefield elevated the status of the common people within the Awakening conceptual system. Here is another location where the revival pushed against the boundaries of the social hierarchy. Features that previously elevated an individual in the social order—birth, education, and wealth—were suddenly subordinated to a kind of piety rooted in the conversion experience.

Political boundaries were stretched as well. If religious doctrine can be understood as foundation for political ideologies, then one should not be surprised to find political fears embedded in what appears on the surface to be a doctrinal dispute.[56] Authoritarian rulers favor an authoritarian-style religion to instill a reverence for leadership in the populace. Thus, the authoritarian Anglican practices found a nice ideological fit with political leanings that supported the monarchy and class hierarchies. The Dissenters could not afford to have their destiny in the hands of a monarchy that, by converting to Catholicism as did the Stuart dynasty, could turn against them. Thus, dissenting churches, which placed an emphasis on parish rule outside the purview of a hierarchy of bishops, embraced the democratic principles of parliamentary rule. And though the New Englanders were distanced from political struggles in England, they did read about them and feel the effects of shifting policies. And as emigration rates rose and renewed conflict with the French approached, the political turmoil of Europe quickly crossed the Atlantic to shape events in the colonies.

The Congregationalists (Puritans) in America had occasionally persecuted non-Puritan elements themselves, forcing many to settle in Rhode Island until the British Parliament passed the Act of Toleration in 1689, ensuring religious diversity throughout the empire. Ironically, the Puritan Congregationalists, who left Europe to sidestep the periodic persecution from the Church of England and the king, began a process of "Anglicization" embodied in the *Massachusetts Proposals of 1705*, which extended privileges of church governance, including voting rights, to those who could not testify to a state of grace.[57] No longer was power consolidated in the hands of the "saints," but now power was shared with other civil-minded people who were nominal Congregationalists. New England's church-state society was evolving into one where the Puritan Church began to resemble the Anglican Church in England, where church membership was no longer determined by piety, where connections and influence enabled a person to climb the social ladder.

Within a democratic society, any religious group that focuses on divisive issues and claims exclusivity to "truth" is eventually marginalized.[58] But the issues on which the revivalists were focusing were legitimate and the growing pervasiveness of the revival made a majority out of the revivalists. The established Congregational and Anglican clergy could not ignore or ridicule them out of the mainstream, forcing a confrontation with the revivalists in the public sphere. For members of the established power structure, everything was at stake. The popularity of revival beliefs and their direct assault on the social order pushed the anti-revival clergy into a corner where they were forced to fight back. The established clergy took the lead to condemn the revival, keeping any partnership they had with the political leadership behind the scenes.

Underneath the religious debate we find political views motivating groups to support or oppose the revivals. To be sure, Whitefield, the Tennents, Edwards, Garden, Chauncy, and other colonial ministers were genuinely concerned for the welfare of the church and true doctrine, but changes in an entire society do not come without political reverberations, especially when empowered by a rhetoric that posits ontic categories of "us" and "them." Whitefield consistently claimed to be a Calvinist, a belief system that provided a strong foundation for Whig interests, perhaps best revealed by John Knox's statement to Queen Mary that "right religion takes neither origin nor authority from worldly princes but from the Eternal God alone."[59] While Calvinist respect for the prerogatives of God could completely displace their deference to a monarch if they were forced to make a choice, the Calvinists could still support and obey a good king who feared God and treated the subjects properly. Ironically, it was Arminianism that truly nurtured the democratic impulse and provided the ideology that would encourage sedition. Calvinism maintained an authoritative theology in which God held all power of determining who received the new birth, as a king who held the power to grant favors. But the Arminian tenet of universal redemption, that all could find the new birth if they chose to approach God and repent, handed the prerogative of salvation over to the individual. This empowerment of the individual strongly bolstered democratic thinking in church membership, in church governance, and in civil governance.

Theologically, Whitefield was more closely aligned with the American denominations than he was with the Anglicans. Yet he consistently built his sermons on Calvinist teachings about the depravity of man and unconditional election, which he supported with selective quotes from the Thirty-Nine Articles of Anglican theology. Nevertheless, due to his outdoor preaching and emphasis on the conversion experience, his critics identified him with the Methodist movement, a charge Whitefield wore as a badge of honor. Arminian or Calvinist theologies notwithstanding, Methodism grew in scope and was continually beset with accusations of social disruption and sedition from the Anglicans. Whitefield was caught in the middle. On the one hand he wished to defend Methodism to support his close Methodist friends, bolster the revival in England, and preserve his own privilege to preach outdoors, while on the other he affirmed the Anglican Church to maintain his official status as a minister. As Whitefield's enterprise evolved, he fashioned a theology with its intellectual roots in Calvinism and its practice in Arminian Methodism. Whitefield, in his paradox-filled enterprise, effectively practiced "universal redemption" in his revival meetings by encouraging "enthusiasm" and then suggesting to his auditors that God's call to election was manifest in their emotional responses.[60] He then offered a choice to his listeners to take action to receive the salvation offered by God. Thus, the occasional accusations against Whitefield for being an Arminian were warranted.

The result of this theology (Whitefield called it *Moderate Calvinism*), which walked a line between uncompromising Calvinists and nominalists, was that Whitefield affirmed the monarchy and the Anglican Church while his preaching served to nourish a democratic impulse in his converts. Whitefield stayed true to this position, preaching up loyalty to the king, which effectively kept him out of trouble with civil authorities, and constantly haranguing his audiences on the choice of new birth. His rhetorical skills helped him to navigate between Calvinism and Arminianism and to fashion his position that supported the government in word while it undermined it in deed.

Recognizing the "us" and "them" categories the revival was establishing, Garden and others could sense where Whitefield's practice was leading. And as the New Lights and New Sides became more politically active, the creation of new discursive contexts combined with an emphasis on individual conversion into a community of "us" ultimately undermined American authority structures by portraying those in power as "them." A situation was developing that can only be seen as explosive. In the final analysis, the implied doctrines of New Light theology would bolster the evolving republican ideology that sought local democratic control of civil affairs and freedom from monarchial or parliamentary intrusion.

# CHAPTER 5

# TOWARD COLONIAL UNIFICATION

As George Whitefield left America to return to England, all seemed
well to him except the conflict with established clergy regarding
enthusiasm and clerical conversion, but the situation rapidly shifted.
The controversy over the revival deepened when subsequent itinerant preachers exacerbated harsh feelings by continuing to reproach
unconverted ministers and encourage their parishioners to join New
Light churches. And as parishioners left established Congregational
and Anglican churches for the New Light congregations, the antirevivalists viewed the defections as the first step in the dissolution of
colonial society. Bonomi reports that "[f]rom the 1740s on, the separating brethren grew in number until Congregationalists throughout
the North joined Presbyterian thousands in the Middle colonies in
open rebellion against the 'spiritual Tyranny' of the traditional church
authority."[1] Whitefield would not be aware of the depth and stakes of
the growing controversy until his return to America in late 1744. But
until then, with Whitefield back in the British Isles for the next four
years, changes both in England and America constrained him to alter
the character and focus of his enterprise, alterations that would subsequently be offered to Christian community in the colonies. Whitefield
held far more influence there than anyone realized, and it would not
take long for shifts in his enterprise to suggest similar directions of
growth in American society.

In this chapter we will examine how Whitefield's enterprise generated controversy with friends and foes on both sides of the Atlantic,
and we will see how he judiciously managed that conflict by fashion-
ing middle-of-the-road positions in theology and politics. It's not that
he completely resolved conflicts with his enemies, but if progress is
measured by retaining his hold on the public mind, he succeeded.
Whitefield's unmistakable and irreversible shift in focus for his enterprise, from a strictly religious focus to one that prescribed a moderate

political ideology to his parishioners, would eventually goad the New Light community a significant step closer to a distinct American political ideology. As this chapter moves the story forward, we will examine how Whitefield, even while absent, kept his name and ideas in the American public sphere. The chapter will also describe the conflict and constraints that forced him to soften his hard-line religious views and adopt an encompassing religious-republican ideology, and will show how these shifts began to influence American colonists.

## A PRESENCE DURING ABSENCE

After his American tour, having left the Awakening in the capable hands of Tennent and Edwards, Whitefield continued establishing parishes throughout the British Isles, but he was largely ignorant of the extent of the growing controversy regarding the American Awakening. In his mind, to maintain the solidarity of his American parish, he needed to ensure he was not forgotten while away in England. Augmenting his sermon publication, Whitefield used two further genres of literature to reveal his persona, explain the new birth, and address perceived problems. First were his autobiographical *Journals*, and second were letters to individuals that he released publicly.

For Americans who did not live in Boston, Savannah, Philadelphia, or other venues where Whitefield regularly preached, the most effective way to know him was through his writings. His intent in publications of sermons, letters of doctrinal defense, and journal editions was to build upon the foundation he established in the 1740 tour. Please recall that it took Whitefield nearly six months from the time Charles Wesley told him about the new birth until he felt he had achieved it. Even though Whitefield offered a choice, he still understood conversion as a process. Knowing that many people were in the midst of conversion, striving to implement the new birth in their own lives, and knowing that many others were struggling to purify their lives from secret sins, Whitefield wanted to facilitate their progress. Whitefield's *Journals* would provide examples of his own successful conversion and regeneration to encourage people to keep striving for the same.[2] In addition to his letters, the journal account clarified his doctrinal positions while defending the legitimacy of his revival meetings.

Just before returning to England, Whitefield had contracted to have his autobiographical *Journals* published throughout America and issued in editions from 1738 to 1744. These were not accounts of his current ministry in England after the second American tour (1741–1744), but of his childhood, education, early ministry, and the story of his coming to America. Released in chronological order, in eight editions, they provided a narrative of his travels and experiences, explained his motivations, bared his character, and argued for his divine anointing. The American public interpreted his *Journals* according to their predisposition toward him. As one author put it, Whitefield "became more beloved to his friends and more despised by his foes."[3] A self-aggrandizing tone permeates the *Journals* to an unmistakable extent. If one were to take it at face value, to oppose Whitefield would be to oppose God. But his critics were skeptical and, of course, interpreted these claims as arrogance.

The *Journals* open with the story of his childhood where he compares his birth to that of Jesus: they were both born in an inn. Whitefield next describes his corrupt youth up to the time of his conversion experience. Along the way he makes references to having a great destiny:

> I can recollect very early movings of the blessed Spirit upon my heart, sufficient to satisfy me that God loved me with an everlasting love, and separated me even from my mother's womb, for the work to which He afterwards was pleased to call me.[4]

Whitefield reveals an early fascination with the clerical profession through his dreams about serving God. Throughout his story Whitefield interprets events as divinely orchestrated to guide him into the ministry, supplying arguments that God ordained his ministry.

The story of his early ministry resounds with providential guidance and blessing. In all the ministry events, God is the agent and Whitefield only does what he is bidden. Laced throughout the *Journals* are brief stories and events that evidence a divine calling upon his work. For example:

> I found uncommon manifestations granted me from above . . . the next day upon my return to London, in the first letter that I opened was a Bank Note of £10, sent from an unexpected hand as a present for myself, this encouraged me to go on doing good to others with a full assurance, that the Lord would not let me want.[5]

In several places he cites the biblical dictum that he must obey God rather than man as a warrant for stirring up trouble by criticizing established ministers. It is probable that Whitefield, already having some experience with controversy, knew he could not convince his critics. Instead, his aim was to convince various public groups to adopt his view. The impartial or naive reader, informed only by Whitefield's account, could easily side with Whitefield if pressed for a judgment.

The account of his conversion is not flattering, but he likely intended it to be an honest example of what anyone might expect who sought a conversion. Whitefield showed how his conversion involved great travail and climaxed at a distinct point in time. With his conversion as a pattern, those who left a Whitefield revival convinced that the new birth was real and necessary, and made the choice to achieve it, could read Whitefield's account and know what they might expect in their own conversion process.

His *Journals* were also crucial for developing a symbolic image, especially as he was normally traveling somewhere else. Rather than being forgotten, they maintained his virtual presence and enhanced his image by reporting his benevolence and successes under the rubric of his ecumenical spirit. He kept publishing the *Journals* through 1742 (issues of which were released as late as 1743–1744) when he intentionally stopped because versions were published without his permission and his forthrightness was liberally interpreted by his religious antagonists. In short, his polemical gain was being negated. A paucity of entries from 1744 to 1745 were written but not published until much later. After Whitefield stopped keeping a journal, accounts of his life must be accessed from his letters or from secondary accounts. He also largely quit publishing new sermons after 1742 and released only a handful after 1746.

Whitefield's *Journals* have been called "pioneering works of genius," and "the ideal vehicle for crafting a public image that could work in his absence."[6] They enhanced the colonists' memories of the 1740 tour to shape his public image into legendary proportions by telling the story of revival in all the other colonies in great detail, casting Whitefield in the best possible light. The *Journals* gave the public a window into Whitefield's personality. Hence, much of his symbolic role as an American icon developed in his absence—in print, through collective memories in an imagined reading community of revived converts.

One does not have to read deeply to see Whitefield's attempts at literary art. His descriptions of crossing the Atlantic are graphically written and were likely intended as a metaphor of the travail of the new birth and entrance into God's kingdom. Immediately after leaving Gibraltar, his ship encountered a storm on the way to Savannah. After the storm broke, Whitefield exclaimed, "Blessed be God, this morning the storm began to blow over, and light broke in upon my soul," echoing his response to his own tumultuous new birth.[7] Whitefield also found illustrations of God's existence and providence in nature for his readers. On one occasion two waterspouts threatened their ship, but miraculously vanished. Whitefield takes the opportunity to declare that God spoke to the sea to be calm and protected the ship's occupants.[8] A society that was familiar with John Bunyan's *Pilgrim's Progress* would have had no trouble interpreting Whitefield's self-described odyssey in terms of Christian conversion.

The community of the ship became a microcosm of society during the Atlantic crossing. Whitefield, the ship's minister, performed all the duties during the three-month voyage that he might if ministering in a parish. On the voyage, he preached regularly to the sailors, encouraging them not to swear or drink, and he expressed satisfaction that during one gale they did not curse as much while handling the ship. Whitefield also conducted three marriage ceremonies, sat at the deathbed of several passengers and sailors, ministered to a condemned sailor convicted of murdering another, and assisted in the discipline of an obstinate lad. Whitefield, with the permission of his "master," ordered the boy tied up until he could repeat the fifty-first psalm, which he did! Near the end of the journey Whitefield even baptized a newborn infant. The archetypal metaphor of the new birth that structures the entire journal story found receptive minds in the American colonists. Whitefield's theology of the new birth eloquently articulated the experience of people who had made the trip to America. Coming to a "new world," they left behind European politics and class structures to enter a land where everyone had to struggle for survival.

## WHITEFIELD AND WESLEY

Of Whitefield's miscellaneous writings published in his American absence, the most widely read was his response to John Wesley's embrace of Arminianism.[9] As defined before, Arminian theology promoted universal redemption, believing that people had a choice to approach God for salvation and that one's own efforts were effectual in regeneration. Even though his exhortations to hearers were pragmatically Arminian—encouraging them to come to Christ and receive salvation—Whitefield perhaps did not see the inconsistency, and he would never support the idea that regeneration could be effected by the individual. Arminian practice stood in stark contrast to the Calvinist doctrine of election, that people were predestined either for salvation or damnation and were powerless to purify themselves. Both theologies were promoted by various ministers in the Methodist movement. Whitefield's response to Wesley is significant in two ways: first, because it represented a defense of his doctrine from charges that he, too, was an Arminian (he usually defied efforts to label his ministry), and second because it distanced him from Londoners who adored the Wesleys. By publicly repudiating Arminian doctrine and evidencing his sincerity by risking the loss of a close friendship, Whitefield was able to silence American critics regarding any Arminian tendencies. But perhaps more importantly, his conflict with Wesley temporarily weakened his standing in England, turning his attention toward Scotland and finally back to America.

Whitefield's thirty-one page letter, written December 24, 1740, critiqued Wesley's sermon *Free Grace*, contending that Arminian doctrine was unscriptural and filled with logical inconsistencies. Whitefield immediately published the letter in Boston at the end of 1740 and then in Philadelphia, Hartford, and Charleston within a year. Although addressed to Mr. Wesley, it is evident that Whitefield intended the letter for the public and his other Arminian critics. If there was any doubt as to whom Whitefield directed the letter, its simultaneous publication all over America and in England attests to the larger audience. In fact, its immediate publication in Boston would have been three months before Wesley, who was in England, could have received it. This letter is typical of how Whitefield disputed with others, addressing a response to a specific individual but always distributing the work publicly.

Within the letter Whitefield considered statements from Wesley's published sermon *Free Grace* and either pointed out a logical fallacy or asserted an alternate interpretation of the scriptures Wesley used to warrant his claims. The letter was not solely intended to dissuade Wesley, but also those in America and England who leaned toward Wesley's position. In fact, Wesley was not moved by Whitefield's appeal, and the two men would not see eye to eye for many years.

In all probability Whitefield was not thinking about the political ramifications of theology as he wrote. The result of the letter was to continue to form his image and promote what he felt was true doctrine. But the political implications of the ensuing break between these two religious leaders would reverberate in the decades to come. Methodism, as a formal organization, would not fully infiltrate America until after the Revolution, after Wesley's English followers had established it as a legitimate denomination. For the time being, America would continue to develop under the influence of New Light revivalism while English religious reform followed the Wesleys. In England, Methodists were subsequently beset with accusations of sedition and had to defend themselves to preserve their right to meet publicly, yet they were careful to maintain the social order and largely stayed clear of English politics. Paradoxically, American New Light theology, following Whitefield's leading, adopted the Arminian practice of choice while it insisted that God had actually predestined the converts and was divinely orchestrating the trajectory of colonial society. And this Arminian *practice*, embedded within Whitefield's New Light theology, furnished a potent democratic impulse.

The release of his *Journals* and the publication of his sermons and other works kept Whitefield in the fore of the "public sphere" during his physical absence, preparing American colonists for a third tour beginning in 1745.[10] Whitefield was no longer the stranger who toured in 1740, but was better known upon his return than when he left. The 1745 tour should have been simply a resumption of the prior one. However, before Whitefield was able to return, events in England forced him to mature, and the shifting religious and political scene in the British Empire invited his increased participation in political affairs.

## WHITEFIELD'S POLITICAL AWAKENING

In late 1739 Whitefield began corresponding with Ralph Erskine, a dissenting Scottish minister in Edinburgh, to schedule a tour of Scotland after his return from America.[11] Not really welcome in London because of his clash with Wesley, Whitefield decided to go to Scotland and initiate what eventually became his most successful ministry venue. However, a serious misunderstanding developed as the time for his first Scottish tour neared. Erskine and the other Scottish dissenters, supposing Whitefield was as religiously and politically radical as they were, expected Whitefield to join ranks with them. In April 1741, Erskine asked Whitefield to become a formal member of the dissenting presbytery (these were dissenters from the Scottish Presbyterians who themselves were dissenters from the Church of England), and as such Whitefield would be required to forfeit his Anglican priesthood and refrain from preaching in any pulpits but theirs. Whitefield recognized the ramifications, both short- and long-term, of joining the dissenters, and politely refused. He wrote back, requesting the use of dissenting pulpits to preach the new birth, hoping to receive support for his ministry as he received from American ministers.[12] On the night Whitefield arrived in Scotland he preached to a large, thrilled audience but afterward was immediately ushered to a meeting with the dissenting presbytery's leaders. Here they grilled him about doctrine and asked him to renounce his Anglican ordination and become a member of their associate presbytery, and again he declined. Whitefield realized that joining their group meant a move away from the mainstream of British Christianity and would ultimately reduce his audience sizes. Also, Whitefield probably weighed the political message it would send to align with the dissenters of Scotland, which had been a political hotspot for decades. He would be viewed as a political radical with sedition lurking in the wings of his ministry.

Erskine respected Whitefield's decision to remain an Anglican, but members of the associate presbytery in Scotland rejected him, perhaps due to anti-British political sentiments. In response, Whitefield allied himself with the established Scottish presbytery, which held a measure of respect, and from that point forward would steer away from linking his ministry with radicals anywhere. His theology, which valued the participation of every saint, presumed the Whig political views that favored a strong parliamentary hand in the affairs of the nation. In Whitefield's view, loyalty to the British Crown was rooted in the Crown's commitment to Protestantism and *religious toleration*, a reform that had been wrested from an earlier king by a Whig-controlled parliament. After clarifying his position with regard to Erskine and his associate presbytery, Whitefield continued the Scottish tour with results that surpassed his popularity and effectiveness in either England or America.

Whitefield necessarily chose middle-of-the-road political and doc-trinal positions in order to hold his widespread appeal. In instituting his ecumenical version of Protestantism as the spiritual expression for an empire, he had to think politically and prescribe a political ideol-ogy that would maintain stability. A nation guided by a parliament would provide the only possibility for groups like the Scots to par-ticipate. A monarchial-controlled government was too risky, especially with "popish plots" afoot and a Catholic "pretender" descended from the brother of Charles II waiting in France for an opportune moment to return to England.[13] An approaching French-backed rebellion led by the pretender would originate in Scotland, and one can wonder if it might have had more support from Scottish Lowlanders if not for the Protestant revival.

In addition to recognizing that the dissenting road led toward the periphery of society and political radicalism, Whitefield faced several other events that helped him to mature and approach his enterprise more soberly. First was his union with Elizabeth James, a widow ten years his elder. After returning from Scotland, Whitefield continued preaching throughout England but was thinking seriously about mar-riage. At the time Whitefield and Elizabeth met, she was in love with Howell Harris, Whitefield's Welsh evangelist friend. But Harris wished to remain single, and knowing that Whitefield was thinking of mar-riage, Harris introduced Elizabeth to him, hoping George would win her affection. After four days of "negotiation," they decided to marry, although love was probably not included at first.[14] They were married within two weeks. One is tempted to ponder Whitefield's motivations in marrying her. The age difference and her name, the same name as George's mother, suggest that his attraction to her might have been founded in a desire for a motherly figure in his life. In addition to the maturation that occurs when a young man marries, undoubtedly she provided a positive influence on him, helping him to face his fears and perhaps reign in some of his penchant for self-aggrandizement.

Elizabeth and George soon had a son for whom George held high hopes of one day inheriting his own ministry, but he died at age four months. It was a significant blow to Whitefield, who wrote:

And then, as he died in the house wherein I was born, he was taken and laid in the church where I was baptized, first communicated, and first preached. All this you may easily guess threw me into every solemn and deep reflection, and I hope deep humiliation . . . yet I hope what happened before his birth, and since at his death, hath taught me such lessons, as, if duly improved, may render his mistaken parent more cautious, more sober-minded, more experienced in Satan's devices, and consequently more useful in his future labours to the church of God.[15]

They never had another child, but Elizabeth's four miscarriages indicated their desire for one. She accompanied him on his next trip to America but remained in England thereafter due to her permanently weakened health after the last miscarriage.

If Whitefield did learn lessons, he soon had use of them. Increasingly vigorous opposition to the revival movement had threatened Whitefield, the Wesleys, and other Methodist preachers with crowd violence.[16] Notwithstanding his Anglican loyalty, Whitefield experienced equal dangers as unruly groups regularly formed on the outskirts of his outdoor preaching events and disrupted the services. From time to time, violent crowds gathered at the house where he was staying and demanded that he come out. Passively submitting, as he supposed the apostles responded to persecution, he turned himself over and reasoned with them on the way to the place of abuse, usually talking his way out of harm. But on one occasion he was thrown into a lime pit (a life-threatening event) and then taken and thrown into a creek (to wash off the lime so he would not die).[17] Whitefield's publicist and financial supporter William Seward was killed by one such mob.

Exacerbating the violence, the London bishops turned a blind eye and were even suspected of conspiring to support the violence since it ultimately met their goal of silencing the Methodists. But a month after the death of his son, Whitefield abandoned his passivity and took several men to court. After a particularly nasty encounter at an outdoor event, he obtained the names of some ringleaders and prosecuted them. During the trial it became clearly evident that political motivations were at the heart of the persecution, not religious ones. The defendants' lawyer argued that the Methodists would "infect and hurt the people," that it was right for any private person to try to stop them, and whoever did so "was a friend to his country." Whitefield's lawyer countered, "Rioters were not to be reformers; and that his Majesty had no where put the reins of government into the hands of mobbers, or made them judge or jury." The judge ruled in favor of Whitefield, reminding the defendants "of the dreadful ill consequences of rioting at any time, much more at such a critical time as this; that rioting was the fore-runner of, and might end in, rebellion."[18] Although minor harassment continued, the ruling, combined with Whitefield's publicizing of it, put an effective end to violent persecutions.[19] After letting his malefactors sweat over a fine of two hundred pounds, he charitably dropped the charges with an eye toward enhancing his public image. Not one to miss an opportunity to advance his cause in the public, Whitefield wrote and published a pamphlet describing the trial to publicize the Methodist victory and thwart violence in other locales. This pragmatic response, contrasting with Whitefield's previous submissive toleration, verified Whitefield's resolve to be more sober-minded in managing his ministry. After forgiving the rioters, the now aggressive Whitefield turned his attention to the suspected source of the persecution: the Anglican bishops.

## Anglican Opposition to Whitefield

The British Anglicans felt threatened by the growing Methodist movement for any number of reasons—jealousy, doctrinal differences, resentment at being charged as unconverted, political differences, genuine fears of sedition—and took actions to frustrate it by associating the movement with seditious movements of the past. The Anglican hierarchy also resented the extempore preaching, the extempore prayers, and the new hymns of the Methodists, all of which were outside the purview of their control, even though the Wesleys and Whitefield were Anglican priests. Through repetitious reinforcement, the liturgy, approved prayers, and hymns of the Church of England all worked to shape the thinking of its parishioners, and the Anglican bishops recognized the threat that new forms of liturgy, prayer, and music held for the authoritarian forms of thought. With their strong ties to Tory interests in British political affairs, their motive for opposing the Methodists was probably rooted in a fear of another civil war rather than clever sectarian tactics.

An anonymous pamphlet was circulated among upper-class circles in 1744 that specifically attacked Whitefield's theology and speculated that his brand of enthusiasm would result in social disorder of the kind Britain experienced when Charles I was beheaded. But Whitefield countered with a publicly released letter to the bishop of London that supplied evidence that one or more bishops authored the pamphlet.

Highlighting the conspiratorial nature of the pamphlet, Whitefield pointed out that it "had been read in the societies of London and Westminster, and handed about in a private manner to particular friends, with strict orders to part with [it] to no one" (i.e., keep it in the hands of the upper class).[20] He explained that the purpose of the pamphlet was "to represent the proceedings of the Methodists as dangerous to the church and state, in order to procure an act of parliament against them."[21] Anxiety that Charles Edward (the Young Pretender) of the deposed House of Stuart would invade England was rising and inflated any supposed threat to political order. There were still many elements in the British Isles that would declare allegiance to the House of Stuart should a deposed heir arrive in the country and attempt a coup. With the nation on edge over political struggles, Whitefield understood the severity of the charges—that more violence could ensue as a fearful populace reacted against the enthusiasts. Worse yet, the danger to order could be realized from another direction as radical dissenters, dissatisfied with the current administration, might become politically active, hoping for a return to a Cromwellian form of government.

In response, as a public figure that held a high degree of influence in the empire, Whitefield publicized his political views. Finding himself between accusations of being a subversive Methodist on one side and his genuine loyalty to the king on the other, Whitefield fashioned a position that would protect his right to hold outdoor meetings while it affirmed his support of the political order. Whitefield set his pen to paper, publishing three times between March and August 1744 to refute the Anglican propaganda.[22] First, Whitefield established that the Methodists were neither a sect nor promoted separatism, declaring them to be *"orthodox, well-meaning ministers, and members of the church of England, and loyal subjects to his Majesty King George."* Countering any claim of personal disloyalty, Whitefield wrote, "I profess myself a zealous friend to his present Majesty King *George*, and the present administration. Where-ever I go, I think it my duty to pray for, and to preach up obedience to him, and all that are set in authority under him, in the most explicit manner." Then he extended that assertion of loyalty to the other Methodists, saying:

> And I believe, should it ever come to the trial, the poor despised Methodists, who love his Majesty out of *principle*, would cleave close to him in the

most imminent danger, when others that adhere to him, only for *prefer-ments*, perhaps might not appear altogether so hearty.

Here is a direct barb aimed at Tory sycophants that reveals the Whig political sentiments of Whitefield. Suggestions of corruption like this resonated with beliefs that many commoners held about members of the upper class.

Whitefield insists that he and the Methodists had ministered within the bounds of the law: "My Lords, I know of no law of the state that we have broken, and therefore we have not incurred the displeasure of the civil power." Then he maintains that they had no intentions of establishing a separate sect: "As yet, we see no sufficient reason to leave the church of *England*, and turn dissenters; neither will we do it till we are thrust out." He underscored their intent to remain Anglicans by a metaphor that characterized their practice as reform: "When a ship is leaky, prudent sailors, that value the cargo, will not leave it to sink, but rather continue in it so long as they can, to help pump out the water."

Whitefield squanders no words in interpreting the intention of the anonymous pamphlet, writing that it portrayed the Methodists as "seditious sectaries, disloyal persons, who, under pretence of tender consciences, have, or may contrive insurrections." He then states that the author may as well "tax the Methodists with high treason." Next, in light of the Act of Toleration, Whitefield contrasts Anglican oppo-sition to Methodism with the leniency that Quakers enjoyed under King Charles. Whitefield asks, "[M]ay not the loyal ministers and members of the church of *England*, nay, protestant Dissenting teachers also, expect under the more gentle and moderate reign of his pres-ent Majesty King *George*, who, as I have been informed, has declared, 'there shall be no persecution in his days.'" Throughout the heart of his response, Whitefield carefully dissected the arguments in the anon-ymous pamphlet, showing the inconsistencies in the writer's logic and offering evidence that refuted the writer's claims. In closing, Whitefield directly confronted the charge that Methodists were turning the com-moners against the king. He writes, "I think it my duty to invite, and preach to this rabble in all places where providence shall send me, at this season; that I may warn them against the dreadful effects of popish principles, and exhort them to exert their utmost endeavors to keep out a popish Pretender from ever sitting upon the *English* throne."

Rather than simply claiming that Methodists were not seditious, he argued that the Methodists encouraged loyalty to the current king in their meetings.

In Whitefield, the bishops faced an able interlocutor who knew enough history and politics to highlight the hypocrisy of their claims and make a case against their motive for opposing the Methodists. And in light of the events in the next two years, when Bonnie Prince Charlie did return from France to make a bid for the throne, one can further wonder if more people might have backed the rebellion had Whitefield and the Methodists not been steering them toward favoring the House of Hanover.

His open affirmation of the established government would continue the rest of his life, though he would fight for reform of his own institution. Yet in defending his freedoms within the Anglican order and calling them to reform, he set an example of resistance that others would mimic; others without the rhetorical skill needed to carve out and maintain a middle position.

## An Assassination Attempt

After this battle of writings, someone attempted to silence Whitefield by other means. In a pub one evening, a would-be assassin boasted that he would kill Whitefield, and had his friends not confiscated his sword, he might have succeeded in the deed. The man came to see Whitefield later that night under the pretense of desiring spiritual guidance. Whitefield admitted him to his room at the inn where he was staying, and they began conversing. But the man soon began to swear and violently beat Whitefield with a brass-headed cane. An accomplice quickly arrived to assist in the murder, but Whitefield's cries and the cries of the landlady and her daughter warded them off. The attack left serious wounds and aggravated his precarious health. It took several months for Whitefield to fully recover.[23] While publicly Whitefield attributed the attempted murder to the devil, it perhaps confirmed in his mind the prudence of supporting the mainstream of religious and civil leadership. His publications stating his political sentiments were still in press at this point.

If we examine the assassination attempt in the context of the summer of 1744, an interesting picture emerges. The crowd violence was generally intended to intimidate and injure, but not to kill. If a Methodist was killed, as was Seward, that was not necessarily part of the plan. A violent crowd could easily dispatch its victim if desired, and any intent to murder would not be carried on in a public setting in broad daylight. Generally, Whitefield was loved by commoners when there was nobody to rouse them with false accusations. It is difficult to support the notion that the would-be assassin was just an offended sinner who didn't like Whitefield's preaching. The assassination attempt was different. It was premeditated. The perpetrator had gone to a pub, likely to get drunk and steel his resolve. He was carrying his sword. Perhaps his guilty conscience, wishing to be foiled, let his tongue slip after a few drinks, and his friends did not like his idea. One has to wonder what the man's motive was. There was an accomplice who apparently was not at the bar but showed up at the crime scene in time to assist with the attempt. This is a strong argument for premeditation and conspiracy. Who might have been behind it? Whitefield had already dropped the charges against the mob ringleaders, so presumably they would have no strong motivation to harm him.

The attempt occurred just a few weeks before Whitefield published a second letter to the bishops defending the Methodists. The compelling evidence and arguments Whitefield presented in the first letter cast the bishops in a negative light, and he rubbed the letter's effect in with a rhetorical force they could not match. Moreover, he published his letters and distributed them nationwide and across the Atlantic while the bishops' anonymous pamphlet only received a limited hand-to-hand distribution. Could a small cabal of Anglican loyalists have conspired to silence Whitefield once and for all before the second letter was released? Any case against the Anglicans is clearly circumstantial and could never be proven. But since this incident so clearly breaks the pattern of previous violence, since the Anglican leaders had already been exposed for inciting mob violence, and considering its timing in the midst of theological and political controversy, historians have grounds to suspect an Anglican-based conspiracy to assassinate Whitefield.

As the arguments in the court case demonstrate, Whitefield's struggle with the Anglicans was clearly not about theology, but about influence over the public mind. Whitefield's letters directly address the civil and political implications of Methodist enterprises. He champions their right to meet publicly and assures his readers their intentions are not seditious. But at this critical point in British history, just a year before the Jacobite Rebellion, the Anglicans had a difficult time believing the Methodists were not a threat.

The sum of these events—Whitefield's recognition of where the dissenting road led, his marriage to Elizabeth James, his son's death, mob and Anglican opposition, the need to support the current political establishment, and the attempt on his life—all contributed tangibly to Whitefield's move away from the radical end of the religious spectrum toward the mainstream of British society. Whitefield had no wish to become a martyr. At this point in his ministry, his goal was to have the largest audiences possible and the highest degree of acceptance among existing denominations and churches. Such a goal would not be achieved if he were identified with the Dissenters—not to mention that he wished to stay alive. His choice to move to the mainstream was pragmatic and did not require that he compromise his beliefs. He could still call Anglicans back to their roots and encourage other denominations to return to their own theological orthodoxy birthed from the Protestant Reformation.

Henceforth, Whitefield stopped generalizing entire denominations as unconverted. He no longer publicly attacked unconverted ministers in general, but only criticized particular threatening doctrines of specific ministers and decried intellectual forays from the Enlightenment that he sensed were permeating and polluting the church. Most importantly, Whitefield would be a vocal supporter of George II and the established government, which, incidentally, was largely under Whig control. Whitefield unwaveringly defended the right of any religious group to hold religious meetings outside the purview and control of established denominational authority. These shifts in his enterprise would serve him well as his future unfolded, but as he returned to America, the colonists were unaware of these changes within his outlook and ministry.

## A THEOLOGICAL AND SOCIAL RIFT

During Whitefield's American absence, Gilbert Tennent, at Whitefield's request, traveled to New England in 1742 for a brief period of itinerant preaching, generating increasing excitement about the revival and further provoking the established clergy with his thundering denunciations. His now-famous sermon *The Danger of an Uncon-*

*verted Ministry* was published the year after Whitefield had censured slumbering and unconverted ministers, and Tennent was admittedly inspired by Whitefield's teachings.[24] Tennent's latent effect was to exacerbate religious division in America by causing members of established churches to forsake congregations led by unconverted ministers and move to other congregations—a situation that greatly alarmed the New England establishment. Their misgivings about Whitefield's teachings were being spectacularly confirmed.

After Tennent returned home, James Davenport also found much popularity in Boston, preaching similar messages, but his excessive enthusiasm caused many Boston clergy and even city officials to cry, "Enough!" Davenport was jailed a couple of times, judged as mentally incompetent, forced to write a retraction for encouraging enthusiastic excesses, and sent back to his congregation in Connecticut.[25] Later Davenport admitted that his actions hurt the revival by providing examples that critics could cite as evidence in their attacks. Tragically, Davenport passed away "believing that the cause of Christ would have been stronger if he had never been born."[26]

As a result of Davenport's excesses, as well as those of many other newly inspired itinerants, the revival came under fire from a faction of Boston ministers led by Charles Chauncy. Alexander Garden's charges against Whitefield had already been reprinted in Boston by 1741, and Chauncy, after a time of careful consideration and research, joined the criticism wholeheartedly in 1742 with the publication of his sermon *Enthusiasm Described and Caution'd Against*. Therein he claims that the itinerants were mistaking their "own passions for divine communications" and that personal responses they supposed were inspired by God's Spirit were actually due to an "over-heated imagination."[27]

Chauncy was delighted by the turn of events centered on Davenport, which vindicated his claims that the revival enthusiasm was ultimately destructive, divisive, and irrational.[28] Chauncy meticulously catalogued the enthusiastic excesses of the Awakening, publishing them fully in September 1743 in a formal treatise titled *Seasonable Thoughts on the State of Religion in New England*. Centered in Boston, the antirevival faction solidified, then wrote and preached against the Awakening, supporting their claims with the excessive enthusiasm of Davenport. Beset by sustained criticism, revival fervor cooled significantly. Moreover, most colonists had already heard and responded to the message of the new birth one way or another. The intense period of the Awakening subsided by 1743, and the war of words over what the revival meant began its conflagration.

In *Seasonable Thoughts*, Chauncy singled out Whitefield as the instigator of all the religious excesses, divisions, and root of the social disorder in New England. He articulated numerous complaints against the enthusiasts, of whom he viewed Whitefield as the chief, and in each instance he demonstrated how every negative aspect of the revival originated with Whitefield, was reinforced by Tennent, stretched to its limits by Davenport, and then placed in widespread practice by other itinerant ministers. Chauncy succeeded in organizing and articulating the suspicions and misgivings of many ministers into a coherent, seemingly air-tight argument, warranted by Scripture, Puritan tradition, and the respected opinions of American and British religious leaders. The widespread revival criticism forced ministers and parishioners across the colonies to reconsider their support of the movement and take a public position. Even though the respected Jonathan Edwards ably defended the revival theology against antirevival ministers, and even though the revival faction held a large majority, the opposition expressed their position forcefully in print, placing the rift at the fore of public religious discussion in the newly developed public sphere.

The controversy over the revival polarized American Protestantism into two distinct factions after the Great Awakening, one supporting and one opposing the revival. The antirevival faction, composed of Puritan Old Lights and Anglicans, generally represented the upper classes, supported authoritarian hierarchies of British society, had ministers who were well educated, and relied primarily on writing to promote their ideas and agenda. The New Light revivalists almost always represented the lower classes, were much more egalitarian, and had ministers who were often less educated but excelled in oral public discourse. The bifurcation was by no means equal. New Lights outnumbered Old Lights and Anglicans by four to one as the youth and lower-class masses attended and affirmed the prorevival churches.[29] But even though America itself was religiously, intellectually, and socially divided, the public controversy goaded groups into bifurcation instead of a mosaic of positions.

Whitefield had heard rumors of the growing rift between the ministerial factions but was unaware that the controversy had reached extreme proportions until he returned to Boston in late 1744. By this time, the revival fires had cooled, ministers and parishioners had largely taken sides, and colonial society was negotiating the shifts in its ecclesiastical and political structure as people were leaving the established churches and joining the New Light congregations. Whitefield's announcement of a third tour exposed the rift by forcing ministers to welcome or reject his arrival. The charges against Whitefield became a challenge that complicated his successful return to America by demanding answers, concessions, and apologies.[30] Although Chauncy's criticisms were largely limited to the religious realm, his belief that the revival posed a threat to social order reveals the political ramifications of the social realignment that was occurring due to the Awakening. Various New Englanders cast charges of sedition through anonymous newspaper editorials as soon as Whitefield set foot in Boston.

## THE PUBLIC TRIAL OF WHITEFIELD

Upon his return to Boston, Whitefield recognized the antirevival faction and complained to a friend that a group of ministers, citizens, and publishers banded together and were opposing his latest New England tour:

> TEMPORA *mutantur;* a confederacy, a confederacy! The clergy, amongst whom are a few mistaken, misinformed good old men, are publishing halfpenny testimonials against me.[31]

The defections from Old Light churches had grown so numerous that Puritan and Anglican leaders were anxious for the future of their churches and their influence in the community. Rumors of a plot to subvert New England's authority structure quickly burst forth from these fears. Upon Whitefield's return, to offer him or deny him a pulpit made a pragmatic statement regarding one's attitude toward the Awakening, affirmed or disowned the excessive practices of the itinerants, subscribed to or rebuffed their theological errors, and revealed one's position with regard to political order. Whitefield's enterprise became the focal point for the upheaval in New England society, threatening the "glorious New England tradition" in either one of two ways: first, as a British Anglican who might encourage the development of Anglican hegemony in the colonies, or second, as one who promoted separatism and the growth of non-Puritan denominations. Either of these mutually exclusive fears threatened colonial political stability, and both provided a rationale for criticism. At one point, even the rhetoric of antipapism was employed against him.

The ensuing struggle between Old Lights and New Lights emanated from the pulpits, flowed from the colonial newspapers, filled numerous pamphlets, and constituted "not so much a debate between theologians" in Heimert's words, "as a vital competition for the intellectual allegiance of the American people."[32] The issues were profound, and the changes that sent tremors through the shifting society promised extensive consequences. Citizens, who were strengthening the communitarian networks amongst themselves, began to question their ministers on ecclesiastical matters in a challenge Old Lights believed led down a slippery slope to anarchy. The fact that there even existed an emerging intercolonial public sphere in which the debate could occur reveals the depth of approaching change. The Old Lights, with a penchant to view matters with a political eye, clearly recognized where the changes could lead. Undermining the theological rationale for the shifts in the balance of power would get to the heart of the problem. Since Whitefield generated the symbols that defined and sustained the Awakening, the most direct way to assault it was to attack him.

All of the propaganda and focused criticism of Whitefield would create an exigency demanding an *apologia*—a public defense of his character and ministry. Whitefield arrived back in the colonies with his wife, Elizabeth, to a cool reception, whereupon Charles Chauncy insisted he leave New England. The *Boston Evening-Post* backed Chauncy by reprinting and disseminating his charges.[33] But the returning Whitefield was not the same rash innovator that blazed through the colonies in 1740. His experiences in England with criticism and controversy prepared him for his defense. Having just defended himself against similar charges of enthusiasm, factionalism, and sedition from the Anglican leadership in England, Whitefield quickly recognized the magnitude of the situation and took quick action to salvage his reputation and consolidate his gains from the 1740 revival. His ecumenical "parish" was divided, and he saw it as his responsibility to suppress the conspiracy propaganda and heal relationships between his parishioners, if possible. Perhaps most importantly, the controversy over the revival had drifted squarely into the political sphere, and Whitefield would leave it there as he attempted to restore his tarnished image and quell the threat to the community.

Whitefield's public image in America was not connected with Methodism in America as it was in England, but he was associated with the separatists—groups that dissented from the dissenters. He wished to completely shed that image and step back into the mainstream of American religious culture and politics. His plan was to apologize to the offended ministers and then back up his apology with practical support of their political system. His chief rhetorical strategy was to adorn himself with what he termed "another spirit" to disassociate himself from his previous image and sever his connection with radical enthusiasts. This move constituted a shift away from either pole of the debate and created a new moderate position in between and removed from either end of a supposed religious continuum. A cynical writer for the *Boston Evening-Post* shows that the term "another spirit" was circulating immediately after his arrival: "It was industriously spread abroad, that Mr. *Whitefield* was now come in *another Spirit*, in the *Spirit of Meekness, Love and Peace; that he declared against Disorders and Separations, and would preach against them, and endeavour to heal our Divisions.*"[34] A key word in this quote is "industriously," which indicates great efforts on Whitefield's part. Helping Whitefield to perform in "another Spirit," and evidencing general change in his ministry, was Elizabeth Whitefield. The Boston newspapers mention her, and undoubtedly her presence altered perceptions of Whitefield in a positive way. Charges of immorality against him were never taken seriously in America and did not enter the respectable side of the debate.[35]

For the most part Whitefield performed in "another Spirit" fairly well, giving his critics nothing new to use against him. Yet perhaps this was not a new performance but a conscious expression of his genuine essence? According to Milton Coalter, Whitefield's apparent shift to the mainstream was not a shift at all but rather indicated differences he held with hard-line Calvinists like Gilbert Tennent that did not immediately surface upon their initial meetings or shared labors in New Jersey and New York.[36] In 1745 Whitefield labored to make the differences public.

In addition to executing his own agenda for promoting "another Spirit," Whitefield faced an overwhelming matrix of accusations, both substantial and contrived. The *Boston Evening-Post* became a convenient venue for anonymous writers to challenge Whitefield and the revivalists, while the *Boston Gazette* voiced the opinions of revival supporters. Arguments in the public debate were published in pamphlet form or appeared in the newspapers in statements that were thrust upon the public for its consideration. The imagined community was becoming manifest in the public sphere to debate this issue. Appropriately, the public would be the judge in this trial of Whitefield's conduct and character, and their attendance at his events after 1745 would cast their vote either vindicating or reproving his ministry.

The religious conflict can be organized around three clusters of accusations directed at Whitefield: (1) attacks upon his character, (2) charges that he promoted erroneous doctrine, and (3) accusations that his ministry was seditious. The single issue that binds each cluster of accusations into a semicoherent whole was Whitefield's criticism of the unconverted ministers. To the antirevivalists this criticism indicated that Whitefield was uncharitable, it exposed his theological shortcomings, and it caused people to realign their religious loyalties and, by implication, their political loyalties. Moreover, England was on the brink of war with France. Rumors of the rebellion by the Young Pretender were not circulating as prominently in New England as they were in London, but the Boston papers abounded with news of British, French, and Spanish ships being hounded and seized by one another's privateers, the goods and ships themselves confiscated, and the prisoners/survivors being swapped at ports like Louisburg in Nova Scotia. As a result, charges of social sedition against the revival supporters were particularly threatening.

Charles Chauncy became the main spokesperson for the antirevivalists. Leading the accusations against Whitefield's character, he charged Whitefield of having "*too high an Opinion* of his own *Gifts* and *Graces*." Furthermore, Chauncy raised the question of whether the large collections Whitefield solicited to support his Bethesda orphanage had been appropriately distributed.[37] In the *Boston Evening-Post,* "Publicola," an anonymous author, accused Whitefield of pilfering orphanage collections for his personal use.[38] But without doubt, "uncharitable" was the most frequent term used to castigate Whitefield's character. Chauncy accuses Whitefield of "Instances of uncharitable Judging," for condemning established ministers as unconverted dupes of the devil. Chauncy wrote:

> The next Thing that is amiss, and very much so, in these Times, is that *Spirit of rash, censorious* and *uncharitable Judging,* which has been so prevalent in the Land. This appear'd first of all, in Mr. W----D, who seldom

preach'd, but he has something or other, in his Sermon, against *unconverted Ministers.*[39]

Justifying this charge, Whitefield had written earlier that the
deceased Anglican archbishop Tillotson, whose Arminian perspectives
had gained some respect among the Old Light clergy, "knew no more
of religion than *Mahomet.*"[40] If a revered Anglican archbishop cannot
meet Whitefield's standard for conversion, then who can? Additionally,
more than one author complained that Whitefield expected others to
attend his sermons, but he would not bother to show up when the Boston ministers preached. Leaders at Harvard were also upset and accused
Whitefield of being "habitually . . . uncharitable, censorious and slan-
derous" because he questioned their Christian character, saying, "Their
Light is now become Darkness, Darkness that may be felt."[41]

Chauncy labeled the second cluster of accusations against Whitefield as the "Spirit of Errors," by which misinterpretations of Scripture resulted in unorthodox practices and teaching, which would
generate ill-advised shifts in social structures.[42] Chauncy asserted that
the enthusiastic practices in the New Light meetings were excessively
impassioned and ventured beyond reasonable scriptural examples,
referring to them as "[s]creamings, convulsion like tremblings and
Agitations, Strugglings and Tumblings, which in some instances,
have been attended with Indecencies I shan't mention."[43] Moreover,
Chauncy insisted that Whitefield and the others claimed to receive
revelations directly from God, but that which they attributed to divine
origin actually proceeded from their own imaginations. The actions
of Whitefield and others could be misdirected acts of piety and genuine service, Chauncy confessed, but he shows how, in each case, the
enthusiasts go well beyond what he considered sensible. However, in
this statement Chauncy charitably offered the revivalists a chance to
save face and make peace. But what if this kind of enthusiasm made
its way into political activism? The extremity of the emotional displays
and their widespread occurrences made leaders nervous that it could
spread to other public venues.

Whitefield's rationale for condemning unconverted ministers was
another aspect of the "Spirit of Errors" frequently cited by his critics.
It was an issue that brought forth frenzied opposition: "As you have
enter'd in the present Paper War, I doubt not you are prepar'd for
all Encounters." This anonymous author employed eleven war meta-

phors in the first paragraph alone.[44] Chauncy's reading of Whitefield interpreted unconverted ministers as "uncapable of being *Instruments of spiritual good to Men's Souls.*" Chauncy countered that New England ministers were not unconverted, but are "a Set of Men, *as found in the Faith,* and of as *good a Life,* as any part of the Christian World are favoured with." He argued that Whitefield's position was unbiblical, and "indeed a downright *popish Principal.*"[45] Here, he invoked the Protestants' traditional enemy as well as England's struggle with the French to attack Whitefield, further hinting at the political fears that lay beneath the surface of the debate.

The third cluster of charges completely unmasked the political fears, asserting that Whitefield was an itinerating, divisive, seditious conspirator who would overturn New England society. American religious leaders had witnessed the splintering of their churches, while the New Lights grew in number and moved beyond their control. Responsibility was cast upon Whitefield, not merely as a symbol of religious disorder, but as the prime mover of the drift into separatism. Thomas Clap, the rector of Yale, exclaimed, "Separatists every where set you up for their Oracle, Pattern and Patron."[46]

Old Light clergy and others who decided to oppose the revivals, in Hall's words, viewed "itinerancy as an engine of social upheaval."[47] Chauncy attributed the separations to the practice of itinerancy, claiming that those who minister outside of an assigned parish "introduce Disorder and Confusion into the *Church* of GOD." Chauncy accused Whitefield of neglecting his own parish in Georgia with his itinerancy and provided a slippery-slope argument to complain that the "entire Dissolution of our *Church State*" would occur should this practice become more generalized. Chauncy then proclaimed the existence of a conspiracy: "It is very just to infer, that there is a Design carrying on to *subvert* and *eject* the *standing settled Ministers.*" But even here, Chauncy again provided Whitefield a means of saving face, hinting that such rash judgments may be due to Whitefield's youth, and that he may mature and his opinions change, "as he has been in some other Instances."[48] And, by and large, Whitefield took advantage of Chauncy's provision.

The hypothetical design of Whitefield's conspiracy, according to Thomas Clap, called for ministers from Scotland, Ireland, and even those trained at Bethesda Orphanage to replace the "unconverted" ministers. Supposedly then, once the ministers had been replaced, the civil authorities would be next on the list. A rumor had been circulating that several students of Yale, expelled for enthusiasm, were told "that there was no Danger in disobeying their present Governours, because there would in a short Time be a great Change in the civil Government, and so in the Governours of the College." Clap even implicated Jonathan Edwards in the plot—an accusation that Edwards quickly rejoined.[49]

When Whitefield administered the sacraments at Dr. Benjamin Colman's church in Boston in December 1744, his critics sounded the alarm because they felt that this was direct and explicit evidence of the conspiracy. In their view, to have an Anglican priest administer the sacraments in a Congregational church symbolized an attempt to establish dominance—a blatant crossing of boundaries far more serious than merely borrowing a pulpit. In Britain's past, taking the sacraments in the Church of England had been a means of publicly identifying with a certain political ideology.[50] Anglicans in England held positions in the House of Lords and used the church as a direct means of controlling the populace through the official state religion. But in New England, Congregationalism was the state religion. As an Anglican priest, Whitefield's administration of the sacraments appeared as an attempt to assert an Anglican presence in New England—a supposed advance of English influence within the arena of religion. There exists an inconsistency in the logic of simultaneously accusing him of promoting separatism and Anglican hegemony. But charges were coming from various voices who did not all share the same perspective, except they all opposed Whitefield. The antirevival faction believed the security of their hard-won dissenter privileges and the order of New England politics were at risk, and thus their most vigorous response was deemed necessary—no holds barred, including adhering to reason.

## WHITEFIELD'S DEFENSE

Whitefield wasted no time in acting once the stakes became clear to him. He met with a group of influential Boston ministers who were concerned about the charges but remained undecided, including Dr. Sewall, Dr. Colman, Mr. Foxcroft, and Mr. Prince. In so doing, Whitefield won over several respected clergymen who would then influence other undecided New Englanders. Whitefield described the meeting:

They were apprehensive . . . that I would promote or encourage separations, . . . I said, I was sorry if anything I wrote had been a means of promoting separations for I was of no separating principles. . . . We talked
freely and friendly . . . by which their jealousies they had entertained
concerning me seemed to be in a great measure ended.[51]

Whitefield's "another spirit" was on display in these statements, and
the ministers were convinced. It is likely that Whitefield's charismatic
personality also helped to smooth these relationships as much as his
responses to their concerns. These ministers then became the core of
a group, absolutely necessary for Whitefield's continued success, that
faithfully supported him during his stay in Boston, even to the point
of having their own characters maligned. Whitefield disseminated
his public responses to the allegations as fast as the presses could produce them. He promptly reprinted a pamphlet he had on hand that
defended his ministry against charges of illegal itinerancy, enthusiasm,
and sedition in England. Then he printed the account of the recent
trial in England to show the opposition "confederacy" that he would
not tolerate violence and that the British courts would back him. Next,
he wrote two largely overlapping letters, one to Charles Chauncy and
one to Harvard, that addressed each accusation. He also continued to
preach almost daily wherever he was lent a pulpit. He wisely stayed out
of the fields for a while.

After the Boston clergy made their case against him, the Boston
press churned out anonymous and authored editorials for and against
Whitefield. The *Evening-Post* came out squarely against Whitefield with
front-page articles deprecating his character, doctrine, and practice,
but the *Boston Gazette* published occasional articles in his support along
with a regular feature of where Whitefield had preached, what the
response to his preaching had been, and where he would preach next.
The debate between the two papers kept a literal scorecard of who
was for or against Whitefield, each one listing the names of ministers
as they took a public stand. On January 8, 1745, the *Gazette* published
a list of 141 ministers from all over the New England and Middle colonies who supported the revival (though not necessarily Whitefield). The
*Evening-Post* countered with a list of eight ministers against Whitefield
(including two from Charlestown) versus eight who were for him from
the Boston area, trying to make the division look more equal. Eventu-

ally fifty ministers from New England signed their names to pamphlets declaring their intention to deny Whitefield admission to their pulpits.

Within the pamphlets and letters Whitefield published during his stay in Boston, he rejoined all three clusters of charges. Regarding the criticism that he was arrogant, Whitefield responded to Chauncy with contrition, his own countercharge, and a veiled plea for forgiveness. "All this, Reverend Sir, might possible have been true concerning me—but have you not prejudged me?" Whitefield complained that he had promised to explain and defend his practice of itinerancy, but Chauncy did not wait for the explanation before publishing, and that was unfair in Whitefield's eyes. Regarding his own attitude, Whitefield insisted he should not be held to a standard of *"sinless Perfection,"* and that God led him from his former attitude into a new one—a clear reference to "another spirit."[52]

Whitefield published an accounting of the Bethesda collections and budget before the end of 1744.[53] He flatly denied extorting money, claimed that the orphanage was in good hands, and stated that his contributors were satisfied with his management of the money.[54] Additionally, Whitefield argued that he could have "made what the World calls a fortune, and set down and nestled quietly," but instead he lived in voluntary poverty.[55] Questions regarding the Bethesda finances quickly subsided as his critics turned to exploit more fruitful issues.

Whitefield defended his conduct against the charge that he was uncharitable by suggesting their opinion of him was too harsh: "But, Gentlemen, does it follow that *Peter* could properly be styled a cursing, swearing man, because with oaths and curses he denied his LORD?" Whitefield claims that one must be "habitually uncharitable" to deserve the epithet, not just guilty of one infraction. Whitefield admitted culpability and apologized with regard to specific uncharitable comments about the state of New England colleges and the Tillotson remark: "I had no idea of representing the Colleges in such a deplorable state of immorality and irreligion." Whitefield admitted that he should have limited his criticism of Tillotson to his theology and not implicated his character.[56]

Regarding the second cluster of charges—the Spirit of Errors—Whitefield did not deny the evidence used against him, especially since they had quoted his own journal. Rather, he asserted that Chauncy and others had failed to make a case out of these facts: "And is there any Thing, *Reverend Sir*, in this that may justly be stiled *Chimerical* or *Enthusiastical?*"[57] Whitefield countered that he was not led by "sudden impulses" but "acted cautiously" and "took time to consider" what he would do in the particular case that leaders at Harvard criticized.[58] Whitefield also claimed it was not "enthusiasm" to interpret dreams and other such instances as God's attempts to lead his people. Overall, Whitefield agreed to disagree, letting God be the judge. Yet on the unconverted minister issue Whitefield acquiesced as much as he could without totally losing face, backing off his *absolute* claim and replacing it with a *conditional* one:

> My settled Sentiments concerning them are these,—That they are sel-
> dom made Use of to convert others I verily believe: but if I have any
> where said what may be construed to imply, that it is *impossible* that
> unconverted Ministers should be Instrumental in converting others, or
> that their Administrations in the visible Church are invalid, as it was not
> my intention, I would revoke it.[59]

Here then is a seemingly small concession from his hard-line position that, combined with his confession of judging New England's ministers, evidenced his desire to heal the breech between religious factions.

To the third cluster of allegations, that he was an itinerating divisive conspirator, Whitefield responded by defending his itinerancy and denying that he desired people to leave their churches or that he was part of a conspiracy to replace the ministers. Whitefield counterattacked, stating that few nonresident ministers in England could give as good an account of their parishes as he, that many led a duplicitous life, while he worked hard at preaching the gospel. Additionally, he "constantly exhorted" the people to attend established churches rather than encouraging the separations that occurred while he was absent.[60] Here again, Whitefield's strategy prospered as his apologies, retractions, and gracious responses, even when he denied charges or disagreed, provided palpable evidence of "another spirit." In his reply to Harvard, Whitefield unequivocally denied any intent to undermine New England's religious structure:

> I am come to *New-England*, with no intention to meddle with, much less
> to destroy the order of the *New-England* churches, or turn out the gen-
> erality of their ministers, or re-settle them with ministers from *England*,

*Scotland*, and *Ireland*, . . . such a thought never entered my heart; neither, as I know of, has my preaching the least tendency thereunto, . . . I have no intention of setting up a party for myself, or to stir up people against their Pastors.[61]

As for being the leader and cause of all the trouble in general, Whitefield said they could only hold him accountable for his own wrongdoing—not the sins of others. For speaking against ministers without personally knowing them, Whitefield admitted he was wrong and apologized: "I thank you, *Reverend Sir*, for pointing out this Fault unto me.—But that I had a Design either in preaching or writing to alienate People's Minds from their standing Ministers, I utterly disavow."[62]

But perhaps the most consequential position that Whitefield took during this debate was manifest in the following statement from his published reply to Chauncy:

That I spake of *unconverted Ministers* in the Lump, as *Pharisees*, *Enemies* of Christ Jesus, and the worst *Enemies* I had, I believe is true; but that I spake of the Ministers of *New England* in this Way, I utterly deny.[63]

Whitefield was not one to avoid conflict or placate his antagonists when he believed he was right. In this statement, he maintained the distinction between converted and unconverted ministers, but confessed that the New England ministers were indeed converted. Here Whitefield's care to only name Anglican clergy in his sermonic attacks paid off. He never publicly named the New England clergy, and while Alexander Garden still had a complaint against him, the New England Congregationalists could not make this charge stick.

So then, Chauncy and many others who denied the privileged place of emotions and feelings in conversion had experienced a legitimate conversion and were genuine Christians after all. Whitefield had made a monumental concession: *the emotional style of the new birth was not the sole means of obtaining salvation*—one could have a conversion experience within the Old Light scheme as well. Whitefield would never soften his stance on other doctrines. He still averred that God was the central agent in conversion and that a person's good works were ineffectual in securing pardon for sins. But by enlarging his definition of how conversion occurs, Whitefield initiated reconciliation between the New Lights and Old Lights. Whitefield had moved to the middle, and as the "Oracle, Pattern and Patron" of the "Separatists," this move would set the example for many prorevivalists. It would take another eight months before ministers from the two factions in Boston would actually meet and try to reconcile their differences—several months after Whitefield left New England—but they did meet, and with some communication and the passing of time the religious bifurcation began to dissolve.

In effect, Whitefield began paving the road for political cooperation between the two factions by conceding that the antirevivalists were not "out" but actually "in" God's kingdom and that both were genuine members of the Christian community. In order to repair the rift, Whitefield expanded the community to include many of the "unconverted" ministers and their congregations whom he was now willing to define as converted. After 1745 the sharp rift between New Lights and Old Lights began to close as initiated by Whitefield's extended hand. Their shared desire for increased piety among parishioners eventually provided ground for peace as the Old Lights also awoke from their religious slumber and focused their rhetoric away from the revivals and toward the increasing French threat. Though other ministers would still debate the meaning and purpose of the revivals, Whitefield moved on to more important issues by including Old Lights in the community, making the controversy a moot point in regard to his own enterprise. New challenges to Whitefield's parish were emerging, and a more mature, sober Whitefield prepared to meet them.

## THE MODERATE FACTION

To his advantage Whitefield found a unified contingency of ministers to which he could appeal, en masse, for reconciliation and thus initiate a cautious amalgamation process between the New Lights and Old Lights. After gaining the support of Dr. Sewall, Dr. Colman, Mr. Foxcroft, Mr. Prince, and others with whom Whitefield met in November, other ministers were won over if not through Whitefield's responses outlined above, then by the pamphlets written on his behalf. Thomas Foxcroft and William Hobby both published in Whitefield's favor, defending him at the expense of their own public images, which were subsequently subjected to ridicule by Boston editorialists who were maintaining the controversy.

After publishing his responses to all the charges in a line-by-line fashion, Whitefield's actions that displayed "another spirit" helped him more than all his arguments and apologizing. The activity of French and Spanish privateers had been increasing as of late, and the swelling conflict with the French displaced the revival controversy from the Boston news. Massachusetts governor William Shirley proposed an expedition to capture the fortified French military port at Louisburg on the coast of Nova Scotia, just six hundred miles northeast of Boston, which offered the privateers a safe haven too close for Boston's comfort. But New Englanders shied away from enlistment after Governor Shirley's announcement of a campaign in the spring of 1745. Frankly, the political leaders of Boston and New England were having difficulty persuading farmers to enlist in the military for what, to some, seemed a remote and uncertain cause. So General Pepperell, who was assigned the command of the Louisburg expedition, appealed to Whitefield to support the enlistment effort by providing a "motto for his flag." After some initial hesitation, Whitefield conceded and coined the phrase *Nil Desperandum, Christo Duce,* i.e., "If Christ be Captain, no fear of a defeat."[64] Then, Whitefield preached a sermon that spiritualized the story of David, exhorting potential enlistees that as soldiers of Christ they were like David's men who found success in their battle against God's enemies. He declined the request that he be the Louisburg expedition's chaplain.

Whitefield played the loyal subject and deployed his ministry to encourage both physical and intellectual allegiance of the people to established British authority. In so doing, he committed colonists' blood to the war effort and began reapplying the us-them distinction in his military sermons to Protestant and Catholic religious orientations, casting the newly expanded Protestant community as "good" and the French Catholics as "evil." After Whitefield pronounced God's blessing upon the Louisburg expedition, enlistment in the military soared, and the fortress fell in six weeks to the delight and encouragement of the New Englanders. Thanksgiving sermons by both New and Old Light ministers responding to the victory displayed a "remarkable unanimity," revealing a diminishing distance in the rift between them.[65] Undoubtedly, Whitefield's support of the New England governor was out of character with being a conspirator and contradicted allegations of sedition. In fact, from this point on through the rest of his career

Whitefield would maintain a voice in public rhetoric regarding war. Shortly thereafter, Whitefield did perhaps the best thing he could to cool the religious controversy in Boston: he took his leave and did not return to New England for two years. Chauncy, Clap, and the other antirevivalist leaders stopped publishing complaints and went back to their normal business.

In Whitefield's absence, the public conflict sustained a couple more turns. William Shurtleff, a respected Boston Congregationalist, issued a pamphlet that voiced a reasonable view, one that promoted the moderate position and promised harmony to the factions. In late May 1745 Shurtleff, without explicitly supporting Whitefield, reasoned that the revival, despite its controversy, had not worsened but actually improved the state of religion in New England. Shurtleff reminded his readers of the profusion of apostasy in New England before the revival and contrasted it with the religious zeal that now abounded—the churches were filled, and ministers were again fervent.[66] Perhaps Shurtleff's perspective supplied the rationale for a meeting of Boston's ministers, scheduled for September 19, 1745, which was convened to resolve the divided state of affairs.[67] Issues of newspapers that might describe the proceedings are missing from the historical record, but one editorial mentioned the meeting, "which has occasioned so much talk and Writing," and noted that a number of troublemakers aimed to disrupt it. Out of the meeting a statement was published titled *Convention of New England Ministers*, which charted out the doctrinal and practical positions of a moderate faction.[68] The twenty-four participating ministers repudiated excessive enthusiastic practices and staked out what they felt was a reasonable position toward the revivals. Chauncy did not sign the statement.

Clearly the Old Light and New Light factions had much more in common than not. As a 1745 sermon by Samuel Quincy testifies, many Anglicans actually held doctrinal positions almost identical to Whitefield's regarding the new birth and regeneration. In his 1745 sermon "Regeneration," Quincy affirmed the necessity of the new birth and agreed that the new birth is a spiritual transformation, requiring a season of growth, authored by the Holy Ghost. He only differed with the enthusiast's position regarding the role of the emotions in the conversion process and the hard-line Calvinist belief in predestination. These were differences with which Whitefield could coexist, judging from his prior concession that the Boston Old Lights were indeed converted.

Though Whitefield affirmed predestination doctrinally in his writings, he was less inclined to impose it explicitly on his live audiences. In fact, Whitefield loosely interpreted *any* impulse leading toward repentance as *evidence* of God's calling upon a person, impulses that he was renowned for eliciting. Clearly, Quincy's sermon was responding to the straw man of the radical enthusiasts, or perhaps a number of lesser known itinerants, rather than the doctrinal reality of moderates, revealing the presence of a middle ground, even from the Old Light perspective. It was on this middle ground that the New Light moderates could be reconciled with Old Lights who were recognizing that they indeed benefited from the revival, just as Shurtleff had claimed. The gap between the two factions was more propaganda than substance, and with time and examination this fact became evident to most.

Thus, emerging out of the New Light faction of the post-Awakening period, Whitefield aligned himself with a growing coalition of moderate ministers who promoted a doctrinal and practical middle ground—ministers who initially embraced the revival but retreated in the face of enthusiastic excesses.[69] This was a middle ground shared by Old Lights like Shurtleff and Anglicans such as Quincy, although some were slow to admit it. Giving advice to a friend, Whitefield wrote, "*Moderate Calvinism* I take to be a medium between two extremes."[70] There would always remain a radical faction that continued to emphasize enthusiasm and never settle the differences, and Whitefield would continue ecumenical relationships with these, but in principle he was a moderate, and he recognized the need for peace with the Old Lights to maintain his popularity as well as social stability.

Where religious apathy had once ruled New England, the Awakening had shaken many people out of their slumber and moved the issue of who was in and who was out of God's kingdom to the fore of public discussion. Shurtleff was right. The Awakening was good for everyone; and through its bifurcation of religious groups, each was unified with those in its respective faction; then both factions admitted and emphasized their shared beliefs and positions via the *Convention of New England Ministers* as they realized that conflict was destructive and their differences could be successfully marginalized.

With Whitefield gone and the war with France developing an American theater, the ministers of Boston began to heal their breaches and were further goaded toward unity by the threat of a common enemy. Now the entire New England religious community could be counted as "us" facing the threat of "them"—French control and its consequent Roman Catholic religious system. The popish plots of 1678 and 1715 were back! With the growing reconciliation of Old Lights and moderate New Lights, the Catholic French were transformed into the new "them," an enemy with malevolent intentions in both religion and politics.

As Whitefield's tour progressed from 1745 to 1747, he led the transformation of the colonial mind in casting the French as the new "them" through the delivery and publication of his martial sermons. Other American ministers soon followed with harangues that castigated the popish French, but nothing was published earlier than Whitefield's *Britain's Mercies and Britain's Duties*. Before long, with an unofficial, moderate religious faction composed of both New Lights and Old Lights providing an increasing degree of unity, religious controversies gave way to civic and martial issues, which were animated by the residual zeal of the Awakening.

## A POLITICAL TURN TOWARD NATIONAL COMMUNITY

Although the relationship between religion and politics in colonial America had always been close, political stability in the early eighteenth century had not demanded activism from the church. For the most part the two existed in a quiet partnership, with the ministers attending largely to spiritual matters unless political exigencies called for their attention. But the Awakening, among other things, emphasized points of tension in the political-religious partnership through the stresses it placed upon it by challenging established authority structures. And just as the religious factions were forming a new balance of power and dropping charges of conspiracy and heresy, Britain's war with France supplied a common threat that would demand their full cooperation. "In the minds of Old Lights," explains Hatch, "images of Antichrist shifted from 'enthusiasm' to the French menace, and New Lights ceased to be preoccupied with the dangers of an unconverted ministry."[71] There is nothing like a common enemy to align squabbling neighbors, and Whitefield's return coincided perfectly to help facilitate their cooperation. It would take a few more months for the middle ground to solidify completely, but the *Convention of New England Ministers* had suggested its blueprint, and it was only a matter of time before harsh feelings abated and the formation of a "Christian Union" began.

If there was any lingering doubt regarding Whitefield's stance toward the colonial authority structure as his tour progressed, he erased it by aligning solidly behind political leaders and lending his polemic weight as the war with the French ensued. Securing martial allegiance from the Awakening community would require the demonization of the secular enemy, and this was no difficult task with an audience who recalled the Inquisition, the persecution of Queen Mary, the plots of the Stuart kings, and recent oppression of Protestants in France. Whitefield associated fears of French control with Roman Catholic ascendancy, which he believed was evil and constituted a palpable threat to Protestant freedoms—and in 1745 it was.

Martial metaphors had been frequenting Whitefield's sermons as early as 1740. Whitefield viewed the Christian community as "soldiers lifted under the banner of Christ" who have "proclaimed open war at our baptism, against the world, the flesh, and the devil."[72] After Whitefield's enlistment sermon for Pepperell brought the resources of the people to the aid of the Massachusetts governor, Whitefield's response to the Jacobite Rebellion of 1745 further displayed the depth of his support of the Crown and traditional authority structures.

As Whitefield's 1745–1748 tour progressed, he displayed "another spirit" wherever he preached. With political connections throughout the colonies, Whitefield stayed near the conflict and occasionally stepped into the fray as needed. Great Britain was embroiled in King George's War in Europe, which did not have a particularly large impact on colonial Americans, although its news filled pages of the press.

By mid-1745 Whitefield decided to tour the Southern colonies and described in his letters to friends how he enjoyed "hunting in the woods after the lost sheep," itinerating in North Carolina and Maryland.[73] As Bonomi emphasized, "[T]he metaphor most commonly used to portray religious conditions in the Middle and Southern colonies was that of scattered sheep without a shepherd."[74] When Whitefield arranged a meeting near a town, he wrote of "preaching to thousands, generally twice a day," showing a continued fervent reception among the people. Now Whitefield was finally preaching to those he had been unable to reach effectively in his 1740 tour. Wherever Whitefield went, almost without exception large crowds attended his sermons, and he would not make the same mistakes he made in the 1740 tour. For him the Awakening was a lifelong event. But now, the more mature Whitefield took care to differentiate between the kind of enthusiasm to which Chauncy objected and a genuine outpouring of God's spirit as Edwards described. Whitefield confessed that "there was much smoke, yet every day I had more and more convincing proof, that a blessed Gospel-fire had been kindled in the hearts both of ministers and people."[75] By the end of 1746 Whitefield declared "the harvest is great in many places."[76]

Whitefield showed people how to chart a moderate position in religion and make peace with his detractors. In England, to thwart the violence, Whitefield turned to the courts and then challenged the origin of the problem. His rhetorical skill and prudence served him in the courtroom where the Methodists did not deny being a type of enthusiasts but insisted that their practice was not seditious, keeping the argument in a sphere where they could win. In writing against the Anglican bishops who were persecuting Methodism, Whitefield used carefully reasoned arguments that were eloquently phrased and then published to hold the bishops accountable for their actions. Likewise, in America, he apologized for indiscretions and actions of which he was guilty and then challenged the other accusations with solid reasoning. He always appeared reasonable, rational, and willing to own up to his faults, *and he always published*. Whitefield recognized that such conflicts were not negotiated in the courtroom or ecclesiastical conventions but in the public sphere where image was crucial and public opinion provided the more powerful judgment.

Whitefield found success making peace in a sphere that has traditionally bred more conflict than any other: religion. He demonstrated a prudential use of practical reason to fashion a middle position that would not alienate anyone, except his "enemies"—those that impinged on dissenter freedoms or threatened Protestantism. By demonstrating how to chart out common ground and negotiate differences in the religious sphere, Whitefield sketched a blueprint for reconciling political differences as well. As we have seen, divergent political positions are typically founded upon contrasting religious theologies. And if the hard case of religious controversy can be negotiated, then the easier case of political disputes can be as well.

Whitefield was the perfect candidate for exemplifying how differences could be reconciled. A walking enigma, he was an Anglican priest, representing traditional authority on one hand, yet on the other he thought and acted like a Dissenter. He was the Calvinist who invited everyone to Christ, as a good Arminian would. He was a Whig, fighting for the rights of Dissenters against a hegemonic Church of England, yet he was unabashedly loyal to George II. Throughout his life and enterprise we see the reconciliation of opposites, an example of *phronesis* that would have pleased even Isocrates. His positions required an artistic touch and personal finesse to win over his detractors, as well as a heavy rhetorical hand when charm would not work. He showed the political and religious world how the rhetorical tactic of taking the best of both positions to fashion a third one transcended mere compromise to form a theology, ideology, or program of action. As his life progressed, Whitefield evolved into a spiritual statesman for the republican ideology, championing the privileges of the people within the bounds of established authority.

## CHAPTER 6

## THE WAR AGAINST ARBITRARY POWER

Whereas from 1736 to 1744 George Whitefield primarily sought to spread the message of the new birth to the entire world, constraints in Great Britain and America compelled him to extend the goals of his enterprise. Whitefield said, "I hope I shall always think it my bounded duty, next to inviting sinners to the blessed Jesus, to exhort my hearers to exert themselves against the first approaches of Popish tyranny and arbitrary power."[1] After 1745 Whitefield viewed his evolving enterprise as having a twofold function: first was his well-known mission to preach the gospel wherever he could find an audience, but second, he felt a call to protect Protestant freedoms as well as British civil liberties: "Alas! alas! what a condition would this land be in, was the protestant interest not to prevail?"[2] His duty to "exhort his hearers" took its most poignant expression in his diatribes against the French and his criticism of Anglican encroachment on dissenters' religious freedoms. Over the course of the next fifteen years Whitefield aimed his polemic arsenal at the French Roman Catholics as England waged war on two continents (the Seven Years War in Europe and the French and Indian War in the colonies). Then, after the wars, he turned his attention to Anglican leaders who continued arbitrarily opposing itinerancy and other dissenter privileges.

Unmistakable republican impulses punctuated his writings from this point until his death. Mark Noll has questioned Bernard Bailyn's theory that the use of republican language became a "contagion" that spread into religion. Instead, Noll asks whether the motion of language use flowed both directions: "Rather than a rhetoric or republican civic humanism spreading out into the religious backwaters of colonial society, the religious backwaters may have been rising to carry republicanism where its leading theorists had not intended it to go."[3] Being a leader in publishing and oral dissemination of ideas, as well as

idolized by many ministers, Whitefield was instrumental in the confla-
tion of republican and religious language use, whichever way it tended
to flow. As has been argued above, religion is a structuralizing factor
for political positions—a situation that, if indeed true, indicates that
the ideological movement occurred more from religion into politics
than backflowing the other direction. Of course, Whitefield was a
product of his times, was heavily influenced by Puritans in his youth,
and expressed clear Whig and republican tendencies. But if ideologies flowed from religion into politics, his influence was certainly at
the fore. As this inquiry has attempted to affirm, Whitefield's role was
more squarely in the motion and dissemination of ideas rather than as
an originator. The following chapter will focus on his increasing use of
republican language and its blending with his theology. In his desire to
preserve dissenter freedoms, Whitefield co-opted the notion of liberty
in his writings. The Revolution was still thirty-one years away, so the
audiences hearing his messages were the parents of those who actually fought in the Revolution. Although Whitefield's influence would
thus be secondary, it held the greater power due to propagation by a
parental source from within one's family.

## GOOD KINGS AND BAD KINGS

England in 1745 found the French-backed effort to overthrow the British Crown finally underway. Charles Edward (the Young Pretender),
the son of James II (the Old Pretender), attempted forcibly to claim the
throne of England for his aging father—a throne he would thereafter inherit. The second Jacobite Rebellion commenced when Charles
Edward landed on Eriskay Island in Scotland on July 23, 1745, with a
supply of friends, money, and arms.[4] The House of Stuart originally
gained power when James I (from a daughter of Henry VII through
the Scottish line) inherited the British throne. Hence, Scotland was
the logical point of departure for Charles Edward to initiate a war
to regain the monarchy. Joined by discontented Scottish Highlanders,
Charles Edward began wresting Scottish cities away from British control, exacting tribute for his war chest with each success. By October
he commanded a force of 4,500, with 400 horsemen, and invaded
England with the hope that the English citizens would welcome the
return of the Stuarts and swell his armies. Upon reaching Derby in
December, only one hundred miles from London, quarrels among his

Scottish officers regarding their ability to take and hold London mired the invasion. Had they known that George II was preparing to flee London, they might have pressed their advantage.

After a disorderly return to Scotland, Charles Edward's army regrouped and gained strength through reinforcement from other clans along with a group of French artillery and engineering experts. But their hesitation and temporary retreat offered the British a chance to regroup and counterattack. On April 15, 1746, a pursuing British force led by Lord Cumberland struck the Jacobite army at Nairn, inflicting heavy losses that scattered his surviving Scottish enlistees. British forces ruthlessly pursued Jacobite rebels and leaders, executing them and committing other atrocities in the aftermath of their victory. After five months of fugitive wanderings in Scotland, Charles Edward escaped to France despite the price of £30,000 on his head offered by the British government.[5] Later a Scottish lord was put on trial for harboring him. Many Jacobite supporters were quickly deported to the colonies, and others emigrated on their own to begin an anonymous life free from the immediate hostility of England.

After a trip down to the Bethesda orphanage in Georgia, Whitefield returned north to Philadelphia whereupon, hearing about the failed Jacobite Rebellion in England, he produced a sermon for a national day of Thanksgiving. Whitefield preached *Britain's Mercies and Britain's Duties* in Philadelphia on August 24, 1746, and had it immediately published. As the topic was time-sensitive, the sermon probably was included in Whitefield's standard oral repertoire just long enough for him to promote it widely in person. Eager buyers quickly gobbled up at least four editions in Philadelphia and Boston. No other American sermon by any writer in 1746 went through more than one edition.[6]

Recognizing a growing body of Scots in America and fearing Charles Edward might be regrouping in France for another opportunity, Whitefield wished to disarm any potential for trouble in America from new immigrants and deportees who were not loyal to the British Crown. Additionally, still smarting from Chauncy's charges of sedition and associations with papism, Whitefield feared his tarnished image in New England might be reinserted into any forthcoming public controversy if these new Scots harbored any rebellious tendencies. It is likely that shiploads of the deported Jacobites were arriving in colonial ports along with less rebellious Scots-Irish immigrants as the news of the final battle crossed the Atlantic.[7] In America, their discontent might fester and stimulate separatists to continue their supposed plot of sedition against the New England authority structure. Whitefield had just completed a tour of Scotland in 1744 where he aligned himself solidly with the Scottish Presbyterians, potentially giving New England conspiracy theorists ammunition to rouse continued fear of his enterprise.

But Whitefield's efforts to stem "arbitrary power" were genuine, and he wished to continue his open support of the British civil authorities. Since the ideology of the Jacobites held that kings were authorized to rule by hereditary succession rather than providential choice, they had rejected the authority of George II and still might be viewed as a threat in the colonies.[8] Whitefield's rhetorical challenge was to steer Scottish and Jacobite allegiance (as well as the allegiance of others not inherently loyal to the British) back to the House of Hanover. If he could do this publicly, his image of "another spirit" would benefit from the hard evidence supplied by his open support of the British authority structure. Thus, to avert renewed criticism, Whitefield seized the opportunity to publicly declare his loyalty to the king and further disarm accusations that his enterprise was seditious.

Whitefield attempted to soften antagonism against the British by associating fears of a Catholic-controlled government with a return of the Stuart Dynasty. The Jacobite immigrants, who were largely Presbyterians, needed to be brought into the British-American fold, and the most effective means to accomplish that task might be to appeal on religious grounds. In this sermon, Whitefield clarified the connection between religious and political spheres and warned of the ramifications of supporting the Stuarts as backed by the French and papism. Whitefield's sermon promoted the idea of religious liberty by speculating on its loss under a Roman Catholic–controlled government. Simultaneously, while affirming the Protestant and British protection of religious and civil liberties, Whitefield's supportive actions would define him as a supporter of King George II once and for all. Hence, with just the right sermon, he could kill two birds with one stone. Moving quickly, he had the sermon published and advertised for sale in Boston within three weeks of its initial oration.[9] In the analysis of the sermon that follows, the reader can see how Whitefield built upon the conceptual system he had been promoting for seven years and how he extended his notions of virtue, as expressed in "good-evil" terms, from individualistic religious status to nationalistic status.

To achieve his ends, Whitefield introduces a temporal distinction (past-present-future) around which *Britain's Mercies* was structured: Whitefield argues that knowing the past helps one to place the present situation in perspective and suggests a future response. In this case, knowing about God's past mercies allowed one to be thankful to God, which in turn would nurture future piety. After Whitefield explained this principle as drawn from biblical stories, he suggests that it applied to Great Britain in the aftermath of the Jacobite Rebellion. For him, the averted rebellion constituted deliverance from a palpable threat, for which thanks must be offered to God to ensure societal piety as well as God's continued favor. Thus the sermon is divided into three major movements: first, Whitefield emphasizes the stability in Great Britain after the Glorious Revolution of 1688; next, he paints a portrait of the instability that could have resulted from a successful Jacobite Rebellion, describing both civil and religious atrocities that would have resulted; and last, Whitefield praises the heroes of the battle and argues that if they deserve praise, then God deserves more. Britain's sustained stability would depend upon appropriately recognizing God as their protector and subsequently fulfilling their religious duty. Whitefield's flowery style contrasts strikingly with other sermons. He says nothing in a blunt, direct manner but employs the grand style of oratory traditionally reserved for the most formal of occasions.

Whitefield begins by asserting that Great Britain has enjoyed a "gentle mild administration" under George II, in which political and religious oppression have been nonexistent, and Britain has prospered financially.[10] He lavishes praise upon George II for his prudent rule filled with justice and civil freedom:

> By thee we enjoy great quietness, and very worthy deeds have been done unto our nation by thy providence. He has been indeed *Pater Patriæ*, a father to our country, and though old and gray-headed, has jeopardized his precious life for us in the high places of the field. Nor has he less deserved the great and glorious title . . ."a nursing father of the church." . . . As there has been no authorized oppression in the state, so there has been no publicly allowed persecution in the church. We breathe indeed in free air.

Whitefield appeals to the observations of anyone attuned to political matters, as if a matter of fact, that George II is "one of the best." Not offering specific examples but general assessments, he extols the condition of peace, resulting in both civil *and* religious liberty, owing to the farsighted actions of the king. Whitefield ultimately attributes agency for the king's beneficent leadership to God and concludes by declaring, "Happy art thou, O England! Happy art thou, O America, who on every side art thus highly favored!"

Abruptly shifting his tone, entering the second movement of the sermon, Whitefield vilifies Charles Edward with a scathing sequence of imagined possibilities had the rebellion been successful: "But, alas! How soon would this happy scene have shifted, and a melancholy gloomy prospect have succeeded in its room, had the rebels gained their point, and a popish abjured pretender been forced upon the British throne!" Whitefield projects a slippery-slope portrayal that defines Charles Edward as *Phaeton*, Apollo's son who "was to guide the chariot of the sun; and had he succeeded in his attempt, like him, would only have set the world on fire." Having introduced antipapism into the argument with the term "popish," he further characterizes the rebellion as a "horrid plot, first hatched in hell, and afterwards nursed at Rome." Supplying evidence for the evil intent of the rebels, Whitefield accuses Charles Edward of ordering his officers to "[g]ive no quarters to the Elector's troops"—that is to say, take no prisoners. Had Charles Edward successfully gained control of the country, Whitefield speculates that Parliament would have soon been impotent, as it had been in previous eras, and that the popish pretender would have shortly ruined the British economy.

Whitefield also employs the term "arbitrary" to typify the rule of the House of Stuart. Whitefield reminds his audience that "for his arbitrary and tyrannical government, both in church and state," the Stuart dynasty "was justly obliged to abdicate the throne" in 1688 "by the assertors of British liberty." In these phrases, Whitefield links images of "arbitrary" and "tyrannical," juxtaposed against the notion of "liberty," all within a church/state context. Whitefield asserts a hereditary succession of evil to Charles Edward, claiming that his lineage provided the hegemonic monarchial beliefs, saying, "Arbitrary principles he has sucked in with his mother's milk."

But Whitefield is far from finished with Charles Edward! Moving from political fears to religious ones, he presses the denunciation forward, speculating on the threat to Protestants, "But, alas! What an inundation of spiritual mischiefs would soon have overflowed the

Church." Then, Whitefield lists his fears in a picturesque, eloquent, climaxing portrayal:

> How soon would whole swarms of monks, dominicans, and friars, like so many locusts, have overspread and plagued the nation; with what winged speed would foreign titular bishops have posted over, in order to take possession of their respective sees? How quickly would our universities have been filled with youths who have been sent abroad by their *Popish* parents, in order to drink in all the superstitions of the church of *Rome*? What a speedy period would have been put to societies of all kinds, for promoting Christian knowledge, and propagating the gospel in foreign parts? How soon would our pulpits everywhere have been filled with those old antichristian doctrines, free-will, meriting by works, transubstantiation, purgatory, works of supererogation, passive obedience, nonresistance, and all other abominations of the whore of *Babylon*? How soon would our protestant charity-schools in *England*, *Scotland*, and *Ireland*, have been pulled down, our Bibles forcibly taken from us, and ignorance everywhere set up as the mother of devotion! How soon should we have been deprived of that invaluable blessing, liberty of conscience, and been obliged to commence (what they falsely call) catholics, or submit to all the tortures which a bigoted zeal, guided by the most cruel principles, could possibly invent! How soon would that mother of harlots have made herself once more drunk with the blood of the saints!

Notice how Whitefield employs the words "our" and "we" in the passage, indicating that he viewed himself as part of the colonial society. The reader can easily imagine how Whitefield might have clothed the passage with indignation and anger through his tone and bodily action. These fears were quite meaningful to the community of Protestant Christians since the Jacobite bloodletting reminded them of England's previous periods of revolutionary and religious turmoil. Moreover, the violence and war of the past two hundred years in Europe—usually resulting from or attributed to religious conflict—made these fears far more potent than they might seem today. Notably here, Whitefield condemns the notions of "passive obedience" and "non-resistance" as "abominations of the whore of *Babylon*." These were central themes that had been debated in British politics for the past century. Their successful refutation was what enabled Cromwell's 1645 revolution and the "Glorious Revolution" of 1688. Yet Jacobites and other Stuart supporters continued to invoke these principles in their efforts to put the Stuarts back on England's throne. These became central issues prior to the American Revolution. They were echoed and expounded upon by Jonathan Mayhew four years later in his sermon that John Adams called the "morning gun of the Revolution." Whitefield ends the section giving thanks to God for preventing such horrors.

Religion was political for Whitefield, and he became increasingly political when religious freedoms were threatened. While Whitefield may or may not be exaggerating the extent of the averted evil, he believed he was not and wanted his audience to believe the same. The community of Christian converts that grew out of the Awakening held inherently political interests that, as their minister, he felt obligated to defend. His purpose was to solidify public support of the current British Crown for the purpose of protecting the free practice of Protestant religion. The Scots were largely Presbyterians with whom Whitefield could build a bridge founded on their common Protestant faith. This particular group of colonists had been constructing an identity, since their initial arrival in 1729, based in reformed Protestantism where, in the words of Patrick Griffin, "religion trumped ethnicity."[11] Whitefield desired to create a deeper sense of unity among the more-recent immigrants by offering a rationale for Jacobite sympathizers to support the political status quo based on their religious heritage. In addition, most of the European groups who immigrated to America were Protestant and could respect his argument. By employing John Knox's argument, that obligation to God outweighs all, Whitefield's policy of protecting religious liberty transcends any impulses to support political upheaval. A change in the king could have replaced the Church of England with Roman Catholicism as the state-supported religion.

But more important, Whitefield provided definitions of a good king and a bad one. On the one hand, he portrayed George II in glowing terms with general examples of his justice and wisdom. On the other, he depicted Charles Edward as a servant of the Antichrist and speculated on the ramifications of a successful invasion with examples of past atrocities. While his speculations may have been fostered by his own personal fears, his portrayal of the gravity of the situation was realistic. Indeed, with better advice, unified leadership within the Scots, and a stronger base of support from the people of Scotland and England, the rebellion might have plunged the empire into another period of bloodshed. Thus, Whitefield distinguished between good and evil leadership in the practical republican terms of action, whether arbitrary and tyrannous, or protective of liberty. And while his definition was intended to draw people closer to God, it supplied, for those who internalized it, a benchmark for leadership in all contexts. In so doing, these definitions would begin to operate as a first-stage rhetorical topic for Revolutionary-era polemicists.

In the sermon's third movement, Whitefield attributes the fortunate turn of events to God's mercy, giving God full credit for Charles Edward's retreat from Derby back into Scotland. He compares Charles Edward's advisors to the biblical character Ahithophel, whose rebellious yet prudent advice to a biblical usurper was thwarted by God's divine intervention.[12] Whitefield points out that because of Charles Edward's retreat to the Highlands and the subsequent amalgamation of all the rebels into one army, Cumberland was able to completely and decisively defeat the rebel threat. Whitefield even argues that it was best for the rebellion to go as far as it did, because the king learned who his friends were, it gave people an occasion to express their loyalty, France was humbled, and an "effectual stop" was put to "any such further popish plot to rob us of all that is near and dear to us."

The "instrument of this victory" deserves notice, and Whitefield personally names and extols individuals key to Britain's success. Whitefield describes Duke William, a younger son of George II, with the terms "nobleness of mind," "courage," "surprising bravery," and "magnanimity," eloquently acclaiming eight aspects of his character or deeds. Also, he lauds others involved in the battle:

> And shall we not say "Blessed above men let his Royal Highness the Duke of Cumberland be; for through his instrumentality, the great and glorious Jehovah hath brought mighty things to pass?" Should not our hearts be towards the worthy Archbishop of Tirk, the Royal Hunters, and those other English heroes who offered themselves so willingly? Let the names of Blakeney, Bland and Rea, and all those who waxed valiant in fight on this important occasion, live for ever in the British annals. And let the name of that great, that incomparable brave soldier of the King, and a good soldier of Jesus Christ, Colonel Gardiner, (excuse me if I here drop a tear; he was my intimate friend) let his name, I say, be had in everlasting remembrance.

He links tyranny with Catholicism in his praise of the battle's victors, who "delivered three kingdoms from the dread of popish cruelty, and arbitrary power." By defending English liberty, and opposing the threatened tyranny of Charles Edward, these men have earned great praise. One can only imagine the vocal punctuation and emotion with which Whitefield was able to adorn the above passage, especially in light of the grand style of oratory, laden with rhetorical devices and even rhyme displayed therein. The passage is somewhere between poetry and prose. If one reads it aloud with attention to its internal metering, alliteration and rhyme, *membras* and *commas*, the passage comes alive! Undoubtedly, Whitefield was at his oratorical and theatrical best. In a *Boston Gazette* editorial published a few weeks later, an eyewitness praised Whitefield and the sermon: "I should have been well pleased that all Men had heard it from the Preacher . . . he was in an Extasy, and every pause was so natural, that the Congregation were charmed with *Silence that spoke, and Eloquence of Eyes*."[13]

Whitefield follows his praise of men with a call for the praise of God. He demands consistency from his auditors; if men deserve honor, God deserves more honor, and such honor can best be proffered through obedience to God's moral law. For Whitefield, a system of civic/religious ordinances, as set down in Scripture and practiced in New England, was far superior to a legal code of any secular origination, and its superiority is self-evident: "Is not the divine image and superscription written upon every precept of the gospel? Do they not shine with a native intrinsic luster?" He continues the discourse by providing a repetition of his argument that God is the agent of their blessings and deserves honor. Finally, Whitefield concludes with a warning for the future, insisting that the danger from the rebels has not ended, that they may be instruments of God intended to scourge England for the neglect of her citizens toward God's law. He argues that as God "dealt with the Egyptians," God might also deal with Britain, and perhaps already has, citing recent epidemics.

The sermon can be read as an inverted jeremiad that reverses the formula of the traditional jeremiad, which is couched in strong and threatening language, painting a graphic picture of current degradation and coming wrath, and concluding with a positive vision of a potential future state, dependent on piety. In contrast, Whitefield argues that people should continue their piety to maintain God's blessings. *Britain's Mercies*, on the surface, appears ceremonial with the purpose of praising heroes and blaming villains (at which Whitefield demonstrates his adept ability) but takes a deliberative turn as he uses the immediate occasion as a spiritual analogue, arguing for the type of people they ought to be.

Whitefield's political sentiments (an aspect of "another spirit") were manifest by addressing a significant military and political event and prescribing a political ideology for his auditors. Conspicuously absent is an invitation to the new birth and any choice for action, which climaxes almost all his other sermons, showing that his goal for the sermon was not spiritual. For one such as Whitefield, this absence of a persuasive invitation to the new birth is significant and must not be overlooked in interpreting his intentions for the discourse. Recalling the distinctions that structured Whitefield's sermon, past-present-future and good-evil, one can presume that audience members, for whom these representations of reality held legitimacy, might embrace his definitions and interpretations—definitions that were grounded in common sense, eloquent, and widely circulated in print, giving them the potential of being influential to open minds. Even his slippery-slope accusations of life under a tyrannical "Popish government" were not without precedent in European history. The actions themselves and descriptions of tyrannical rule in general created a vivid definition of a tyrant by which other rulers might be compared. Moreover, Whitefield praised the opposition to potential tyranny, even though Charles Edward had a legal claim to the throne according to the practice of hereditary succession. He lauded the individuals who fought in the battles and established the notion that "opposition to tyranny is just." Technically, Whitefield presented a rhetorical reality, to be employed by his audience for the interpretation of states-of-affairs in American society that could generate first-stage rhetorical topics useful for both personal and collective deliberation regarding courses of action.

Whitefield was drawing upon an older tradition to vilify the French through their link with papism. Antipapal rhetoric had been employed for at least a century in English political upheavals as "coded language for constitutional fears of over-powerful monarchy."[14] But according to Nathan Hatch this tradition was not grounded in "Puritan fears that Rome pulled the strings for Stuart puppets," or from Enlightenment thinkers that accused Rome of keeping people ignorant that they might be more easily controlled; instead this tradition was derived, in Hatch's words, from a "view of history that had come to define the struggle between Protestants and Catholics as one battle in the larger war between liberty and arbitrary power."[15] By portraying the

Catholic French as "them"—the enemy of genuine religion (which now included moderates from both the New Light and Old Light factions)—and blending the religious vocabulary with political terms, Whitefield further insinuated religious activism into American politics. He prescribed a political ideology—palpable support of the British Crown—to the religious community, and they accepted it and became involved in the war effort. This political shift suggested a precedent for American religion and politics: that the church should support (with blood if needed) the government that will ensure religious liberty and oppose the government that would oppress its people through arbitrary power. Whitefield reiterated and reinforced this notion for the rest of his career.

As Whitefield's tour progressed, he was explicitly aware of the radical message in *Britain's Mercies* and was concerned for the reception of its published version. In a letter to the Welsh evangelist Howell Harris, Whitefield confided that he wished to "know what effect my sermon on the rebellion has had" back in England. Calling it "much blessed in these parts," Whitefield also expressed his anxiety for ecclesiastical unification in New England, saying, "I shall be glad when the great Head of the church unites dear brethren again."[16] Whitefield also hoped that the sermon would make a definitive public statement regarding his own loyalties and contribute to the rehabilitation of his public image. To another friend Whitefield later wrote, "My *State Sermon* has gone through two editions. They have also my five last sermons, which have convinced my friends that I am firm to my principles."[17] His efforts seemed to work. The *Boston Gazette* dedicated the front page of September 23, 1746, to an editorial penned by "Methodistus" supporting Whitefield: "The Gentlemen at the Head of the Administration . . . have given it as their Opinion, that the *Methodists* in general and Mr. *Whitefield* in particular, are great Friends to his Majesty, and all that are set in Authority under him." The writer went on to say, "*I DOUBT NOT but everybody in the British Dominions will*, upon reading that Sermon, *be convinced* (if any one ever stood in need of such a Conviction) that *Mr.* Whitefield *is as zealous a Protestant, as a warm a Friend to Liberty, and therefore as dutiful a Subject to his present Majesty*, as any Man living."[18] Whitefield's public image was well on the way to recovery.

## Civil Millennialism and Unification

The millennial theology of the Christian community has traditionally consisted of the belief that Christ would one day return from heaven, destroy all who do evil and cause sin, and then reign over a kingdom of saints for a thousand years until the final judgment and the creation of a new earth. Hence, the Awakening was viewed by Protestant leaders such as Jonathan Edwards as a final outpouring of God's grace and calling of people into his kingdom that would immediately precede Christ's return. But Christ did not return as soon as expected, creating a delay that exerted pressure to revise their doctrine. To resolve this problem, the ministerial community mused, "Perhaps Christ was already at work in setting up his kingdom and making war on evil by more visible means. Perhaps Christ and the devil were already at war with one another through existing governments." It follows that if these were indeed the reasons for the delay, then the right polemic discourse could redefine the community of believers and goad them to align politically with the established colonial governments. Thus began a blending of religion and politics that evolved into what Nathan Hatch has termed "civil millennialism," an "amalgam of traditional Puritan apocalyptic rhetoric and eighteenth-century political discourse." This blend forged a tenacious link between religious piety and liberty![19] As Hatch explained:

> In picturing the struggle of liberty versus tyranny as nothing less than the conflict between heaven and hell, the clergy found their political commitments energized with the force of a divine imperative and their political goals translated into the very principles which would initiate the kingdom of God on earth.[20]

Asserting that the expectations of Edwards and other New Light theologians had to be modified when the Awakening failed to usher in the millennial reign of Christ, Hatch placed the development of civil millennialism between 1744 and 1754, setting it in place just in time to empower the French and Indian war rhetoric. Yet Hatch sheds little light on the intellectual origins of civil millennialism, merely pointing out that it could not have directly evolved from post-Awakening theology and that it first appeared in sermons by New Light ministers after the Louisburg expedition. By the mid-1750s, ministers, including Old

Lights, were preaching that "an extensive French-Catholic conspiracy" was "linked directly to an apocalyptic interpretation of history in which the French were accomplices in Satan's designs to subjugate God's elect in New England."[21] According to Hatch, this initial form of civil millennialism was developed and expressed by Jonathan Mayhew and other ministers. But prior to Mayhew's publication, Whitefield's sermon *Britain's Mercies* explicitly connected the French, papism, and Antichrist in the "horrid plot, first hatched in hell, and afterwards nursed at Rome" that he believed inspired Charles Edward's attempted coup. Whitefield's connection of virtue with liberty predates Hatch's first exemplars of the apocalyptic plot by eight years and establishes an effective argument field to attack arbitrary power. Again we find Whitefield resurrecting an older ideograph, situating it on the leading edge of an intellectual transformation and disseminating it throughout the colonies.[22] Whitefield was the agent most able to sponsor notions of civil millennialism among the colonists. Few ministers of the period had sufficient popularity to sell their published sermons beyond their immediate spheres in the same way that Whitefield could. He provided an eloquent rhetoric and a network of dissemination that accelerated the spread of this notion throughout the colonies.

In practical terms, civil millennialism resulted from transporting the us-them distinction from strictly religious grounds into political grounds. Such a shift was precisely what Whitefield was seeking to help him recover his sphere of influence, which had been curtailed during the post-Awakening conflict. Having distanced himself from the radical enthusiasm of other dissenters, Whitefield's emphasis upon tangible threats to the American Christian community served to refocus colonial eyes upon the political sphere, thus easing criticism against him.

Whitefield was back in Maryland in 1747, continuing to range the woods for sinners, but was prevented from going into Virginia by a recently passed anti-itinerant law. In spite of his published defenses of itinerating, Whitefield did not challenge the law, preferring instead to bide his time. Moreover, New England might not have been ready for his return, perhaps due to the heavy loss of life while garrisoning Louisburg for the winter. He did not yet sense a welcome mat laid out for him, writing, "I am afraid that many ministers and the heads of the people would not bear it."[23] But since thousands in the South had not yet heard him, he decided to continue his ministry there: "Nobody goes out scarcely but myself."[24] So he continued his touring of the Middle and Southern colonies throughout 1746 and early 1747. At this time, the message of the new birth fully permeated the South as it had New England seven years earlier. By June 1747 Whitefield was planning a return to Boston in order to say goodbye to his friends there, and he was certainly optimistic that his reception would be better than the one three years earlier. He was not to be disappointed.

The *Boston Gazette* began reporting Whitefield's whereabouts as his tour neared New England again. Every week through the early summer the paper reported where he had last preached and speculated on when he would arrive. After hearing that Whitefield was becoming increasingly ill in New York and had cancelled his trip, the paper ceased its reports. But in early August, Whitefield announced that his health would permit a trip up to Boston after all, and the paper reinstituted the progress reports. He arrived two weeks later and immediately began preaching all over town: Coleman's church was first, then he preached at various places—Presbyterian, Congregational and Baptist, all to large crowds. Within a week he preached his farewell sermon on a cemetery hill at the edge of town. According to the newspaper, "The Hill with its Avenues were covered with People; and some tho't there were Twenty Thousand."[25]

In a letter to Gilbert Tennent, Whitefield summarized his reception: "I can now send you good news from the Northward. My reception at Boston, and elsewhere in New-England, was like unto the first. . . . Congregations were rather larger than ever, and opposers' mouths were stopped."[26] Whitefield was so encouraged that he was reminded of the revival in 1740 before all the controversy ensued: "The gathering of the people, and the power that attended the word seemed to be near the same as when the work begun seven years ago." Then, in a move that would have been foolhardy had there remained any controversy, Whitefield invited Tennent to come up to Boston and continue the revival as he had in 1741: "Will you now take another trip? I believe it would be blessed to the good of your own and many other souls."[27] The breach was at least partially healed. The *Convention of New England Ministers* had apparently initiated a shift in the majority of attitudes. Fears about Whitefield and conspiracies abated, and radical enthusiasts such as Davenport had been marginalized, leaving Edwards, Whitefield, and Tennent in the mainstream of the Christian community. Tennent would help to reunite the split among Presbyterians in the next decade. Although the New Light and Old Light clergy still held some doctrinal and practical differences, they had ironed out a working partnership that would be called to duty in the next two decades in the fight against the French and to defy the scheme to establish an Anglican episcopacy in America, which, as people feared, might undermine the authority of colonial governments.

Whitefield traveled back south after leaving Boston, describing his visit as a "pleasant journey," and spent much of the fall and winter in Georgia before he set sail for Bermuda, where he stayed several months recovering his health. He left for England in June 1748 and employed his hand revising his *Journals*, removing the portions that Old Lights used against him in the paper war of New England three years earlier. Reflecting on the last several years, Whitefield seemed honestly to regret the trouble ascribed to him and accepted responsibility for his role. In a letter to a minister friend in England, Whitefield lamented:

> Alas! alas! In how many things have I judged and acted wrong.—I have been too rash and hasty in giving characters, both of places and persons. Being fond of scripture language, I have often used a style too apostolical, and at the same time I have been too bitter in my zeal. Wild-fire has been mixed with it, and I find that I frequently wrote and spoke in my own spirit, when I thought I was writing and speaking by the assistance of the spirit of GOD. I have likewise too much made inward impressions my rule of acting, and too soon and too explicitly published what had been better kept in longer, or told after my death. By these things I have . . . hurt the blessed cause I would defend, and also stirred up needless opposition . . . I bless him for ripening my judgement [sic] a little more, for giving me to see and confess, and I hope in some degree to correct and amend, some of my mistakes.[28]

Whitefield arrived in England in July 1748. Having attended to his American parish, it was time to visit his parishes in Scotland, Wales, and England. He had been absent from the British Isles for nearly four years by the time of his return.

### Chaplain of a Countess

A couple of months after Whitefield's arrival in England, Lady Selina, the Countess of Huntingdon, recently widowed and now in command of great wealth, invited Whitefield to deliver a sermon at her home to members of England's nobility.[29] Duly impressed, she appointed Whitefield to be one of her private chaplains, an arrangement that would continue to the end of Whitefield's life. From this point he regularly preached in her home to Britain's aristocrats. Attendees included Lord Chesterfield, Lord Bolingbroke, and Beau Nash, among others, and though they appreciated Whitefield for his oratorical skill, their open conversion was not to occur. Yet, more than once an Anglican bishop attended a sermon at Lady Huntingdon's home, hidden in a curtained bishop's seat dubbed "Nicodemus' corner" by a woman who used to help them slip in to hear without being seen.[30] Through these parlor sermons and in subsequent conversations, Whitefield established connections with British political leaders. After one parlor sermon Whitefield wrote:

> On Tuesday I preached twice at Lady Huntingdon's to several of the nobility. In the morning the Earl of Chesterfield was present. In the evening Lord B____ [Bolingbroke]. All behaved quite well, and were in some degree affected. Lord C____ thanked me, and said, "Sir, I will not tell you what I shall tell others, how I approve of you," or words to this purpose. He conversed with me freely afterwards. Lord B____ was much moved, and desired I would come and see him the next morning. I did; and his Lordship behaved with great candour and frankness.[31]

Such relationships attest to Whitefield's genuine shift into the mainstream and his deepening relationships with British aristocrats of a Whig temperament. Bolingbroke had been known for his own oratorical abilities early in his career. A Jacobite at the time of the first attempted coup, he lost his position and subsequently regained it. Afterward, an apparent conversion to Whig sentiments was evidenced by his publication *The Patriot King* in 1740, as well as his unsympathetic response to the 1745 rebellion. Though Bolingbroke died in 1751, Whitefield certainly maintained relationships with his peers. Information he later shared with American ministers regarding the Grenville Program and the efforts to establish an American bishop support the belief that he *likely* discussed political matters with Whig leaders in London before or after his parlor sermons and that his contact with them certainly kept Whitefield abreast of London's political currents.

Whitefield's appointment as chaplain to the Countess of Huntingdon exemplifies the ironic and precarious balance of his enterprise and is a tribute to his ability to create a stable position between divergent religious or political ideologies. Although he was an admitted Methodist who publicly defied Anglican leaders and policies, he had Anglican bishops sneaking in to hear him preach. The person who introduced shifts in communication practices that facilitated the overturning of class structures in the American colonies, whose teachings were irreversibly shaping the American mind into one capable of rebelling against any leadership that began to limit their privileges, was now financially subsidized and approved of by the British aristocracy. And this enigmatic situation could not be due to ignorance. British leaders had recognized the threat of Whitefield's ministry to the social structure since its early years. But Whitefield's ability to maintain and repair relationships and to rhetorically construct moderate ideological and theological positions allowed him to continue his enterprise while soothing the fears of the established order. Maintaining such a balance required great rhetorical skill and continued adjustments. One can view examples of it in the genuine self-effacing, ingratiating tone of his letters to the Countess of Huntingdon, the bishop of London, and others who held a higher social position. He admits his faults and thanks his critics for pointing them out, yet he argues confidently on doctrinal issues and other areas where he had expertise. The apparent inconsistencies of his enterprise ultimately served to demonstrate to his contemporaries the art of reconciling opposites, inventing middle ground, and fine-tuning one's position in response to blows that would shatter less flexible ideologies.

## DISCOURSE CONCERNING UNLIMITED SUBMISSION

In 1750, while George Whitefield was making effective use of his connections with British nobility, a young Boston minister named Jonathan Mayhew delivered and published a sermon titled *Discourse Concerning Unlimited Submission and Nonresistance to the Higher Powers*. John Adams praised the sermon as the initiation of the American Revolution and its pages provide evidence that the Awakening conceptual system had begun to influence the thought of emerging American leaders. The conceptual distinctions and first-stage rhetorical topics Whitefield had introduced and popularized find generous expression in Mayhew's famous sermon.

Mayhew enrolled at Harvard in 1740 and initially embraced the Awakening during a trip to Maine where he heard testimonies of heavenly transports during an outpouring of God's Spirit a few months earlier. But he quickly repudiated his support and spent the rest of his career formulating a theology that would disavow enthusiastic excesses. Although their theological beliefs still differed, by 1750 Mayhew and Whitefield found themselves both in support of the civic and religious status quo in New England and were making similar arguments regarding politics.[32] Mayhew's political perspectives mirrored Whitefield's as he drew upon common argument fields and employed an inventional rhetorical topic that Whitefield resurrected and disseminated to make his own case.

Mayhew's sermon was specifically directed not at George II but at Anglican support of "hereditary succession" and "unlimited submission," doctrines promoted by the SPG (Society for the Propagation of the Gospel—the Anglicans' missionary arm) to enhance the memory of the House of Stuart. Mayhew reports writing the sermon in response to a "strange sort of frenzy" among American Anglicans who were "preaching passive obedience, worshiping King Charles I, and cursing dissenters and puritans for murdering him."[33] These determined SPG missionaries constituted a threat for Mayhew by lauding Charles I, combined with their requests to London to establish an American bishop and consequent episcopal system. Later, Mayhew would lead Americans in the struggle against establishment of a bishop.

Mayhew's sermon employs an argument field used in *Britain's Mercies and Britain's Duties* by making a distinction between genuine and counterfeit leadership. He argues that corrupt clergy forfeit their right to minister and that opposition to tyranny is just. After a lengthy exposition of scriptures germane to the relationship between Christians and civil authorities, in which he explains the scriptural foundation for the notion of passive obedience held by his theological critics, Mayhew attacks the current practice of "passive obedience" as a misunderstanding of Scripture:

> And if we attend to the nature of the argument with which the Apostle here enforces the duty of submission to the higher powers, we shall find it to be such an one as concludes not in favor of submission to all who bear the title of rulers in common, but only to those who actually perform

their duty of rulers by exercising a reasonable and just authority for the good of human society.[34]

Mayhew distinguishes between title and actions, between those with the legal title who do not rule appropriately and those who do. This position parallels Whitefield's opposition to the return of Charles Edward, who had forfeited his commission to rule a Protestant nation by his promotion of Catholicism, even though he had as much right to the throne as George II. Further defining the actions of an evil ruler, Mayhew continues:

> If rulers are a terror to good works and not to the evil; if they are not ministers for good to society but for evil and distress by violence and oppression . . . instead of attending continually upon the good work of advancing the public welfare, they attend only upon the gratification of their own lust and pride and ambition to the destruction of the public welfare—if this be the case, it is plain that the Apostle's argument for submission does not reach them.

Here Mayhew offers a concise description of arbitrary power in the self-gratification of the ruler at the expense of the governed. As in Whitefield's argument, the unrighteous deeds and attitudes of the evil ruler negate any scriptural dictate supporting passive obedience. Mayhew then says:

> Suppose, farther, that a number of *Reverend* and *Right Reverend Drones*, who *worked not*, who preached, perhaps, but *once a year*, and *then* not the *gospel* of Jesus Christ, but the *divine right of tithes*, the *dignity of their office as ambassadors of Christ*, . . . spending their lives in effeminacy, luxury, and idleness . . . would not everybody be astonished at such insolence, injustice, and impiety?[35]

Mayhew reminds the audience that even ministers have a duty to their office, to faithfully minister to their parishioners, just as the king has the duty to establish justice and liberty for Englishmen. For all practical purposes, here is an argument against unconverted ministers that reiterates Whitefield's and Tennent's preaching. Mayhew then directly challenges the doctrine of the divine right of kings: "Rulers have no authority from God to do mischief. . . . It is blasphemy to call tyrants and oppressors God's ministers. They are more properly the messengers of Satan to buffet us." Mayhew's claims mirror Whitefield's accusations against the House of Stuart for "arbitrary and tyrannical government, both in church and state."

On identical grounds both Whitefield and Mayhew condemned tyrannical government (and church leadership) and asserted that such government originates with Satan, not God. Here, as in Whitefield's sermon *Britain's Mercies*, the character of leadership was defined in terms of actions that uphold the spirit of freedom and liberty—rather than any imputed, inherent qualities. Just as one was not a Christian due to baptism or church attendance but through the new birth and "laboriously striving" for an inward change of heart, one does not merely pay lip service to liberty but must uphold traditional rights of Englishmen.

Mayhew concludes: "Common tyrants and public oppressors are not entitled to obedience from their subjects by virtue of anything here laid down by the inspired Apostle." This was a critical first principle extended from Whitefield's thought on titular unconverted ministers. With the widespread publication and acceptance of this argument, civil leaders who condemned opposition to the government on scriptural grounds could no longer do so. Policies that upheld liberty were henceforth to be the basis for a right to rule.

Looking back after the Revolution, John Adams said that Mayhew's sermon was "read by everybody; celebrated by friends, and abused by enemies."[36] However, at the time of its first printing, few readers recognized its radical message. The sermon did not take on its full significance until after the Grenville Program was implemented by Parliament (1764), whereupon it gained an entirely new meaning as it evolved from a diatribe against the martyrdom of Charles I into a statement that obliged Englishmen to oppose tyrannous rulers. For the time being, Mayhew's sermon stepped aside and let other issues move to the fore until its republication in 1775. Although revolution arguably was not Mayhew's ultimate intent, many historians regard his sermon as the initial expression of revolutionary propaganda by alerting colonists to the danger of passively submitting to unrighteous rulers.[37] Bernard Bailyn regards Mayhew's sermon "as a classic formulation of the necessity and virtue of resistance to oppression" and that its publication increased Mayhew's reputation as a spokesman for republican ideas within the colonies.[38] But perhaps Bailyn's accolades for Mayhew should be shared with Whitefield. Mayhew's sermon was prefigured by Whitefield's earlier, more primal message in *Britain's Mercies*. Many of the themes in Mayhew's sermon were first articulated by Whitefield. Mayhew's ostensible contribution was to extend Whitefield's principles from opposition to Charles Edward to rulers in general, not knowing where that extension would lead.

Whitefield remained in the British Isles preaching regularly from July 1748 until September 1751 when he traveled to Georgia with several orphans, but he immediately returned to England to secure the renewal of Bethesda's charter from officials in London as its expiration neared. Most Americans never knew he was in the country. A year later Gilbert Tennent and Samuel Davies visited London to raise money for the New Jersey College (Princeton), and they likely turned Whitefield's attention back to America as he entertained them for dinner one evening. He immediately arranged a fifth trip, which began in May 1754 and lasted about a year. The purpose of the trip was to take twenty-two additional children with him to the orphanage.[39] His return to Boston would be the first visit since 1747, and the former animosity was all but forgotten. Time had healed the wounds of the post-Awakening breach as far as Whitefield's enterprise was concerned. Gillies wrote, "Prejudices subsided; some of the rich and great began to think favourable of his ministrations."[40] Whitefield made further headway into Virginia and Maryland on this trip. Samuel Morris had made Whitefield known to many Virginians by reading his sermons, and other ministers such as Gilbert Tennent, William Robinson, John Blair, and Samuel Finley had visited Virginia as well, spreading the new birth with the Awakening conceptual system.[41] Thus, Whitefield was enthusiastically welcomed in these two colonies, and crowds turned out at his revival meetings.

While other itinerant preachers settled down to tend local parishes, Whitefield continued to travel and preach to vast crowds as if the revival was still going. As far as Whitefield was concerned, the revival never really ended. After an uneventful fifth tour, about which Whitefield says little, he left, feeling it was God's will for him to return to England.[42] Perhaps the approaching war caused him to long for the safety of England.

## THE WAR FOR AN EMPIRE

The English and French, traditional enemies for centuries, renewed their hostilities in Europe in the mid-1750s. Although various and complex issues drew other countries into the conflict, from 1756 to 1763 these two nations, in their efforts to dominate Europe and America, engaged in what many historians refer to as the first genuine world war. Whitefield's concerns during this period were to protect his parish—the whole world—as it faced renewed threats from French-Catholic control.

As the conflict with the French spiraled down into outright war, Whitefield revived his antipapist discourses and expressed his apprehension for the colonists: "O *America*, how near dost thou lie upon my heart! GOD preserve it from popish tyranny and arbitrary power!"[43] In such statements Whitefield revealed his millennial theology that connected the natural world with a spiritual one—that evil political ideals were manifestations of Antichrist in the hearts of people. In the context of his duty to preach against arbitrary power, Whitefield wrote, "O that we may be enabled to watch and pray against all the opposition of *Antichrist* in our hearts.[44] He viewed arbitrary power as the behavioral manifestation of Antichrist, Roman Catholicism as its religion, and the nation of France as its political face. So thoroughly did Whitefield believe that papism should be resisted that he even left, in his will, a list of "Subjects for Annual Prizes at the Orphan-house" for oratorical contests among the orphans and students. For one contest Whitefield rewarded the best "oration on the glorious Revolution, and the infinite Mercy of GOD, in delivering *Great Britain* from Popish Tyranny and Arbitrary Power."[45] He wished the children in his care to learn British history, develop an explicit connection between the civil and religious spheres, and to understand the role that arbitrary power played therein.

In 1754 George Washington led a failed attempt to capture a French fort at Pittsburgh, initiating the American theater of the conflict known in the colonies as the French and Indian War. By 1756 both nations, England and France, were aggressively executing their designs, but not all colonists were passionate about the war effort. New Englanders found little relevance of the war to their lives, and Presbyterians of the Middle and Southern colonies seemed to care little, if anything, about the conflict.[46] Requiring recruits to man its armies on both sides of the Atlantic, Parliament and the king had a sizable problem in the colonies. Returning to London, Whitefield went to work as a propagandist in the war effort by publishing an enlistment sermon, which was released concurrently in Boston, Philadelphia, New York, Edinburgh, and London in 1756. Since Whitefield had granted General Pepperell's request for an enlistment sermon a decade earlier to promote the Louisburg expedition, it is not unreasonable to suggest that Whitefield's noble acquaintances in London may have drafted his voice to support the war. Thus, Whitefield's sermon, *A Short Address to Persons of all Denominations, Occasioned by the Alarm of an Intended Invasion, in the Year 1756*, played a role in motivating the religious community to make the war their business. The sermon went through five editions and was the number two best seller in the American colonies behind William and Elizabeth Fleming's gripping account of their capture and escape from Native Americans.[47]

Whitefield opens *A Short Address* with a humble request to add his voice to public discourse concerning the recently declared war with France. Whitefield applauds the calling of a public day of "humiliation" and defends it as a reasonable and effectual response to the French military threat. The first section of the sermon provides an analogical argument, building upon a biblical example, citing how a plot against the Jews while they were in subjugation was thwarted by a public fast. Appealing to the consistency of God, Whitefield reasons that if the Jewish public fast brought God to their cause, then a public fast would do the same for Great Britain. Next, Whitefield lays responsibility for the war at the feet of the French for breaking a treaty. He reminds his listeners that God once honored the prayer of a Turkish general who fought against the Crusaders after they broke a treaty. How much more would God support a Christian nation after their evil enemy broke a treaty? This is followed by pointing out the efficacy of other historical figures that prayed and fasted before battle.

Apparently directing his persuasive efforts at Christians in his audience who would not support any war effort, Whitefield counters pacifism by asserting that God is no pacifist and that people who eschew war must view the situation from a jurisprudential perspective:

> For if God himself is pleased to stile himself a Man of War, surely in a just and righteous Cause (such as the *British* War at present is) we may as lawfully draw our Swords, in order to defend ourselves against our com-

mon and public Enemy, as a civil Magistrate may sit on a Bench, and condemn a public Robber to Death.[48]

Whitefield attempted to recast the terms of the war with the magistrate/robber metaphor. If he could convince his audience that indeed the French were acting illegally, then the metaphor provides a rationale for action. He further reasons from authority, reminding his audience of the Anglican dictum that Christians may serve in wars at the command of the king. Moreover, he warns of the consequences of neglecting to serve: if the French are not joined in battle, they may steal Pennsylvania from Britain's dominion.

Since the French initiated the war, and since "civil and religious liberties are all, as it were, lying at Stake," Christians were obligated to defend their country and would incur the "curse of Meroz" should they fail to espouse the war effort. Herein begins a very revealing passage of the sermon. The "curse of Meroz" refers to a biblical curse pronounced by the prophetess Deborah upon the inhabitants of the Hebrew town of Meroz whose men refused to fulfill their duty to join in battle against the enemies of Israel: "Curse ye Meroz, saith the angel of the LORD, curse ye bitterly the inhabitants thereof, because they came not to the help of the LORD against the mighty."[49] The curse served multiple purposes in colonial American history, and its use here further identifies Whitefield as a leader in shifts in public patterns of thought. In 1742 Jonathan Edwards introduced the curse to eighteenth-century Americans by invoking it metaphorically against antirevivalist New England clergy and parishioners. He criticized those questionable Christians who failed to support the revival. But here, Whitefield applies the curse literally, viewing the British as God's chosen people and the French as God's enemies. He applies the curse to those who would be pacifists. This use appears to be the curse's initial application in a martial sense in the eighteenth century. Samuel Finley, a Log College minister, made the curse the theme of an entire sermon published a year later in 1757, and Samuel Davies, another Presbyterian dissenter, drew upon it as well.[50] Both of these men were friends of Whitefield and likely had his sermon in their libraries when preaching its themes. Even if Davies or Finley first applied the curse in a martial sense (and there is currently no evidence that they did), their sermons were not immediately published, and their influence was limited to their locale.[51] Eventually, the curse would empower the rhetoric of American revolutionaries. As one rhetorical historian concluded, "When fighting on the side of God against the devil, even the most extreme measures of defense are not only sanctioned but mandated in the appeal to natural law or God's law."[52] Whitefield's use of the curse appears to be its first instance making a literal appeal to fight the French, and certainly he was the first to publish and widely disseminate what became "the favorite text of the Calvinist ministry in the wars of the Revolution."[53]

*A Short Address* hinges on the "curse of Meroz" as Whitefield holds it over the head of his audience and expounds the Christian's obligation to fight God's enemies. As the argument progresses, Whitefield further justifies the war with France by reminding his audience of the political links of France to papism. He repeats his arguments from *Britain's Mercies*, that papism was the earthly manifestation of the Antichrist. Whitefield exclaims that dying in battle would be a better fate than "hearing that a *French* Army, accompanied with a popish Pretender, and thousands of *Romish* Priests" had conquered Britain.

The next section elucidates Whitefield's attitude toward arbitrary power, which he claimed a self-appointed duty to expose and resist. Whitefield begins the section by praising George II (using similar language as in *Britain's Mercies*) for twenty-eight years of a "mild and gentle Administration." Whitefield again labels George II a "Nursing Father to People of all Denominations" and claims that he deserves the title "GEORGE THE GREAT" for his benevolent rule. Whitefield's portrait of a good ruler is to be contrasted with those seeking arbitrary power—power with no responsibility toward the governed. Whitefield decries "men of lax Principles, loose Lives, and broken Fortunes" who would "break through all Restraints of Gratitude, Loyalty and Religion" to support any shift in power that would advance their own personal financial or social standing.

From this point, Whitefield links the papists with evil, fusing them together with graphic terms such as "savage Popish Priests," a "cruel Popish Queen," "cruel Papists," "voracious Popish Priests," and phrases such as "*Rome*, glutted, as it were, with Protestant Blood," "ravenous Wolves pursuing the harmless and innocent Flocks of Sheep," and "their bloodthirsty and cruel Hands." Whitefield finally amalgamates them all in a full expression of civil millennialism at the end of the sermon, saying, "We need not fear what *France* and *Rome*, and *Hell*, with all its united Force, can do unto, or plot against us." Lastly, Whitefield adjures his audiences, if they put their trust in God, to fear not "the malicious Efforts and Designs of Men and Devils."

In addition to disseminating the sermon through his network of publishers, Whitefield personally spread themes voiced in *A Short Address* as he began to tour England and Scotland in 1756, frequently and explicitly preaching his martial message. As Gillies recounted, Whitefield unmasked "the miseries of Popish tyranny, and arbitrary power . . . exhorting his hearers to loyalty and courage at home, and . . . stirring them up to pray for the success of his Majesty's forces, both by sea and land abroad."[54] Thus, such sermons were no peripheral part of his ministry. In fact, *Britain's Mercies* and *A Short Address* were his two best-selling sermons after 1742. Whitefield's messages were fit for the occasion, as their popularity testified. Once again, Whitefield had eloquently reinforced the us-them distinction between Catholics and Protestants, and French and English, and disseminated his prescriptions through his network of publishers.

In spite of the French proximity and accompanying dangers as the French and Indian phase of the war progressed, the political situation in the American colonies was becoming relatively stable as moderates from both New Light and Old Light factions worked together in the war effort, and the colonists remained largely satisfied under British rule until after the death of George II. Talk of the separatists overturning the glorious New England tradition had ceased, and in its place ministers exhorted their parishes to support the war effort. Whitefield's backing of the war was critical to American development by virtue of his role as an opinion leader. French control was unacceptable, and many American ministers, following Whitefield's lead, threw their weight into the effort as a chance to bring down the papal Antichrist and to serve the "*Publick Good*." Gilbert Tennent exhorted people to "Let the WELFARE of so many of your fellow subjects, the welfare of the PROTESTANT INTEREST, the welfare of the CHURCH OF CHRIST, animate your hearts."[55]

Not only among the Protestant community did the war tend to unite the British colonies against the French, but other polemic networks had begun to promote unification as well. In 1754 Benjamin Franklin published a famous editorial cartoon depicting a snake, chopped into sections, each representing a colony or region, with the caption "JOIN, or DIE."[56] We should recall Whitefield's close friendship with Franklin when considering Franklin's increasing immersion in American politics. Whitefield normally lodged at Franklin's home whenever he was in Philadelphia, and Franklin likely appreciated the calls to form societies and the political involvement that he saw in Whitefield's enterprise.

Whitefield had been calling for unity among churches and ministers in America for seventeen years at this point. He understood how divisions between denominations would ultimately hurt the cause of Christ. These important themes found similar expression by Franklin, who translated them directly into political appeals. The famous saying attributed to Franklin, "We must all hang together or we will all hang separately," also reveals the us-them distinction as it evolved in Franklin's mind as the colonial crisis neared. One could speculate that Franklin and Whitefield found much to talk about as Whitefield's connections with British nobility and his involvement in British public opinion deepened.

After 1756 Whitefield became increasingly devoted to his duties in London with a church he established at the Moorfields, funded by Lady Huntingdon, and with his regular sermons to England's elite, fulfilling his duty as her chaplain. The Bethesda orphanage was prospering on secure financial ground and did not need his close attention as it did earlier. He also itinerated throughout Scotland, Wales, and England in the next few years and opened a second chapel in London on Tottingham Court Road, also funded by Lady Huntingdon. Here, Whitefield began preaching regularly, much to the consternation of the carnival entertainers and the theater community, drawing their paying audiences away and soliciting donations from them. As a result, a public conflict ensued in which Whitefield warned against the evil of attending plays, and members of the theater community regularly disrupted his meetings. Finally, Samuel Foote, the comic playwright, wrote *The Minor*, which lampooned Whitefield and his followers. In response Whitefield proudly remarked, "Satan is angry. I am now mimicked and burlesqued upon the public stage. All hail such contempt!"[57] Nevertheless, Foote had begun an effectual campaign of satire that eventually caused Whitefield to close the Tottingham Court chapel. But Whitefield soon found another theater that required his polemic efforts.

## DOMESTIC ENCROACHMENTS ON FREEDOM

After 1760 the Anglican Church and British Parliament began to prod Americans in sensitive areas. George II, the *Pater Patriæ* and "nursing father of the church," was dead. His reign had provided a stable climate in which Whig interests dominated British politics. The twenty-two-year-old George III succeeded him to the throne, and accompanying him were profound changes in the British government's approach to domestic and colonial governance. Determined to regain control of the country from the Whigs, George III took aim at their power and began undermining it. His chief tactics in the bid for increased control were to cause division within the Whig ranks and to solicit patronage through appointments and pensions. Whig control of the nation would gradually decrease as the next decade passed and the American colonists, who had grown accustomed to managing most of their own affairs under a Whig-run system, began to suspect plots to undermine their liberties emanating from the new Tory-led administration. But to have control of the nation's subjects, especially in the colonies, the Tories needed the Anglican Church to regain supremacy from the Dissenters. The intellectual allegiance of the people was the grand prize, and through the control of religious thought this allegiance could be effectively secured and shaped.

Whitefield remained steadfastly loyal to the monarchy after 1760, but gone were flattering acclamations of the king, and he spoke of loyalty to George III only in general terms. By 1764 he would be opposing the Tory plots against liberty, especially where the church was involved. He had plenty of opportunities as the Anglicans tried to slow the Methodist movement in England and increase their presence and power in the colonies.

Up to this point the SPG had focused its missionary efforts on the American frontiers and toward converting Native Americans, steering clear of the jurisdictions of New England Congregationalists. The Anglicans' efforts were hampered, however, by the lack of an ecclesiastical authority figure, a bishop, with the power to ordain new ministers. Talented young men, seeking ministry positions within the Anglican Church, had to travel to England for ordination, and important decisions had to be made in England as well. Thus, the SPG was seriously handcuffed and prevented from accomplishing all it wished. Important decisions and permission could not be secured in a timely manner, and

occasionally aspiring priests were lost at sea on their sojourn for ordination. In the 1760s the American-Bishop issue moved to the fore as
Thomas Secker, the archbishop of Canterbury, decided the time was
right to extend the episcopacy into America.[58] Concurrently, the SPG
turned its interests increasingly away from the Native Americans and
back toward Anglo-American colonists, welcoming excommunicated
Congregationalists and proselytizing separatists and Puritans alike into
the Anglican Church. Understandably, the Congregational ministers
became alarmed.

The Anglican Church itself had been tolerated in the colonies,
but with aggressive SPG missionaries, the potential for an American
bishop, and the establishment of an episcopal system, colonists espied
a Tory intrusion into their world that had been free from such influences since the founding of their colonial charters. American ministers
feared that Anglicans were seeking control of colonial affairs in both
civil and religious spheres through the office of a bishop. Just as the
Old Lights had suspected a Dissenter plot to take civil control in 1745,
the Christian community now suspected that ecclesiastical courts,
mandatory tithing, and Anglican political appointees would soon follow the episcopacy.[59] Each of these practices, which were standard fare
in England, smacked of arbitrary power for the colonial leaders.

In America these possibilities were not viewed as encroachments on *religious* liberties per se, but on liberty in general. Republican notions pervading the intellectual climate erased any distinction
between civil or religious liberties in the New England mind. Hence,
the non-Anglican ministers of America initiated a public conflict that
exceeded the scope of the Awakening controversy fifteen years before.
Jonathan Mayhew emerged as the leader against the establishment of
the Anglican episcopacy in America, spearheading vigorous resistance
to Anglican scheming throughout the period, urging his peers to keep
a vigilant watch for the sake of their civil and religious liberties.[60] After
the Treaty of Paris had been signed in 1763 ending the French and
Indian war, Archbishop Secker redoubled his labors to establish the
American episcopacy. But Mayhew and his New England associates
effectively frustrated the effort at every turn by informing the citizens
of their designs and organizing active public and private resistance.

As Whitefield would have wished, the moderates among American ministers continued to define themselves by seeking an increasing
degree of colonial unity. Ezra Stiles, a dedicated Whig and Old Light

from Rhode Island, called for the Protestant churches of America to form a voluntary consociation to protect religious liberties of all Americans. Stiles published an influential sermon titled *A Discourse on the Christian Union*, which articulated his recommendations for the structure of an anti-episcopal consociation of Dissenters.

Stiles points out that the enthusiasm of the Awakening was "piously meant, and honestly intended, and proceded [*sic*] from a zeal for the cause of God."[61] Additionally, the Awakening brought an "augmentation of 150 new churches" to New England, founded not on "separations," but "natural increase." He goes on to argue that the religious disparity between Arminianism and Calvinism is founded more upon "jealousies" and "mistake" than upon practical differences:

> And I find both reputed calvinists and arminians, especially of the clergy, agree in admitting the depravity of human nature in all its powers and affections—the absolute inability to faith and holiness, without the special influences, assistances and operations of the spirit on the human mind . . . that to his enlightening energies is to be attributed the principle of regeneration. . . . And I am persuaded if all would freely and candidly compare their sentiments to this rule [an appeal to the inspired writings], they would be very soon found not very variant.

Stiles wishes ministers to examine their doctrine and compare it to the "reality" of others, not the straw men each side had portrayed, confident that any genuine differences can be mitigated by "honorable and benevolent concessions." Once Christians saw that their differences could be downplayed, Stiles believed that churches could form consociations for "fellowship only, and not for dominion." Upon a common challenge to the church, they could elect a council to address it, but such councils would be dissolved once the matter had subsided. In the midst of these recommendations and arguments, Stiles makes a clear reference to the plan for an American episcopacy: "You are very sensible, that there is a formal attempt on the chastity and order of our churches, which is vigilantly to be guarded against, at present, till our churches grow into one cemented, large, pure, defensible body." Based on an appeal to a moderate ground between unrestrained "liberties," which lean toward "anarchy," and complete "dominion," which leads to "tyranny," the final passages of the sermon exhort the reader to lay aside prejudices and take steps toward unification of the churches.

Additionally, Stiles unmistakably reveals the growing distinction between "us" and "them" with no less than nine references to "our churches," voluntarily united against mandatory jurisdictions that create a "perpetual DICTATOR," referring to the intended Anglican bishop. Hence, in Stiles's view, Christians could find sufficient common ground for the voluntary union of America's churches, the purpose of which would be to resist tyrannical encroachments on their liberties. For the forty-six-year-old Whitefield, a consociation of churches would fulfill a life's dream and reassure him that religious liberty would be preserved in America. Not all ministers embraced Stiles's vision, especially those who still believed that pure evangelicalism would redeem American society. But after 1750, even "wild enthusiastical people," such as the Baptists led by Isaac Backus, were being "restored to the Edwardean fold" as they rediscovered Edwards' lofty "vision of the redemption of both church and society."[62] Led by Whitefield's example, American separatist churches were moving from the periphery to the center. Old Lights were now suggesting cooperation with New Lights and vice versa. Although the New Light churches had numerous theological strains, each was becoming more mainstreamed and more unity-minded as they affirmed common ground with other American denominations in the face of the Anglican threat. The *Convention of New England Ministers*, along with Stiles's sermon *Christian Union*, evidences the increasing impulse toward unification. As Stiles wrote of Arminians and Calvinists, "I cannot perceive any very essential real difference in their opinions respecting the fundamental principles of religion."[63]

The Tory and Anglican bids for increased power were two sides of the same coin; and as colonists were beginning to recognize the menace posed by the Church of England and its plans for a bishop, and as Ezra Stiles was calling for a "Christian Union," politically minded writers worked to expose initial instances of arbitrary power and tyranny in America. The critical eye turned toward British governance can be linked with the new vistas provided by blended republican and religious discourse. Tellingly, these writers employed arguments invented by Whitefield that drew upon the Awakening conceptual system for intelligibility and force. Both New Lights and Old Lights had been arguing for two decades that ministers who held their offices by virtue of their connections, or ministers who abused the privileges of their offices, were unfit. This pattern of thought—that one's qualifications for office depended upon one's ability and faithfulness in the execution of duty to the people—functioned as an inventional resource for anyone who wished to argue against corrupt leadership. Arguments generated by this resource sought to uncover behavioral and ideological inconsistencies, not just among unconverted ministers but public servants as well.

## A LETTER TO THE PEOPLE OF PENNSYLVANIA, &C

As both Whitefield and Mayhew had argued, even a king was subject to the duties of his office, and arbitrary power on his part was to be condemned. Inevitably, the new perspectives made possible by this inventional resource pointed out parallel inconsistencies in the political realm. In particular the behavior of colonial judges emerged as the initial issue that inflamed Americans to call for justice. Officeholders who abused their power would eventually be identified as part of "them," one of the tyrants, along with all the ramifications that identification carried.

In 1760 Joseph Galloway, a Philadelphia lawyer and a friend of Whitefield, published a pamphlet titled *A Letter To the People of Pennsylvania, &c* that suggested Parliament was undermining the judicial system that protected English liberty.[64] The thirty-one-year-old Galloway was associated with the antiproprietary faction, also known as the Franklin-Quaker Party. His pamphlet was widely circulated and served as a paradigm for later pamphlets regarding the tenure of judges. It was upon notions first articulated in Galloway's pamphlet that Thomas Jefferson drew to argue in the Declaration of Independence that an independent judiciary was essential to protect the rights and liberties of the people.

At issue was Parliament's refusal to end the practice of colonial judges serving at the king's pleasure. In September 1759 the Pennsylvania Assembly passed a law regarding the tenure of judges, prescribing that judges and justices in the colony would serve their "several and respective commissions and offices aforesaid, *quadiu se bene gesserint* [as long as they conduct themselves properly], and that their respective commissions shall be granted to them accordingly."[65] The Pennsylvania statute was meant to end the practice of allowing colonial judges to sit *durante bene placito* [at the king's pleasure], but Parliament immediately overturned it. Pennsylvanians were incensed. The resulting controversy moved the judicial issue to the fore in other colonies as they recognized the inconsistency between English and American legal practices. Judges in England were elected. Because colonial judges were appointed, the colonists felt cheated. In response, Galloway argued that citizens of the colonies should be allowed to elect and remove their own judges, as practiced in Great Britain, to ensure protection of their liberties as Englishmen. This exemplar of oppression remained a consistent grievance until 1776.

Colonial identity surfaces as an issue in the pamphlet as Galloway posits a distinction between "we" the Pennsylvanians and "them" the British, a use of pronouns that evidences an increasing self-awareness as a people. The distinction is legitimated by Parliament's "evil" act of enforcing a double standard that afforded English liberties to the Britons but not to the Americans. Up to this point the many colonists had understood their identity as British, but the inconsistency between colonial and English practice affronted their self-conception. As Breen explained, "The extraordinary bitterness and acrimony of colonial rhetoric requires us to consider the popular fear that the English were systematically relegating Americans to second-class standing within the empire."[66] Since Parliament's restriction impinged on British American privileges, Galloway judged their action as evil. And according to the implied doctrine that rulers are to be evaluated by their behavior and adherence to duty, Galloway was justified in condemning Parliament's suspension of the Pennsylvania statute.

The pamphlet begins by arguing that the chief end of government is to "secure the persons and properties of mankind from private and domestic oppression."[67] The central means of providing this benefit to the people was an independent judicial system, free from the influence of both the people and ruling officials. Galloway claims that judges will invariably become corrupt (displaying his Calvinist belief in human depravity), leading to a governmental system of slavery and tyranny. Galloway provides examples directly from British history to support his predictions and then traces the evolution of *quadiu se bene gesserint* to demonstrate its British origin.

To denounce parliamentary suspension of the Pennsylvania statute, Galloway reminds his readers of the "popery" of previous reigns: "Where then is the difference? If Charles and James dispensed with penal statutes in order to introduce popery, your former g----rs have dispensed with the laws and fundamentals of your liberties and privileges in order to introduce slavery." Thus he compares Parliament's action to the "Papists'" tactics—a strategy quite persuasive with Protestants. Echoing Mayhew and Whitefield, he continues by saying:

> Can you doubt that human nature, wearing the yoke engraved with the motto DURING PLEASURE, will not hold and practice the doctrine of *passive obedience* and *nonresistance* with respect to the destruction of your rights and privileges? . . . will not the same cause ever produce the same effect? Will that which was once destructive now change its nature and become harmless and innocent? Has the poison of the asp ever lost its virulent quality?

This passage draws upon the religious sphere, through the inventional resource of behavioral consistency, to argue that similar arbitrary behavior in the judicial sphere should be opposed. Galloway's reference to "human nature" bolsters the argument with the tenet that humanity is incapable of good without God.

Next, Galloway reasons with his audience to abandon the practice of "during pleasure" and support the practice of *"independent of power,"* finally taking the ideas out of their obscure Latin terms and translating them into terms that people could easily grasp. He then moves into a highly polemic section at the end of the essay that reinforces the implicit distinction between us-them, saying, "Consider my countrymen, farther, are the *Pennsylvanians* men of more independent fortunes or of greater abilities . . . and are they less liable to influence and corruption than the people of *England?*" By posing the question in this manner, Pennsylvanians are distinguished from those in Great Britain even while their similarities are being highlighted. He goes on to bring the distinction closer to home, using the pronoun "we": "Are we not subjects of the same King . . . and have we not the same God for our Protector?" Then he addresses pacifists:

> Let me ask those enemies to your welfare, how much thereof are you entitled to? Who will measure out and distribute your poor pittance, your short allowance? . . . Ye who are not willfully blind to the advantages of this beneficial law, who for want of a little reflection have spoke derogatorily of its merits, let me rouse you from your lethargy and prevail in you to see through the perspective of truth and your posterity's danger and approaching misery.

Although he argues that Pennsylvanians have the same rights as natural-born English, he clearly distinguishes between them as the letter concludes: "to the people of Pennsylvania in the same free and
constitutional manner as your sovereign grants them to his subjects in
England." Herein "us" and "them" are consistently distinguished with
"us," favoring the Pennsylvania statute, and "them," opposing it and
being identified with "his subjects in England." "We" are those who
support liberty, and "you" are those who promote tyranny.

Galloway's reasoning was made comprehensible by drawing on
earlier inventional resources popularized during the Awakening, bolstered by blended republican and religious vocabularies. The elements
and arrangement of his argument—the king, Parliament, and judges,
who assaulted liberties—bear a structural resemblance to the pope,
Roman Catholicism, and their "foreign titular bishops" who oppressed
Christendom. Additionally, Galloway's argument draws intelligibility
from the Church of England's appointment of "unconverted ministers" who misused their offices. Likewise, judges (ministers), who served
at the pleasure of the king (bishop), were cast as corrupt (unconverted),
guilty of exercising arbitrary power (religious tyranny), while independent judges would be virtuous (converted), leading the nation toward
liberty (freedom from sin). Just as the Holy Spirit was the common
privilege of all believers for Whitefield, the rights of Englishmen were
to be common to all British subjects. Galloway argued that anyone
who claimed that the colonists did not possess the same rights as
natural-born Englishmen was guilty of arbitrary power and was an
enemy to English liberty. Thus, in his effort to protect civil liberty, Galloway built upon the us-them distinction as it imbued the religious and
political spheres to construct a case that echoed notions reinforced by
fifteen years of continuous New Light preaching.

Evidence of shifting identity lurks in this text as well. Galloway
distinguishes between "we" Pennsylvanians and "you" who support
British policies, and highlights the ramifications of good and evil that
attend the distinction. Galloway rightly asks that if "we" do not share
the rights of Englishmen, then are "we" *really* Englishmen? Cultural
theorist Greg Urban points out that the use of such pronouns indicates
that notions of community are becoming part of everyday expression in the development of culture.[68] Tension regarding this question began to permeate the Revolutionary propaganda increasingly
throughout the rest of the colonial period, becoming more explicit as

the decade passed, surfacing even more pointedly in later Revolutionary pamphlets.

The rhetoric directed at parliamentary intrusion and Anglican aggression was simultaneously cast to the public with pamphlets displayed side by side at booksellers' shops and excerpts intermingled in the colonial papers. Whitefield's publications would be among the best sellers, reinforcing the patterns of thought that were now finding widespread usage. Politicians were complaining about Parliament, and the ministers were complaining about the Church of England. As the decade progressed, other political concerns would soon replace the *durante bene placito* issue, but the possibility of an American bishop continued as a bone of contention. "A succession of happenings," explains Carl Bridenbaugh, "nearly always involving Anglican missionaries, intimately took on for suspicious dissenters—and not without reason—the semblance of an ecclesiastical plot connected with the policy of the ministry, which culminated in the Stamp Act."[69] Although he had remained rather silent (in print) for several years, very soon Whitefield would surface again in the center of the Stamp Act crisis.

## CHAPTER SEVEN

# THE DEEP-LAID PLOT

As the French and Indian War came to a close in 1763, the new British administration sought to raise funds from abroad to ease the national debt, recovering some of the costs of the war from the colonists whom they viewed as the central beneficiaries of the victory. In 1763 George III replaced the Earl of Bute with George Grenville as the new prime minister, who promptly began a program of taxation and increased British control known as the Grenville Program. Soon, the colonists faced a two-headed threat that challenged colonial autonomy in both the religious and civil spheres, a threat that quickly ushered in social unrest. Carl Bridenbaugh explained, "To long-standing religious grievances fresh civil ones were now added, and it was the conjunction that produced the crisis."[1] Colonists, who had been struggling against Anglican hegemony, saw the new taxes as further encroachments upon their freedoms. In their view, liberty was being simultaneously assaulted on at least three fronts: by ecclesiastical hegemony, by a faulty judicial system with Parliament refusing to allow Americans to fix it, and by the Grenville Program that levied new internal taxes without the consent of colonial legislatures. And in a land where civil millennialism shaped the thinking of many, where republican vocabularies and notions were strengthening, the assault took on Armageddon-like proportions.

After the fear of French Catholic control subsided, Whitefield recognized a renewed threat to religious liberty from his own Anglican denomination. Persecution had largely ceased in 1744 after the trial and Whitefield's two pamphlets, but once George III took the throne, the Anglicans renewed their efforts to discredit the Methodists. Additionally, submersed fears of a conspiracy to overthrow New England's religious tradition were revived, but this time the culprits were Anglican instead of Separatist. As Whitefield added his opinions to the protests, for Americans, Whitefield's *direct opposition to his own denomination* defined the Anglicans as the new "them" who would impinge on

religious freedoms with their planned bishop. This reorientation of
"us" versus "them"—from Protestants versus Catholics to Dissenters
versus Anglicans—served as an essential step in the progression of the
colonial perspective that led to revolution!

William Warburton, bishop of Gloucester, had just published a
pamphlet accusing the Methodists of being seditious enthusiasts. Taking the role of an advocate, Whitefield counterpublished, suggesting
that Anglican efforts to suppress the Methodists would be replicated
in America with efforts to suppress all non-Anglican churches if a
bishop were appointed. Whitefield's opinions were already influential
in America, and since he was an Anglican with well-known connections with British nobility, many Americans might presume that he had
inside information regarding British designs. Whitefield had to express
himself carefully to keep out of trouble with Anglican leaders in Britain, but he wished to take a public stand and cleverly accomplished
it by opposing Warburton, his own local bishop, on theological and
practical grounds. Whitefield published his views in a pamphlet titled
*Observations on Some Fatal Mistakes* and had it promptly printed in London (three editions), with one edition each in Edinburgh, Philadelphia,
and Boston.

In Whitefield's publication, he positioned himself as a reformer
whose interest was in promoting "true Christianity" and resisting those
who were not genuine Christians, even if they were Anglican leaders. Herein Whitefield applies the us-them distinction directly to his
own denomination, identifying those who suppressed religious freedom
as out of God's kingdom. As usual, Whitefield opens by justifying the
need for his publication, forwarding an *a priori* argument that as Paul
and Jesus opposed the Pharisees, professors of a dead religion, the same
should be opposed today:

> Hence it is, that when they come to touch upon the internals and vitals
> of Christianity, they are quite grappled, and write so unguardedly of the
> all-powerful influences of the Holy Ghost, as to sink us into a state of
> *downright formality*; which, if the Apostle Paul may be our judge, we have
> need as much to be cautioned against, as of fanaticism, superstition, or
> infidelity itself.[2]

Here Whitefield identifies his moderate middle ground, between
"formality" and "fanaticism." Evidencing his moderate theology and

practice, the mature Whitefield does not promote the enthusiastic version of the operation of the Holy Spirit, of which he approved during the Awakening, but describes a version much closer to that explicated by the Old Light Samuel Quincy. He establishes the parameters of true Christianity and points out that they are defined by one's beliefs regarding the operation of the Holy Spirit. Whitefield explicitly excludes the professors of a formal Christianity from God's kingdom, making them members of the devil's kingdom. Whitefield echoes Paul in accusing leaders such as Warburton of "[h]aving a form of godliness, but denying the power thereof," and warns true believers, "from such, turn away; and to use the words of our LORD, Publicans and harlots enter into the kingdom of GOD before them." He could not have more explicitly declared that the bishop was unconverted! Whitefield further clarifies the spiritual condition of the bishop: "Surely, was the Apostle *Paul* to rise from the dead, and read over, or hear of such strange positions, his spirit, as once at *Athens*, would again be stirred in him; to see a writer thus attempting to erect an altar for the public worship of an unknown GOD: I say, an unknown GOD." Here Whitefield forcefully emphasizes that in his view Warburton does not even know God! Whitefield goes on to declare that "he is not a real Christian, who is only one outwardly; but he alone is a true Christian, who is one inwardly."

Next, Whitefield points out Warburton's internal inconsistency—that the bishop relies on God's Spirit to discern that God's Spirit has been withdrawn from man. Whitefield asks rhetorically, since human reason (in Warburton's view) is sufficient to understand spiritual matters, why, in all the oaths of ordination, do the Anglicans call upon God's Spirit for wisdom and guidance if it is no longer needed? Whitefield criticizes Warburton for establishing an *"external rule of faith"* to replace an internal indwelling of God's Spirit. His consistent use of antithetical phrasing to compare and contrast his theology with Warburton's endows the pamphlet with an eloquent and powerful voice.

Turning to attack Warburton's character, Whitefield quotes the bishop: "truth is never so grossly injured, or its advocates so dishonoured, as when they employ the foolish arts of sophistry, buffoonery, and personal abuse in its defence." Then he exclaims, "By thy own pen thou shalt be tried, thou hapless, mistaken advocate of the Christian cause." He goes on to compare the bishop to the "witch of Endor," describing how Warburton tainted the ghosts of the *"good old Puritans,"* falsely characterizing them as subversive independents responsible for the political turmoil of the Cromwellian Revolution in an attempt to associate the Methodists with analogous sedition. Whitefield also accuses the bishop of "heraldic, genealogical fiction" and asserts that he would prefer the zeal of the Puritans to the formalism of the current Anglican leadership. In a subsequent letter to an American friend, Whitefield pointed out that he defended the Puritan tradition in this pamphlet, suggesting that he inserted this reference to the *good old Puritans* to appeal to his American readers.[3]

Next, Whitefield accuses the bishop of duplicitous motives, saying, "The design our author had in view in drawing such a parallel, is easily seen through. Doubtless, to expose the present Methodists to the jealousy of the civil government." Thus, Whitefield's countermove is to assure the British government that Methodists and Dissenters are not seditious and that they should be allowed to practice their religion without civil restraints, just as he asserted in the trial transcripts he published in 1744. Finally, in classic polemical fashion, he judges Warburton: "My dear friend, if this is not gibbeting up names with unregenerate malice, to everlasting infamy, I know not what is."

Not coincidentally, Warburton was active in the Anglican propaganda effort for the American bishop and was accused of castigating the history of America to justify the need for an American episcopacy.[4] Thus, to discerning readers abreast of the bishop issue, Whitefield aligned himself in opposition against an American episcopacy, and he would directly state his views upon his arrival in America in 1763. Perhaps recalling the assassination attempt last time he published a pamphlet against Anglican leadership, Whitefield wisely left England as his pamphlet against Warburton was going to press.

Concerning the appointment of an American bishop, Whitefield's name was under consideration. Ironically, the American bishop was a post for which Whitefield was perhaps best qualified and one for which many Americans supported his appointment, even though the suggestion irritated many Anglicans in America.[5] However, Whitefield makes no mention of desiring the post in his own writings, and from this point on in his ministry he was continually at odds with various Anglican leaders and worked to advance American political interests.

Understandably, being an Anglican himself who always made public appearances in his priest's attire, Whitefield was not the opinion leader on the bishop issue in America. Yet by siding with the Americans, he encouraged a bandwagon effect and legitimated colonial fears of what the Church of England was really planning. By attacking War-burton, as a representative of Archbishop Secker and tyrannical Angli-cans in general, Whitefield damaged the Anglicans' public image by implying the American episcopacy plan really would serve to oppress dissenting churches in the colonies. Here was an Anglican accusing the Anglicans of what American writers had suspected all along.

Fighting to protect the liberties of dissenters was tantamount to maintaining the Whig's ability to increase the spread of republi-can thought. Warburton was not the only Tory to dredge up Crom-wellian epithets to castigate the Whigs. Samuel Adams reveled in being called a Roundhead by Tory propagandists later in the decade. As the bishop issue goaded yet another conflict, Whitefield defined the sides in unequivocal terms by providing evidence that the highest Anglican leaders could and were acting arbitrarily, which by now was equiva-lent to accusing them of manifesting Antichrist! But while Americans were sorting out the levity of Galloway's assertions, and while the noise and clamour pitched at the establishment of an American bishop was intensifying, forthcoming parliamentary legislation overshadowed both issues. George III and George Grenville began implementing their taxation program with the first of several new taxes.

As the Grenville Program began to unfold, Whitefield, who now had his finger on England's political pulse by virtue of his connec-tions with lordly friends, became even more deeply involved in oppos-ing increased British domination of Americans. Whitefield landed in America in 1763 and promptly published his critique of Bishop War-burton in Philadelphia and Boston, letting British Americans know exactly how he felt about anyone who would challenge religious liberty. Even the casual reader could not miss the deeper political implications of the religious conflict.

Shortly after his arrival, with contributions of money and books, Whitefield assisted Harvard in rebuilding its library that had burned down. So endeared did he become in New England that Boston issued Whitefield a public statement of thanks. On one occasion the students of Yale begged their president to let Whitefield preach for another fif-teen minutes, a request approved by none other than Thomas Clap, Whitefield's nemesis of 1745.[6] Then, if there were any lingering doubts where he stood in regard to colonial interests, they were completely erased when Whitefield met in the spring of 1764 with Dr. Samuel

Langdon and Samuel Haven, Congregational ministers in Portsmouth, New Hampshire, who were active in opposing the bishop and later would be Whig leaders. Whitefield directly informed them of the Tory intentions:

> I can't in good conscience leave the town without acquainting you with a secret. My heart bleeds for America. O poor New England! There is a deep laid plot against both your civil and religious liberties, and they will be lost. Your golden days are at an end. You have nothing but trouble before you. My information comes from the best authority in Great Britain. I was allowed to speak of the affair in general, but enjoined not to mention particulars.[7]

Here we see strong evidence of a growing division between America and Great Britain entering Whitefield's own thought. Undoubtedly, he still conceived of the empire as a whole, but his repeated use of the pronouns "your" and "you" betray the budding distinction. He did not mention that these same civil and religious liberties were under siege back in England (the struggle between Anglicans and Methodists was common knowledge), but he seemed only concerned for their vitality in America.

Dr. Langdon subsequently repeated what Whitefield had told him to the New Hampshire General Assembly. Without doubt, a rumor such as this would travel fast in New England. Moreover, Whitefield the itinerant had spent his life delivering the same messages wherever he traveled, thus it is reasonable to presume that he met with moderate ministers throughout America where the plot would exert an impact and that he told them at least as much as he told Langdon. As Langdon considered Whitefield's warning, he believed the "deep laid plot" included such provisions as "general taxation of the colonies, alteration of the chartered governments, the introduction of bishops, tithes for the support of the Anglican clergy, and public offices for Anglicans only."[8] Each of these provisions constituted an act of arbitrary power and thus could be resoundingly condemned through republican or civil millennial lenses by Protestant colonists. John Adams later emphasized the connection between parliamentary aggression and the fear of the episcopacy:

If any gentleman supposes this controversy to be nothing to the present purpose, he is grossly mistaken. It spread an universal alarm against the authority of Parliament. It excited a general and just apprehension, that bishops, and dioceses, and churches, and priests, and tithes, were to be imposed on us by Parliament. It was known that neither king, nor ministry, nor archbishops, could appoint bishops in America, without an act of Parliament; and if Parliament could tax us, they could establish the Church of England, with all its creeds, articles, tests, ceremonies, and tithes, and prohibit all other churches, as conventicles and schism shops.[9]

But what the common people believed and what upper-class lawyers and politicians of 1765 were willing to publish were not the same. Without hard evidence, few of America's civic leaders participated in the noise and clamour of the bishop debate, which was spearheaded by ministers as conspiracy theories circulated around the social circles of commoners. Instead, political activists participated with opposition to the Sugar Act and Stamp Act, arguing on grounds they could support without citing rumors.

## THE PROPAGANDA BARRAGE

Passage of the Revenue Act (the "Sugar Act") in 1764 and the Stamp Act in 1765 provided sufficient evidence of the plot needed to inspire civic leaders to unsheathe their pens. The Revenue Act provided taxes on various goods imported into the colonies via England to raise the costs of supporting an army in America as well as securing trade with the colonies and discouraging smuggling. The Stamp Act was a thirteen-thousand-word document requiring a tax (with an accompanying stamp to prove the tax had been paid) on almost any imaginable legal, ecclesiastical, or business document that authorized or recorded public and private transactions. At one level or another, nearly all domestic goods and services were affected; even the sale of cards and dice now required a stamp. In response, American writers filled the newspapers with letters and articles denouncing the Acts and calling for their repeal. In the colonial mind, liberty faced an unprecedented assault through the internal taxation levied without the consent of colonial legislatures. Two particular writers summed up Americans' official responses to the acts. First, Oxenbridge Thacher, in *The Sentiments of a British American* (1764), investigated the oppression of English rights and privileges through the passage of the Revenue Act. And although Thacher employs a family metaphor to characterize British and American relations, the pamphlet expresses an anxiety over identity by bemoaning increasing exclusion from the British family. For Thacher, inherited British citizenship was insufficient to guarantee liberty, bringing the issue of civic identity to the fore of the conflict. Subsequent pamphleteers could no longer presume full English identity as did Whitefield, Mayhew, and Galloway, authors of initial antityrant and anti-British propaganda. The second important response was Stephen Hopkins' essay *The Rights of Colonies Examined* (1765), analyzed more closely below, which supported and extended Thacher's claim, asserting that if British-Americans are not afforded their inherited family privileges, they must be deemed slaves. Hopkins recognized Americans' declining social status and would not accept slavery. In this way Hopkins placed the issue of British American identity squarely in the public sphere for consideration and redefinition, a redefinition influenced by the implied doctrines of the Awakening conceptual system.

Stephen Hopkins, a Rhode Island son, was born in 1706, making him a few years older than Whitefield, though any relationship to Whitefield or the Awakening is obscured by silence. But Whitefield did itinerate regularly through Hopkins' locale and it follows that Hopkins would be familiar with his ideas. Hopkins' pamphlet, *The Rights of Colonies Examined*, used an underlying structure that mirrors the New Light assertion that Christianity cannot be inherited, that the new birth was required to obtain spiritual freedom. Drawing upon this first-stage rhetorical topic, Hopkins argued that since a British political inheritance was failing to provide civil and judicial freedoms, a reorientation was called for to establish an identity that would honor and protect freedom—not unlike a new birth.

Hopkins opens by citing a first principle: "Liberty is the greatest blessing . . . and slavery the heaviest curse that human nature is capable of. This being so makes it a matter of the utmost importance to men which of the two shall be their portion."[10] He uses the next five pages to argue that the "inherent indefeasible right" of British Americans should match the privileges of "natural-born subjects of Great Britain." Hopkins claims that Britain's past dealings with the American colonies traditionally recognized these rights. Hopkins also characterizes the past relationship with the familial metaphor and declares that colonists' loyalty and devotion to Great Britain was displayed by their support of the war with the French. Next, Hopkins argues that the British empire is a collective entity, thus dependent upon the economic health and a freedom of its parts: "for what good reason can possibly be given for making laws to cramp the trade and ruin the interests of many of the colonies, and at the same time lessen in a prodigious manner the consumption of the British manufactures in them?" After employing economic arguments, he returns to the notion of slavery: "They who are taxed at pleasure by others cannot possibly have any property . . . can have no freedom but are indeed reduced to the most abject slavery."

Hopkins' argument hinged upon a clear definition of identity. If Americans were not equal citizens, then they must have been slaves and by implication were not members of the British family. Hopkins referred to the "mother country" three times as he asserted that the colonies had done everything deserving of inclusion in British citizenship, and he closed with the term "filial dependency" to describe the appropriate relationship of Great Britain to the colonies. Notably, Hopkins claimed that anything less than full privileges and representation in Parliament constituted "slavery." Hopkins' pamphlet nicely exemplifies James Darsey's summation:

> In the opposition maintained by Whig rhetoricians, there is no incremental freedom; one is either free or one is not . . . "Freedom" and "Slavery" and their derivatives functioned in Whig rhetoric dialectically as "God terms" and "devil terms," radically dividing the world into good and evil, between them a great yawning void.[11]

Here we see the structure of the Awakening conceptual system shaping Hopkins' political thought—a structure that lacks middle ground on selected issues. From this all-or-nothing perspective, which was sharpened by Parliament's lack of response, the Awakening conceptual system constrained Americans to see themselves as "out" of the British family, even while Hopkins futilely argued that they were still part of it. The resulting cognitive dissonance invited a reconstruction of national identity. By this time British identity in England had been increasingly associated with George III as the icon of national identity. A free people with a love and respect for the notion of liberty cannot accept the con-

dition of slavery, and it is at this juncture that their experience during
the Great Awakening provided a pattern of thought that would help
reinterpret their circumstances and suggest an appropriate response.

It was not that Hopkins was a proponent of the new birth in explicit
national terms, but by implication, he pointed out a need for *something*,
and the widespread New Light teaching about identity in Christ furnished a convenient and logical solution. All that was needed was to
secularize the spiritual concept into republican terms as colonists had
already been doing regarding war and political leadership. In addition
to the religious function of the new birth, it came to symbolize a transformation in secular identity as well—from European to American. As
Whitefield had portrayed in his *Journals*, travel across the Atlantic stood
as a metaphor for the new birth. Thus, the reconstitution of American
identity, in an American family, was augmented by a preexisting familiarity with the notions and vocabulary of the Protestant community.
Consequently, in the decades that followed, republican-minded ministers "increasingly confused civic virtue with piety and, finally, political
enthusiasm with the joy of conversion," and colonists were "converted"
from Tories to Whigs as they aligned themselves in defense of liberty.[12]
Here were born the structures of thought that became so much a part
of American culture that Abraham Lincoln could say a hundred years
later that "this nation shall have a new birth of freedom."

## WHITEFIELD'S CONTRIBUTION TO THE CAUSE

As the Stamp Act regulations commenced and while the colonial propagandists flexed their muscles in the press, Whitefield felt it was time
to return to England and commented on the state of American affairs
as he left: "I fear I must embark for *England*. Well may I say *I fear*;
for indeed words cannot well express what a scene of action I leave
behind. Alas! my American work seems as yet scarce begun."[13] Other
than a few glimpses into conversations with people like Dr. Langdon,
the historical record lacks an account of what Whitefield was up to
during his sixth American tour. Since he had been so successful at
converting colonists, and since he specifically mentions the colonial
turmoil, we can presume that his "*American* work" referred to the second duty of his ministry—to resist arbitrary power in whatever form
it took. Probably owing to his ecumenical spirit and strong connections to England, Whitefield never completely distinguished between

Americans and British in the same way that American writers did. Yet a few references to Americans that differentiated them from the British begin to populate his writings as early as 1749, when, just as above, he referred to his "*English* or *American* work."[14] By 1766 Whitefield sporadically refers to "Americans" and the "American church" vis-à-vis the British.[15] These distinctions indicate an increasing demarcation for Whitefield after his visit to America in 1765. His impending death circumvented the evolution of a complete division between Britons and Americans in his mind.

Whitefield left America in June 1765 to be present in Bath for the opening of a chapel financed by Lady Huntingdon, but he apparently left with more on his mind than merely religious duties in England. In November 1765 Samuel Adams, the prolific New England polemicist, along with Thomas Cushing, wrote two letters to George Whitefield enjoining him to utilize his connections with British nobility on behalf of the colonies. Here was an opportunity to continue his "*American* work" while in England, where it could make the most difference. Adams opened a rather formal letter to Whitefield, stating:

> Our good friend Mr. Jonathan Mason has communicated to us in a Letter which he received from you, wherein you very kindly express your Regard for the People of New England, & your Desires to serve our civil as well as religious Interests—We need not inform you that we are the Descendents of Ancestors remarkable for their Zeal for true Religion & Liberty.[16]

In these lines, Samuel Adams reveals part of the letter-writing network of people working on behalf of colonial interests, indicates his perception of Whitefield's mission to further religious *and* civil interests, and attempts to identify with that mission. Clearly, Whitefield's duty to oppose arbitrary power was common knowledge. The lion's share of the letter is spent convincing Whitefield that New England and the colonies are indeed loyal, affectionate subjects of the king, but that the Stamp Act and Sugar Act will harm the trade of the colonies, ruining them financially and ultimately harming the nation. "Money is the very support of Trade; & if the Trade of the Colonys is beneficial to Great Britain, she must herself very soon feel the ill Effects of a measure, w[hich] will consume the very Vitals of that Trade."[17] Adams closes with a request: "It would add very great Weight to the

Cause of the distressed American Subjects if their Circumstances could be fully known to a nobleman of his Lordships' great Integrity & Understanding."[18]

Adams decided to spell out his request more directly in a second letter written a few days later. Adams and Cushing write, "The free access which I am informed you have with some eminent Personages, may put it in your Power to do us Offices of singular kindness." The second letter was more direct. Referring to the Earl of Dartmouth, Adams writes, "We stand in great Need of some such Advocate in England," politely implying that Whitefield might direct his efforts toward persuading him to America's side. Within the two letters, Adams summarizes the American perspective of the economic and political fallout of the Acts, provides pertinent information, and lists the most effective politically based lines of argument one would need for speaking against the Stamp Act were he inclined to do so. Moreover, Adams hints that the colonies might be forced to pursue independence if England "shall exert her power to destroy their Libertys." At the heart of the issue was internal taxation without sufficient representation in Parliament. History does not record whether or not Whitefield quoted or used Adams' views to win a nobleman to their cause or whether he might have testified before Parliament, but he did, by several accounts, lend his polemic skills to the cause.

While Whitefield was journeying back to England, groups of New Lights in America decided they also would take action regarding the Stamp Act. Using the terms "marked or stamped" repeatedly, the Act generously lent itself to a literal interpretation by Protestants as the "mark of the beast," fulfilling the biblical prophecy that nobody in the end times could buy or sell without having the mark. Consequently, associating the Stamp Act with Antichrist and perceiving the stamps literally as the mark of the beast inspired protests against it by colonists. For this religious community, the perceived danger of the situation was enormous. Leading the popular opposition to the Stamp Act, according to Joseph Galloway, was "an union of the congregational and Presbyterian interest." He described the appointment of a "standing committee of correspondence" that transformed the separate congregations "of little significance" into a consequential body of men. Recalling the events fifteen years later after he sided with the English, Galloway labeled the body a "dangerous combination of men whose principles of religion and polity were equally adverse to those of the established Church and Government."[19] Armed with the organization and means of communication to promote their interests, this body began systematic opposition to the Stamp Act.

A Connecticut New Light mob burned the Stamp Act in effigy (as Antichrist), demonstrating the depth to which they believed that Satanic forces were motivating the Grenville Program.[20] In August 1765, after Whitefield's departure, a Massachusetts mob (the Sons of Liberty) was convened by hanging an effigy from a tree representing Andrew Oliver, the man appointed distributor of stamps for Massachusetts. Beside it hung a boot from which protruded a devil's head.[21] These symbols linked the Stamp Act, the British government, Oliver, and the devil together to animate the mob to violence. The boot/devil icon specifically referenced, through a play on words, the previous prime minister, John Stuart, the Earl of Bute (pronounced "boot"). The icon's continued use beyond 1763, after Bute resigned, indicates that it had become a convenient and widely recognized symbol of the prime minister's office. The devil inside the boot made severe implications about the officeholder. By the end of the evening, the aggressive mob (led by Ebenezer Mackintosh) destroyed a business property owned by Oliver and completely demolished his home.

A few months later, in the tradition of field preaching, an orator at the Liberty Tree in Boston encouraged an economic boycott of stamped goods and explicitly accused Grenville of manifesting the Antichrist:

> He has ordained that none amongst us shall buy or sell a piece of land, except his mark be put upon the deed and when it is delivered, the hands of both buyer and seller must infallibly become branded with the odious impression: I beseech you then to beware as good Christians and lovers of your country, lest by touching any paper with this impression, you receive the mark of the beast, and become infamous in your country throughout all generations.[22]

We notice the free intermingling of ideas with reference to "his mark [Grenville's] be put upon" and then defining that mark as "the mark of the beast," which could be acquired by merely touching a document with a Stamp affixed. If resistance to the Stamp Act were merely founded in its economic ramifications, such appeals to persuade the public would be ludicrous and ineffective. In reality, the Sons of Liberty, and New Lights in general, increasingly viewed the prime minister's office as one through which the Antichrist was operating, so much so that a boot/devil icon could conveniently symbolize it, and so much so that they believed they could employ the hyperbole of "damnation by touching." While such themes continually resurfaced in public oratory and editorials in the New England press, they were not themes that could be used by lawyers and politicians to argue against British legislation. Clearly, the discourse of rational thinkers like Hopkins served a different purpose and did not accurately represent the heart of early Revolutionary rhetoric. As Gordon Wood confirmed, "There is simply too much fanatical and millennial thinking even by the best minds that must be explained before we can characterize the Americans' ideas as peculiarly rational and legalistic and thus view the Revolution as merely a conservative defense of constitutional liberties."[23]

These New Light mobs that roamed New England, burning effigies and harassing stamp-duty officials, did not exemplify the kind of society Whitefield promoted or with which he participated, but he undeniably had a hand shaping their members, as this entire study has argued. With his move to the mainstream Whitefield participated in more respectable ways. Benjamin Franklin, along with Whitefield, who had received Adams' letters by this time, led the American diplomatic effort for repeal. Taxes were nothing new to British Americans. They had been paying tax on all sorts of items imported from Great Britain for decades. However, in testimony before the House of Commons in 1766, Franklin explained American opposition to the new taxes on legal and rational grounds:

> An *external* tax is a duty laid on commodities imported; that duty is added to the first cost and other charges on the commodity, and when it is offered for sale, makes it part of the price. If the people do not like it at that price, they refuse it; they are not obliged to pay it. But an *internal* tax is forced from the people without their consent if not laid by their own representatives. The Stamp Act says we shall have no commerce, make no exchange of property with each other, neither purchase nor grant, nor recover our debts; we shall neither marry nor make our wills, unless we pay such and such sums; and thus it is intended to extort our money from us or ruin us by the consequence of refusing to pay it.[24]

Obviously any argument that the Stamp Act constituted the mark of the beast would not be taken seriously by Parliament, and Franklin probably did not believe this anyway. So he founded his case on republican notions of freedom and slavery. Whitefield accompanied Franklin to London on this diplomatic effort and though nothing of what Whitefield said, or to whom, was recorded, perhaps Samuel Adams' letters inspired whatever assistance he lent. Whitefield was a persuasive man, and with a narrative of economic facts and a list of arguments at his fingertips (as provided by Adams), undoubtedly he could encourage open minds to pause and reconsider. It is most likely that he limited his assistance to private discussions with British nobility, but his symbolic presence with Franklin before Parliament made an unequivocal statement that held profound implications. Whitefield, a proactive synecdoche of the public mind in America, had embraced the cause of the colonists. Whatever was his direct participation, in conversation or testimony, the Stamp Act was overturned in 1766, causing Whitefield to write, "*March* 16, 1766, Stamp Act repealed, *Gloria Deo.*"[25] In addition to whatever pressure the threat of boycotts provided, Nathaniel Whitaker, a colonial leader who visited Whitefield in London shortly thereafter, recalled that Whitefield "was greatly concerned for the liberties of America" and that the repeal of the Stamp Act "was in no small measure owing to him."[26]

The Stamp Act provided an issue that reveals the intermingling of religious and civil perspectives to unite American civic leaders, ministers, and mobs of citizens in a common cause. Davidson pointed out that "the experience of working together, the ideas that were inculcated during the movement, and the sense of accomplishment resulting from united efforts were indispensable. The agitation of each period, in fact, made easier the work of the next."[27] Lawyers, politicians, and uneducated dissenters were all working together to repeal the acts; respected citizens worked through the press; the mobs operated through graphic public demonstrations and personal attacks. Colonial representatives opposed the act through the legal and diplomatic channels. In resistance to the Stamp Act, colonial leaders forged patterns of organizational cooperation to oppose the Townshend Acts, the Quebec Act, and other arbitrary assaults on American liberties.

Whitefield also helped Franklin avert public criticism after his testimony before Parliament. Many colonists felt that Franklin did not faithfully represent their interests by making a distinction between internal and external taxes, when both were viewed as illegal. Franklin's critics complained loudly in America over the explanation quoted above, and at Joseph Galloway's request Whitefield helped to rehabilitate Franklin's image by employing his letter writing and publicity network on his behalf, praising Franklin's efforts in England.[28] Again, Whitefield's popularity provided a strong influence as criticism of Franklin soon waned.

## FURTHER GOADING BY GREAT BRITAIN

In the American colonies, just when one crisis seemed to be averted, another would quickly replace it. Although repeal of the Stamp Act served to settle colonial upheaval somewhat, the SPG renewed their efforts to establish a bishop and roused American ministerial fury. It did not help the SPG that eleven of the thirteen Anglican bishops in the House of Lords opposed the repeal of the Stamp Act. By 1766 American ministers made no distinction between religious or civil liberties; "LIBERTY itself faced extinction" and colonial ministers marshaled a defense through renewed opposition to the establishment of the Anglican episcopacy.[29]

Jonathan Mayhew's untimely death in 1766 left a void in leadership in the bishop struggle that Charles Chauncy stepped in to fill. Now, Chauncy and Whitefield, old theological enemies, were working on the same side. Chauncy published no fewer than 710 pages, in three treatises, arguing against establishment of the bishop. Chauncy and others characterized episcopacy supporters as "High-Church men and Jacobites, not always averse to alliances with the greatly feared Church of Rome."[30] As the debate continued, the American propagandists firmly attached the label "Tories" to the SPG missionaries; they persuaded many American colonists that increased tyranny would accompany a bishop, and they successfully associated papal plots with the Grenville Program and the Anglican bishop issue.

Aggravating the situation, parliamentary acts extending favors to Canada infuriated American colonial leaders and propagandists. Contrasting with the strong hand Britain was using to manage the seaboard colonies, Quebec, which was won from the French in 1763, found the British government indulging their wishes. Before Americans had time to adjust to the repeal of the Stamp Act, they heard that Britain was allowing a Roman Catholic bishop to be installed in Canada. No news could have goaded the factions such as the sons of Liberty or the New

Lights more. Coupled with redoubled efforts to establish the American bishop, colonists perceived this news as direct evidence of a popish plot. They believed that after the establishment of an American epis-copacy, Britain would allow Roman Catholicism to infiltrate America. An editorial from 1768 in the Boston press signed by "The Puritan" exclaimed, "To say the truth, I have from long observation been appre-hensive, that what we have above all else to fear is POPERY."[31] A verse printed in the *Boston Gazette* a month later summed up the sentiments of many:

> But if he from Rome greater Profit had hop'd
> He who now is be-bishop'd, would have been be-pop'd
> And equally run, to avoid being Poor,
> To the arms of the church, or of Babylon's Whore.[32]

Since many Southerners, where the Anglican Church was strong, sup-ported the idea of an American bishop, the fear of Roman Catholi-cism was essential to motivate them to the cause. The renewed fear of Roman Catholic aggression served to provide Americans in all the colonies, New England, Middle, and Southern, a common complaint against Great Britain. Colonial propagandists would increasingly rely upon the dread of "POPERY" as the crisis deepened.

## WHITEFIELD CONTENDS WITH ANGLICANS AGAIN

Although Whitefield spoke his mind frankly regarding the Roman Catholic threat in sermons such as *Britain's Mercies* and *A Short Address*, being a loyal Anglican himself, he never directly wrote an extensive opinion on the American episcopacy issue, but he did reveal his senti-ments indirectly as he wrestled with Anglicans to preserve his enter-prise. Whitefield found himself struggling with Archbishop Secker in London for control of a proposed college for ministers in Georgia. Whitefield's intent was to educate his orphans and train them to be ministers and public servants for the colony. He had already secured permission from Georgia's governor to establish a college, had obtained land as well as the financing to erect buildings, and only needed official permission from London to move forward. But seeing the opportunity to strengthen the Anglican cause, the archbishop required that the new college conform to the Anglican Articles of Faith and have an Anglican headmaster, requirements with which Whitefield was unwilling to comply. Due to the broad-based financial support of Bethesda, largely provided by northern dissenters, Whitefield promised his contributors that neither the Anglicans nor the Georgian government would control the college. By November 1767 Whitefield was at an impasse with his Anglican superiors and became morose and pessimistic, "NONE but GOD knows what a concern lies upon me now, in respect to *Bethesda*. . . . At present, as to this particular, I walk in darkness, and have no light."[33]

In the winter of 1767 Whitefield took his request over Secker's head to the king, who promptly sent it back to the Anglican leaders to obtain their recommendation. Archbishop Secker suggested to the king that the college's head should be an Anglican and that extempore prayers should be disallowed. Defeated in his attempt to trump Secker and unwilling to give the Anglicans any control, Whitefield decided to withdraw his request for a college for ministers, and instead he sought to establish a public academy to serve all the people of Georgia. Insinuating that the archbishop's influence upon government officials had tainted the decision (implying an influence upon the king), Whitefield wrote Secker again, announcing his change of direction: "And as your grace's and his lordship's influence will undoubtedly extend itself to others, . . . I intend troubling your grace and his lordship no more about this so long depending concern."[34] Whitefield had abandoned plans for a college rather than submit to Anglican control and instead proceeded with designs for a school to serve the public rather than the church.

Stinging over his defeat and wishing his benefactors and donors to know the details, Whitefield published his correspondence with Archbishop Secker regarding Bethesda, and in so doing, Whitefield bolstered Revolutionary propagandists' efforts against the British. The American press recognized the significance of the struggle between Whitefield and the Anglican hierarchy. Understanding that common enemies indicate an alliance, a Boston paper reprinted the correspondence and other colonial newspapers reprinted select portions of Whitefield's letters to show the colonists how Anglican leaders had exercised arbitrary power over Whitefield and the dissenter supporters of the Bethesda college project. His struggle with Archbishop Secker demonstrated the depth to which Whitefield chose liberty over tyranny—he chose to let go of a personal dream instead of betraying his dissenting supporters.[35] Ultimately, colonists interpreted Whitefield's personal clash with

Secker over control of Bethesda and the intended college within the larger scope of Anglican control of the colonial religious scene.

The following year, Whitefield again blew the whistle on arbitrary practices by Anglicans by publicizing the expulsion of six students from Oxford University. According to the college administration, the students were guilty of extempore prayer, singing, and working in the trades before college! Whitefield contended that they were really expelled for being Methodists. He published a letter to Dr. Durrell, the Anglican vice-chancellor of Oxford, criticizing him for the biased decision, denouncing the unfairness of the hearing, and warning of the negative fallout that Oxford and the Anglican Church would soon experience.

In *A Letter to the Reverend Dr Durrell*, Whitefield considers the charges against the youths and systematically refutes them with scriptural examples and natural reasoning, citing examples of honored Anglicans and biblical characters "guilty" of the same offences. Aware, no doubt, of the habits of some students and perhaps leaders within Oxford as well, Whitefield opens the letter sarcastically by pointing out the hypocrisy of expelling the students for extempore prayer:

> It is to be hoped, that as some have been expelled for *extempore praying*, we shall hear of some few others of a contrary stamp, being expelled for *extempore swearing*, which by all impartial judges must undoubtedly be acknowledged to be the greater crime of the two.[36]

The Anglicans were especially indignant at extempore prayer, recognizing that their forms of liturgy held powerful sway over their parishioners' conceptual system. The liturgy ensured that official Anglican views were consistently and repeatedly espoused during times of prayer and worship. Extempore prayer and the singing of hymns, most likely hymns written by Dissenters, could potentially introduce another rhetoric into their venues, allowing dissenting or Methodist ideas to influence their parishioners.

Whitefield asserts that their hearing was unfair, that the students were hissed at in the hall where the hearing was held and were treated worse than common criminals in London's courts. Though he takes great care to note the hypocrisy of Oxford's decision and undermines their stated reasons for the expulsion, he does not speculate on their motive for doing so. Rather, Whitefield hypothesizes on how news of the expulsion will alter the Anglicans' efforts to establish a bishop in America:

> I fear it will follow, that a society, which since its first institution hath been looked upon as a society for propagating the Gospel, hath been all the while rather a *society for propagating episcopacy in foreign parts*: and if so, and if it ever should appear, that our Right Reverend Archbishops and Bishops do in the least countenance and encourage the unscriptural proceedings at *Edmund-Hall*, how must it increase the prejudices of our colonists, both in the islands and on the continent, against the establishment of episcopacy!

Again, an Anglican accusing Anglicans that the SPG's sole purpose was to settle an American bishop further confirmed the suspicions of many colonists. Whitefield indicated that rather than being an honorable organization to further the Christian cause, the SPG had evolved into a tyrannical group working to advance arbitrary Tory and Anglican designs to increase their level of influence in America. The letter was reprinted in Boston immediately, and certain portions were cited and disseminated throughout the American newspapers. For the colonists, Whitefield exposed the Anglicans' true colors, providing evidence of their continued oppression of religious liberties. Yet Whitefield skillfully avoids any accusations that he was anti-Anglican, appearing to serve long-term Anglican interests by asking them to change, to cease their hypocrisy, and to stop acting arbitrarily. Whitefield has again found a position that walks the line between rebelling against his denomination and supporting it by playing the reformer. His discursive message affirmed Anglican loyalty, while his symbolic message identified him with the American churches. The careful Whitefield provided no statements that could be used as evidence to accuse him of betraying the Church of England, but the fact that he published the letter, both in England and America, identifies it as a direct confrontation of the Anglicans' arbitrary actions.

## LETTERS FROM A FARMER IN PENNSYLVANIA

By late 1767 John Dickinson, an educated farmer and lawyer who was also active in the campaign against the bishop, wrote the next significant political response to the changing relationship between America and Great Britain.[38] Dickinson's *Letters from a Farmer in Pennsylvania* also evidenced the growing identity tension between Americans and Britons. Like Hopkins, he also compared the relationship between America and Great Britain as slaves to a tyrant, revealing his Protestant conceptions of good and evil as determined by concrete actions. Although the letters are largely legal and economic, for their intelligibility they rely upon, as well as reinforce, the us-them distinction of the Awakening conceptual system.

Dickinson published his series of twelve letters in the weekly *Pennsylvania Chronicle*. They were reprinted in nineteen of the twenty-three English language newspapers in the colonies and issued in pamphlet form as well.[39] The reception of these letters was both enthusiastic and cool on both sides of the Atlantic. His *Letters*, according to Forrest McDonald, were "unapproached by any publication of the Revolutionary period except Thomas Paine's *Common Sense*" in terms of their impact.[40] All completely composed prior to publication, the letters were released to "welcome" the arrival of new customs commissioners to the colonies to enforce the Townshend Acts—a set of external duties, to replace the Stamp Act, levied on glass, paint, paper, and tea imported to the colonies, reaffirming Parliament's right to tax them.

From 1760 to 1767, George III had labored to minimize Whig power in the British administration and set his own choices in the House of Commons through the implementation of unreasonable methods of election.[41] The Tories had regained control of England and subsequently desired to extend that control to the colonies, a bastion of Whig ideology. Dickinson's contribution to the body of Revolutionary propaganda was to clarify the imbalance of power between Parliament and the king, and to argue that the lion's share should abide in Parliament. As long as the nature and distribution of power remained ambiguous, the various governmental entities of the empire had tolerated each other. But Dickinson hastened overt opposition by pointing out that the arbitrary acts of George III's Parliament were incommensurable with American desires to protect liberty. Dickinson performed a critical task in the letters by characterizing the British Parliament and king as "radical innovators" in terms of interpreting and implementing the British legislative system, while he simultaneously identified the Americans as "defenders of the ancient tradition."[42]

Dickinson begins each letter addressing "my dear countrymen," and, like Jefferson several years later, he applies the title of "British

Americans" to distinguish the colonists from the British.[43] He consistently reveals a distinct American identity by using the terms "we," "our rights," and "an American character." Later in this first letter, Dickinson explicitly unifies the colonies:

> I say, of these colonies; for the cause of *one* is the cause of *all*. If the parliament may lawfully deprive *New York* of any of *her* rights, it may deprive any, or all the other colonies of *their* rights.[44]

Thus, Dickinson presents a united view of the colonies *vis-à-vis* Great Britain at large. Perhaps the distinction comes into focus most clearly when Dickinson writes, "Resistance, in the case of colonies against their mother country, is extremely different from the resistance of a people against their prince." By implication, he is saying that resistance does not constitute rebellion because the two entities are so completely separate. Dickinson also employs the family metaphor that Great Britain is a "mother country," and he says of the colonies, "We are but parts of a *whole*,"[45] and "[l]et us behave like dutiful children who have received unmerited blows from a beloved parent."[46] But here the family metaphor begins to encourage independence. Children grow up and cut the apron strings, severing the control their parents legally have over them, as they reach adulthood. Although Dickinson displays his reconciliationist sentiments, he finds a balance that provides a rationale for distinction and resistance; the metaphor itself suggests that any reconciliation would be only temporary, that independence would be natural and inevitable.

Dickinson also metaphorically employs a slave-tyrant distinction to characterize the motive of the parliamentary acts. Recalling a parallel situation from the Carthaginian oppression of Sardinia, he suggest that Great Britain is a tyrant who drains the wealth of her "miserable" and "oppressed people" whenever they attempt to assert their liberty.[47] He later provides a polemic warning of how this generation of British leadership will be recalled:

> It seems extremely probable, that when cool, dispassionate posterity, shall consider the affectionate intercourse, the reciprocal benefits, and the unsuspecting confidence, that have subsisted between these colonies and their parent country, for such a length of time, they will execrate, with the bitterest curses, the infamous memory of those men, whose pestilential ambition unnecessarily, wantonly, cruelly, first opened the forces of

civil discord between them; first turned their love into jealousy; and first taught these provinces, filled with grief and anxiety, to inquire—*Mens ubi materna est?* Where is maternal affection?[48]

Dickinson called Great Britain's arbitrary leaders "pestilential," "wanton," "cruel," "ambitious," and the instigators of the political rift. This was the type of language that had been formerly reserved for papists! As in all the letters, Dickinson opened with rational arguments backed up with relevant examples from British or classical history. Then each letter took a polemic turn near the end, introducing powerful metaphors that forcefully articulated the situation as he viewed it, exploiting us-them and good-evil distinctions for rhetorical impact.

Moreover, Dickinson's arguments and his conceptual system were guided by the pattern of thought for judging leadership that emerged from the Great Awakening. He pointed out that the British government failed in its responsibility to ensure liberty and was leading the American people toward slavery, just as Awakening-era ministers claimed the unconverted clergy failed in spiritual leadership and led their parishioners to damnation. Thus, as the New Light community became the "defenders of the ancient tradition" for the Church against dead religion and various heresies that threatened to subvert true Christianity, Americans would defend English liberties from the "radical innovators" who ruled Britain and were eroding liberty through their exercise of arbitrary power.

From whatever argument field—economic, legal, natural rights, or the duties of leadership—each contention articulated by the civil pamphleteers drew upon the Awakening conceptual system for intelligibility. Their argumentation was derived from first-stage rhetorical topics established a generation before. Dickinson's pamphlet exhibited no argumentative exceptions that transcended the pattern of thought established by the Awakening movement. Additionally, the farmer's voice used by Dickinson suggested an author sufficiently removed for perspective, possessing the pastoral common sense of a practical agrarian.[49] Stephen Browne explains that the personal nature of each letter allows it to balance "the volatile demands of immediate action and the serene remove of the contemplative world," highlighting "the ideological character of its arguments."[50]

The Awakening conceptual system provided hermeneutical lenses that allowed this interpretive community to respond favorably to the farmer's voice and to easily judge certain actions as good or evil. Colonial leaders had viewed themselves not as Americans but as British citizens, Englishmen, and members of a British family their entire lives. Before 1765, to suggest they were not in the British family was radical and unnatural. Rhetoric such as Hopkins' and Dickinson's called upon deep beliefs in the colonial mind. The Awakening conceptual system had been identifying certain groups as in or out of God's family and promoting conversion into that family by one's attitude toward religious liberty. Hence, pamphleteers such as Dickinson were able to draw upon two decades of seeing people as in or out of God's family in order to argue that one could be in or out of the British family.

## WHITEFIELD BURNS OUT

After fighting for repeal of the Stamp Act, after publishing the account of his struggle with the Anglican archbishop regarding the hoped-for seminary, and after accusing Anglican leaders of arbitrary power, Whitefield turned his attention toward his London Chapel duties where he often described the pulpit as his "throne." In between bouts of illness that would leave him bedridden, Whitefield continued to preach on a regular schedule at various English venues. In letters to friends he often wrote of death and his anticipation of a promotion to heaven. His wife died in August 1768, about which he made no immediate mention in his letters, though he later remarked, "I feel the loss of my right hand daily." One might presume from his comment that he missed her assistance as a scribe and publicist as much as her companionship, since due to his travel schedule he spent so little time with her throughout their marriage.

Whitefield made one last American tour in 1769–1770, his seventh, which pushed his worn-out body too far. He arrived in Charleston and traveled down to Bethesda, where he began construction of two additional buildings for the public academy. Although his published concerns revolved around the orphanage and preaching the gospel, his letters revealed an awareness of the deteriorating political situation: "O for a spirit of love and moderation on all sides, and on both sides the water!"[51] Other than a few similar comments that show his desire for reconciliation, Whitefield concealed any overt participation in public affairs. Perhaps the necessity of taking sides at this point in the conflict was too difficult a decision for him, causing him to focus his efforts upon his first calling of winning sinners to Christ.

After spending the winter in the South and feeling better than he had in years, Whitefield departed for the North, arriving in Philadelphia in May. He planned to itinerate in the North throughout the summer and then return to Georgia in the fall. Both Anglican and Dissenting churches welcomed him, with no closed pulpits: "So many new as well as old doors are open, and so many invitations sent from various quarters, that I know not which way to turn myself."[52] Even in the days preceding the Revolution, thirty years after the Great Awakening, Whitefield was as popular as ever, drawing large crowds wherever he went.

Since his health was temporarily strong, Whitefield began several rigorous preaching circuits, one of five hundred miles. He slowly worked his way further north, arriving in Boston in September 1770, where he commented on the importunity of New Englanders who desired him to stay there: "Never was the word received with greater eagerness than now."[53] But Whitefield also commented on the political unrest, writing, "The season is critical as to outward circumstances."[54] Whitefield attracted crowds in Boston equal to those of 1740 as both Tories and Whigs listened between the lines of his preaching to support their side of the political debate. Whitefield's strategic ambiguity allowed the Tories to applaud his calls for submission to authority, while Whigs stressed his support of liberty.[55] Although his events were well attended, his visit in 1770 did not generate much editorial comment in the newspapers because Bostonians focused their attention on local political issues. In the final letter before his death, Whitefield commented on the British Government's move to dissolve the Massachusetts charter: "Poor *New-England* is much to be pitied; *Boston* people most of all. How falsely misrepresented! What a mercy, that our *Christian charter* cannot be dissolved!"[56] These were among the last published words of Whitefield.

During the early-morning hours of September 30, 1770, an asthma attack ended George Whitefield's life at age fifty-six in the home of a minister friend, Jonathan Parsons. His final act was exhorting believers as he stood on a staircase holding a candle. Speaking until the candle, a foreshadowing metaphor, burned down to the socket, he then retired to bed and suffered his attack at about 5:00 a.m. Refusing to turn Whitefield's body over to anyone else, Parsons entombed Whitefield in a chamber beneath his pulpit in the Presbyterian church in Newburyport, Massachusetts. As news of Whitefield's death spread, the public mourning across America reached dramatic proportions. Public funerals, attended by thousands, were conducted throughout the colonies as well as Great Britain. Numerous ministers wrote and published their memorial sermons. American papers even suspended their coverage of political events to eulogize Whitefield.

Although Whitefield himself had longed for death, the tragic loss was especially painful for Americans. They had lost an agent of awakening and a person who provided identity definitions to an evolving society. But perhaps more significantly, they had lost a voice that had explicitly guided and solidified America's response to religious conflict, external conflict with the French, and internal conflict with the Anglican Church. Although Whitefield expressed his apprehensions about the struggle between the British and Americans, he consistently and assiduously worked on behalf of the colonies, causing later Americans to claim him as a true patriot.

Compelling and fascinating evidence of his widespread, cultic following is revealed by visitations to his body after his death. Five years after Whitefield's death a Revolutionary chaplain and several officers, among them Benedict Arnold, opened Whitefield's casket in Newburyport to view his body. They removed his clerical collar and wristbands, in which he had been entombed, and passed them among their soldiers preparing for a Revolutionary battle. The soldiers cut them into small strips and tucked them into their clothing to take Whitefield into battle with them.[57] As the years passed, Methodist ministers were the customary visitors to his tomb, making pilgrimages to view him. These viewings continued until well into the nineteenth century. In 1789 Jesse Lee wrote, "Removing the coffin lid, [we] beheld the awful ravages of 'the last enemy of man. . . .' How quiet the repose, how changed the features." Abel Stevens, another Methodist minister of the 1820s, wrote that he "took his skull . . . and examined it with great interest." A Freewill Baptist minister, David Marks, who visited the tomb in 1834, described that "the coffin was about one third full of black earth, out of which projected a few bones. The skull bone was detached from the rest and was turned over."[58] At one point his skull was temporarily removed, and two hundred replicas were made and sold.

Along with Whitefield's death, 1770 saw the climax of the agitation regarding the American bishop. As in the debate over the revival in 1740, what appeared on the surface to be religious haggling between moderate colonial ministers with the Anglicans over ecclesiastical control was, in effect, a struggle for social control in general. And on these terms the fight for ecclesiastical control was much more about politics than religion. Indeed, all parties involved realized that the key to widespread social control was to shape the dominant religious institution. American leaders understood, at least implicitly, that "forms, not spirit, sustained them in their own position of authority and determined the course of their society."[59] American ministers recognized the latent threat to civil freedoms that a bishop and strengthening of the Anglican Church in America could bring and fought against it tooth and nail. The struggle continued until independence made it a moot issue. The bishop issue was not tangential to the Revolution, but a central facet of it. Astute New Englanders recognized the depth of connection to the point that humorists could draw upon it. A sarcastic writer after the war pointed out a tax levied by Massachusetts and the appointment of Samuel Seabury as the first Episcopal bishop, "TWO WONDERS OF THE WORLD—a Stamp Act in Boston and a Bishop in Connecticut."[60]

The religious and political spheres in colonial America, as well as Great Britain, overlapped significantly with contrasting religious theologies providing the implied doctrines for Tory and Whig power structures. Thus, resisting the English Anglicans as "them" for threatening religious freedom was part and parcel of resisting the Tory-led British administration and the monarchy. Whitefield never directly articulated the essence of political resistance in his writings, but he did communicate his position symbolically through the controversy over control of his Bethesda orphanage/college project. Perhaps better than any of his contemporaries, Whitefield understood how to establish, through symbolic actions, public positions that spoke louder than words ever could. By decrying arbitrary power in whichever sphere it manifested itself, Whitefield showed Americans how to resist one's own institutions as a reformer, not a rebel. By instituting a form of resistance and reform combined with the establishment of a conceptual system that demanded conformity to a person's very core, Whitefield nudged American society down a path that would lead to Revolution. The Revolutionary pamphleteers would continue to impel America toward independence by following this path—the pattern of thought established by thirty years of Whitefield's religious and ideological prescriptions. They would draw their most potent arguments from the very argument fields Whitefield and the other Awakening ministers introduced and promoted, organizing their world with dichotomies of good and evil.

# CHAPTER 8

# A BLUEPRINT FOR REVOLUTION

As 1770 drew to a close and George Whitefield was laid to rest in Newburyport, Massachusetts, whether colonists had recognized it or not, Whitefield's influence on the development of the colonial mind had been profound. Beginning with the personal sense of identity of all those who had been directly awakened by a conversion experience and extending to those who began to think in the bifurcated terms that the Awakening popularized, Whitefield articulated the elements of a conceptual system that established a collective view of the colonial world. In the preceding chapters we have traced the evolution of that system and observed it shaping and structuring the discourse of even legal arguments against the tenure of judges and internal taxation.

In large part Whitefield's influence depended upon his popularity. Whitefield was truly the world's first international celebrity.[1] One could not have lived in colonial America (except perhaps on the frontier) without being exposed to Whitefield. Anyone born and raised in America inherited the Awakening conceptual system to one degree or another, and those who came over to help the Revolutionary cause, like Thomas Paine, figured it out quickly enough. Analysis of several more pamphlets published after Whitefield's death will complete our story, showing how the Awakening conceptual system helped make the republican ideologies of the period more intelligible and natural.

During the revolutionary era one was not born American, but British, Scottish, German, Dutch, or something else, and required conversion from a Tory to a Whig. Ebenezer Cleaveland depicted one good example of such a conversion in 1774 as he preached on the "conversion and call of Matthew the Publican" and gave "application in terms of the delight experienced by a Crown revenue officer who joined the Sons of Liberty."[2] What an astounding story! So intertwined had the deep structures of religious belief and republican ideology become that the tables had completely turned. Here a minister is attempting to explain religious conversion by comparing it to something he felt his audience understood better: a political conversion!

With the conversion from Tory to Whig came the spirit of liberty to regenerate one into a lover of freedom. Americans subjected public officials to a strict standard that upheld English liberties and demanded they be guiltless of corruption, virtuous, and defenders of liberty, and that they advanced into office based on qualifications rather than connections. By 1776 genuine patriots resented the sycophants of George's court and embraced the promise of a free, self-governing society that would preserve "American liberties." Such patriots viewed reconciliation with Great Britain as a compromise with evil.

By the sense of personal and national identity engendered through the conceptual system the Awakening had provided, Whitefield hastened the comprehension and adoption of republican sentiments in the development of American politics. Explanations for the colonial struggle most intelligible to people were those that viewed the political factions of the British Empire in a millennial struggle between "us" and "them," good versus evil, in a context of slavery or freedom. From 1770 to 1776, colonists could not have viewed the conflict on any other terms. They had no other frame of reference. In fact, not until after Thomas Jefferson wrote the Declaration of Independence can there be found widespread textual evidence of significant extensions and alterations of the boundaries Whitefield had set. Deism and science eventually displaced the church as the leader in intellectual influence, but this transformation did not fully mature among the wider population until after the Revolutionary War. Since persuasive discourse must depart from notions that "the people" accepted, propagandists had to build ideas that currently reigned.

Through the 1760s, the propaganda directed against Great Britain showed a degree of deference for Parliament and the king, but that was not the case when opposing the Anglicans and the SPG. For fear of being arrested and tried for rebellion, propagandists kept their political arguments logical and polite, always *implicitly* charging British leaders with arbitrary tendencies as their rights were violated, knowing that *explicit* accusations might get them in trouble.[3] But Parliament continued to pass laws undermining colonial freedoms and by their actions further exacerbated the British-American identity question. Who were these Americans now if they were not members of the British family? Their parents, George III and Parliament, were disinheriting them, pushing them out of the family. The solution to this dilemma would be the rejection of England and the embracing of American nationalism to crystallize their inheritance of both civil and religious freedoms. The decision to embrace the rebellion was a personal choice that each person would have to make. Breen and Hall argue that citizens had been acclimated to making private choices with regard to a range of issues, and Breen reasons elsewhere that the American embrace of "natural rights" as a component of Lockean liberalism was a fundamental argument field for colonials needing intellectual ground to justify rebellion in the years just before independence.[4] The present study has contended that a necessary precursor of the colonial ability to grasp the spirit of Lockean natural rights was their comprehension and embrace of the concept or the "common privilege" of mankind to partake of the Spirit of God that Whitefield and others preached up throughout the Awakening period. Each of these influencing factors—religion, republicanism, liberalism—required a conscious choice from the colonists, and each required the rejection of the authoritarian conceptual system that dominated European and American thought up to that point in history. Each colonist had to privilege his private concerns over the whole of English society in making that choice, and in that action he adopted an American identity that integrated each "convert" into a new civic community, sometimes imagined, and sometimes reified as membership in a colonial militia.

Overt opposition to the British government was a short step that Whitefield never took, but his contemporaries quickly did. Shortly after Whitefield's death, the colonial conceptual system naturally extended the us-them distinction to contrast "evil" Tory oppression of civil freedom with "good" Whig protection of natural rights. Again, one's stance toward common privileges and liberty predicted group membership. Next, the king himself was cast into the "them" category through his "evil" failure to protect the English citizens' privileges.

The Protestant colonists were law-abiding by nature, so all that remained for revolution to occur was to justify rebelling against Parliament and the king on moral and legal grounds. Jonathan Mayhew, echoing Whitefield, began that process ideologically; Thomas Paine completed the justification pragmatically, coming full circle to religion, revealing an audience remarkably sensitive to and highly motivated by religiously based arguments. If there is any suspicion that the Awakening influence on the colonial mind had faded in the decade before the Revolution, Paine's argument strategy reveals that it pervaded the mainstream of America without apology.

## THE PAPISTS ARE COMING!

With the firm linkage in place between civil and religious liberties in the minds of colonial Americans, to argue against the arbitrary power perpetrated by Parliament was to implicate their meddling not just in civil affairs but in religion as well. Even writers like Samuel Adams, in *The Rights of the Colonists*, blended religious and republican notions in his discussion of rights. Establishing a major premise for his argument, Adams asserted in 1772:

> "Just and true liberty, equal and impartial liberty" in matters spiritual and temporal, is a thing that all Men are clearly entitled to, by the eternal and immutable laws of God and nature, as well as by the law of Nations, & all well grounded municipal laws, which must have their foundation in the former.[5]

Samuel Adams continues by invoking Locke to argue that Catholicism cannot be considered a religion that is either tolerant or compatible with liberty. Thus, one of America's most prolific propagandists incorporated central religious themes into even his most formal writings. In addition to fears of papal domination, other writers supplied the newspapers with virulent editorials that were even more outspoken regarding civil and religious connections.[6]

Whitefield's antipapist rhetoric, his illumination of instances of how arbitrary power could be exerted, his symbolic role in defining American identity, and his articulation of a proper way of being an American provided a volatile formula lacking just one element that, once added, would prompt Americans to react aggressively against England. Americans had turned against the French with the addition of that same element, and it was quickly manifested in parliamentary actions interpreted as the encroachment of Roman Catholicism. After the defeat of the French, colonial fears of papal plots subsided for a time, but the propaganda assault led by Samuel Adams was quick to reintroduce these fears to align American Dissenters with staunch American Anglicans against a perceived common threat.

A Roman Catholic bishop in Canada was bad enough, but Parliament's passage of the Quebec Act in 1774 stoked colonial fears of papal infiltration into the colonies. The Quebec Act provided a civil government for the French Roman Catholics of the Quebec province, extended their territory to include present-day Michigan, Wisconsin, Ohio, Indiana, and Illinois (effectively halting the needed westward expansion of the Northern and Middle colonies), and granted political privileges to Roman Catholics. Warnings of the "plot" had occasioned the popular press since 1765, but the Quebec Act reanimated colonial propagandists to claim that the *highest leaders* in Britain were working to steadily undermine American liberties. Allegations abounded that the newest prime minister, Lord North, embraced Catholicism and that the Parliament and the king intended to establish Roman Catholicism over the entire American continent.[7] Whitefield's initial diatribes against the Roman Catholics never linked Anglican or British leaders to such plots, but the fear of Roman Catholic hegemony over the Protestants, which he vigorously promoted among colonists, provided the perfect foundation upon which later propagandists would build. Paul Revere skillfully played on these fears with an engraving titled *The Mitred Minuet*, which portrays the devil hovering behind and whispering in the ear of the Quebec Bill's author, Lord North. Lord Bute plays the bagpipes next to him while four mitred Anglican bishops dance around a copy of the bill. In this instance, the mitres upon the bishops' heads served as a synecdoche for Roman Catholic authority.

The Quebec Act drew public responses as acrimonious as did the Stamp Act for fear that it was a direct step in the spreading of papism across the colonies. The French had been decisively defeated, and the military threat of Catholics ended, so why would any rational colonist fear that the English government, of all parties concerned, would promote the establishment of the Catholic Church in the colonies? Not because Roman Catholicism was powerful, explained Nathan Hatch, but because it was weak: "Revolutionary ministers were afraid that . . . power-hungry ministers would exploit the papal hierarchy for their own designs" and thus continue the advance of arbitrary power against the civil and religious liberties of the colonists.[8] Now what was feared was a power structure that could facilitate the rise of sycophants and tyrannous ministers. The Quebec Act and fears of Roman Catholic infiltration, whether they were valid or not, were added to an already combustible America in a generation who had personally fought or lost immediate family members in the French and Indian wars. The religious rhetoric that vilified Roman Catholics was brought to bear against England herself, and America's civil millennialism perceived its old adversary, Antichrist, newly embodied in Parliament and the king. Now even colonists from the Middle and Southern colonies had something to fear as the papal threat unified American Anglicans and Dissenters alike. England herself increasingly became vilified as "them" as colonial propagandists called Americans to unity against this supreme enemy. Whether Lord North and the king were actually closet Catholics was irrelevant. American propagandists claimed they were and construed the Quebec Act as evidence that convinced many Americans.

## "RESPECTABLE" PROPAGANDA

By 1774 a collection of reasons to resist Great Britain motivated Americans: the bona fide fear of an Anglican episcopacy, a perceived fear of popery, economic oppression through a series of various acts, the insult of increased liberties for Canadian colonies, and an increasing perception that Parliament and the king were initiating changes illegally. Moreover, outright violence against Americans in Boston was publicized and used to call for resistance. But while the popular press was disseminating political conspiracy theories—warning of popery and inspiring citizens to arms against Britain—respectable thinkers were further exploring Parliament's illegal legislation through the lenses of republicanism and Lockean liberalism. Such writers produced America's Revolutionary propaganda best recalled by historians who focus on formal written treatises. While a superficial reading of the propaganda in the popular press quickly yields ample evidence of the Awakening conceptual system and requires little examination here, an evaluation of the more dignified writings reveals a similar conceptual system at an implicit or structural level. Americans, in spite of their religious, educational, and class differences, shared many conceptual components; and for the shrewd propagandist producing an audience-centered message, the Awakening conceptual system was an extremely useful point of departure. The effective pamphleteer understood that many American audiences held strong, specific religious beliefs and also recognized the types of arguments required to persuade particular groups.

## James Wilson: The Official Vilification of Parliament

James Wilson eventually became one of the first Supreme Court justices in the newly founded United States. Born in Scotland in 1742, he was raised in a rigorous Calvinistic environment where his parents felt him destined to become a minister.[9] In preparation for the ministry he was educated in Scotland at St. Andrews in the midst of the Scottish Renaissance. The ambitious Wilson never became a clergyman but immigrated into America where opportunities abounded, and began a career in law under the tutelage of John Dickinson. Confirming the presence of a mind influenced by the implied doctrines of the Awakening, Wilson's pamphlet *Considerations of the Nature and Extent of the Legislative Authority of the British Parliament* reveals structural congruencies with Awakening perspectives.

*Considerations* was composed in 1768, but perhaps recognizing its potential for inflaming the public, Wilson did not publish it until 1774. He was the first writer to clearly conceptualize an efficacious relationship between the Crown and the colonies, a type of relationship that was officially adopted by Great Britain seventy years later and credited with preserving the empire in the aftermath of the American Revolution.[10] Featured in Wilson's pamphlet is the notion that colonial loyalty is legally only due the king of Great Britain as a "father" to all English people, but not to Parliament. Similarly, Whitefield's discourse affirmed and recognized the monarchy but resisted Anglican hegemony. Wilson structurally duplicated that position by supporting the king but opposing parliamentary control. In this pamphlet, Wilson formally assigns "them" status to Parliament on legal grounds, extending Whitefield's religious distinction squarely, and *legally*, into the political sphere, providing law-abiding colonists grounds to resist Parliament.

In the pamphlet's opening paragraphs, Wilson supplies a perspective of the entire conflict, that it is a struggle between the prospect of liberty or slavery and that it involves inclusion or exclusion from the British family. He shows Lockean tendencies by establishing a major premise that governments exist by consent of the people to enlarge their happiness. He then lays out a rational case, arguing that the House of Commons, in contrast to a king or the House of Lords, is the most likely legislature to avoid corruption and ensure the well-being of the people due to its accountability to the electors: "At the expiration of every parliament, the people can make a distinction between those who have served them well, and those who have neglected or betrayed their interest." Wilson's fear of corruption in Parliament reveals a confidence in the "depravity of man," that "long parliaments will naturally forget their dependence on the people," and once this representative dependence is "forgotten," corruption follows, "England will lose its liberty," and the nation is in danger of perishing. Calling colonial resistance "a righteous cause," Wilson sets his discourse in the mainstream of colonial beliefs.

In addition to the loss of parliamentary accountability, Wilson is equally distressed by undue influence from the church or the "barons." Antipapism is included in the pamphlet when, alluding to Roman Catholic constraints on the Stuart dynasty, Wilson writes:

> They looked upon the prerogatives of the crown as so many obstacles in the way of their favourite scheme of supreme ecclesiastical dominion; and therefore seized, with eagerness, every occasion of sacrificing the interests of their sovereign to those of the pope.

Wilson also castigates the House of Lords as "capricious and inconstant," often aiding the "king in his projects of tyranny; and, at other times, excited the people to insurrections and tumults." In his mind, those who advance to power invariably become corrupt.

The second section of the pamphlet presents arguments for the supremacy of the House of Commons. Wilson praises its ability to reward good princes or check "the progress of arbitrary power" in evil ones. With the premises established that Americans deserve freedom and representation in the House of Commons, Wilson demonstrates that Americans actually have no representation in Parliament. He dismisses the "virtual representation" consistently cited by Tories as an "absurd principal" and then proceeds to transcend that argument by undermining Parliament's jurisdiction altogether.

Wilson illuminates situations that provide a legal precedent for limiting parliamentary jurisdiction. In terms of a progression of logic that led to the Revolution, here is the most important argumentative element of the pamphlet as he makes representation or "virtual" representation a moot point. He cites three legal cases wherein the court determined that Parliament lacked the jurisdiction to legislate for Ireland, Jamaica, or Virginia. In lands where Parliament does have authority, it is granted by representation or "a title by conquest." Since the colonists effectively have no representation, Wilson sarcastically asks, "How came the colonists to be a conquered people?" The right of conquest cannot be applied to America, and it is the only other right besides representation that affords jurisdiction. With no grounds for parliamentary control, established Wilson then concludes that the colonial tie to the British Empire hinges upon monarchial loyalty.

Parliament's authority to pass laws affecting the colonies is completely undermined, and their legislative actions subsequently become irrelevant and illegal. In Wilson's view, while the king might still be one of "us," Parliament is not, and he defines them out of the community that loves liberty. Thus, Parliament excludes itself from the community by the illegal suppression of English liberty (as New Lights objected to the Old Light suppression of the Holy Spirit). Tellingly, Wilson's concluding argument was drawn from a first-stage rhetorical topic of the Awakening system.

## THOMAS JEFFERSON: AMERICAN LOYALTY AND THE MONARCHY

Americans needed to redefine themselves as a nation in a way that would defend the privileges of English liberty while still affirming the unique religious identity many had adopted. The pattern of thought promoted by Whitefield provided the conceptual apparatus to accomplish that task. Just as Dissenting churches had separated themselves from traditional ecclesiastical authority to maintain "undefiled" worship, Americans at large could do the same to maintain their liberties. American zeal to promote English liberties would empower a redefined national identity. By the time Thomas Jefferson composed "A Summary View of the Rights of British America, 1774," the national connection with British identity continued to deteriorate and a new conception of American identity replaced it. In fact, one of the purposes of "A Summary View" was that Jefferson hoped to instruct his Virginia colleagues, in Stephen Browne's words, in "what kind of language and comportment should be expected of Americans at this juncture in the crisis of identity."[11] The reformation of political relationships that one writer asserts was the ostensible intent of American protest up to this point was giving way to open rebellion.[12] If America could not be reformed, it would be reborn; identity would be redefined. One way or another, liberty would prevail.

Thomas Jefferson and George Whitefield could not have been more opposite, especially in their personalities. Jefferson struggled with extreme stage fright, was a poor orator, and perhaps did not even read aloud the Declaration of Independence himself. In fact, hoping that Patrick Henry might read "A Summary View," Jefferson became conveniently ill on his way to the Virginia convention.[13] Yet Jefferson evinced an unambiguous sense of uniquely American identity, equally as clear as Whitefield's conceptions of "altogether Christians" and "almost Christians," and he employed the Awakening conceptual system to frame his ideas about citizenship and liberty.

"A Summary View" opens with Jefferson's republican definition of the role and limitations upon the office of the king. As "the chief officer of the people," the king was "subject to their superintendance," and as such the people could demand that the king terminate the parliamentary oppression.[14] After asserting the people's rights and demanding the king put an end to the oppression, Jefferson recaps the development of the sovereignty of the Saxon people, arguing that since their ancestors were not subject to European monarchs after emigrating out of Europe, the American British were not legally subject to monarchs from the British Isles. They have a right to self-government as did their forefathers, implying that they are a distinct people. His narratives of the Saxon conquest of Britain and recent "conquest" of America construct "a sustained conflict between freedom and tyranny, the rhetorical function of which is to leave the colonies with no choice but to embrace the former by resisting the latter."[15]

Next, Jefferson turns attention toward the "deep laid plot" by pointing out eight instances of arbitrary power in a succession of parliamentary acts. Jefferson calls the instances "a series of oppressions . . . pursued unalterably through every change of ministers" and concludes that the passing of the acts evidences "a deliberate and systematical plan of reducing us to slavery." It is the consistency, in spite of a turnover in prime ministers, that convinces Jefferson of the deep roots of this plot, likely originating in the king.

Jefferson then labels the entire British governmental system tyrannical and points out that it is "removed from the reach of fear, the only restraining motive which may hold the hand of a tyrant," by its distance from America. Jefferson implies that the king could do something about the "oppressions" if he chose, but veiled behind the polite deferential language of the pamphlet, Jefferson implicates the king in this "systematical plan." Even if the king grants America's request for redress, Jefferson will not be satisfied: "Yet this will not excuse the wanton exercise of this power which we have seen his majesty practise on the laws of the American legislatures."

Near the end of the pamphlet, Jefferson challenges the common belief that the British king actually owns all the land of the empire and grants proprietorship to whomever he pleases. In contrast, Jefferson asserts this notion to be a "fictitious principle" that was foisted upon the nation. To make his case, Jefferson returns to British history, summarizing the origin of laws and the present situation, leading him to conclude that the people are the rightful sovereigns of the British Empire and have entrusted the king to rule in their behalf. So Jefferson then asks, "Can he erect a power superior to that which erected himself? He has done it indeed by force; but let him remember that force cannot give right." Jefferson repeats his republican claim that "kings are the servants, not the proprietors of the people." At the end of the pamphlet Jefferson unveils the first-stage rhetorical topic that has generated his arguments, that corrupt leaders betray their commission. Jefferson writes, "The great principles of right and wrong are legible to every reader. . . . The whole art of government consists in the art of being honest." Republican virtue demands honesty and faithfulness from its leaders. In Jefferson's view, dishonest rulers, guilty of arbitrarily oppressing the people, are unfit to lead the nation, just as unconverted ministers are unfit to pastor churches. Jefferson has used the term "arbitrary" seven times in regular intervals throughout the pamphlet, wielding it to assert that Parliament and the king were tyrants, even enemies to liberty. Jefferson then closes by reminding the king that arbitrary leadership will not prevail: "The God who gave us life gave us liberty at the same time; the hand of force may destroy, but cannot disjoin them." Jefferson inseparably links God with liberty, and liberty will overcome this attempt to enslave Americans, thus the king should grant their request to correct the usurpations of power. He draws the lines between good and evil, between slavery and freedom, and positions God on the side of liberty. Jefferson ends with a feigned appeal for reconciliation, saying this is "the fervent prayer of all British America!"

Jefferson's treatise was submitted to the Continental Congress for adoption, but it was declined in favor of milder sentiments and language. Subsequently, Jefferson had the pamphlet printed and distributed in Virginia where it became an important statement articulating the rationale of a voluntary submissive relationship between America and Britain. Yet Jefferson arguably hoped that the pamphlet would prompt Americans closer to a choice for independence if hopes of reconciliation were to falter. As Browne noted, "[A] relationship established by choice, could be disestablished by choice, which is precisely what Jefferson aimed to effect."[16]

Jefferson claimed that British Americans had a true understanding and practice of natural rights, as Whitefield claimed the revivalists had a true understanding and practice of genuine Christianity. In addition, each man charged that status quo leadership had lost their grasp of their respective issues—rights or religion—and thus forfeited any legitimate claim to power. Each cited the abuses of power and warned of the proclivity of leaders to exploit the people under their authority. Jefferson clearly distinguished American identity in terms of us-them throughout the discourse. He had no identity tensions about who Americans were; they were "Americans" who had emigrated from England and Europe, who conquered a new land and who were distinct from the Europeans. Importantly, Jefferson extends accusations of arbitrary power to the king himself. Where Wilson and previous writers focused their criticisms on Parliament, Jefferson, beneath his deferential style, implicates the king. While Jefferson likely owed little intellectual debt to the Awakening, the parallels in logic and reliance on identical first-stage argument topics greatly accelerated the public embrace of his perspective.

## THE POPULAR PROPAGANDA

By 1774 Americans shouldered their arms to defend religious and civil liberties. Since violence had already sporadically erupted in various locations, ministers and civil leaders began to mobilize militias to fight the British. One of the motivating factors spilled out of a mature manifestation of civil millennialism excited by the Protestant belief in the prophesied Armageddon, just as it had during the wars with the French. This religious impulse was no peripheral phenomenon and was centered in New England. One British official complained that the people of rural Connecticut were "all politicians and Scripture learnt."[17] Explaining the public opinion that facilitated violence, the British sympathizer Peter Oliver blamed it on "Mr. Otis's black regiment, the dissenting clergy."[18] In Connecticut, the Awakening conceptual system and civil millennialism had so insinuated itself into the colonial mind that in 1774, after receiving an erroneous letter declaring "that Admiral Graves had burnt Boston, and that General Gage was murdering old and young," Joseph Bellamy and Israel Putnam called together an army of forty thousand "*Sober Dissenters*" (excluding Presbyterians) that began marching to Boston the same day.[19] Connecticut's total Anglo-male population in 1774 (age ten to seventy) numbered sixty-three thousand, thus the army must have been composed of every able-bodied man and many from neighboring colonies, especially since no Presbyterians joined them.[20] Even if the person who numbered this army was a poor judge of crowd size, the size of an army one-fourth that number in colonial America is still astounding. Believing that British tyranny constituted no less than a manifestation of Antichrist in the final days before the millennium, Bellamy inspired this huge army to arms with the "curse of Meroz."[21] They believed they were going to fight the battle of Armageddon. The next day the marching army received word, of course, that there had been no attack, so they returned home and disbanded. This account evidences the pervasive reach of the Awakening conceptual system among rank-and-file colonists—at least in New England. Clark opined that such a quick mobilization of colonial forces in a time of need provides "evidence against religious imagery being mere rhetoric."[22] No doubt many of these recruits were not entirely motivated by religious reasons, but Bellamy, knowing his audience, effectively chose this particular text to rouse what he believed to be the majority.

Bellamy's pronouncement of the curse of Meroz reveals the perceptual shift occurring, where the British have become "them"—the enemies of God—while the *Sober Dissenters* represent the new "us." In Massachusetts, Nathaniel Whitaker called upon the curse of Meroz in 1777 to rouse Bostonians against the British and attempt to convert American Tories into Whigs.[23] Mark Noll concludes that, "In their shared efforts, both political and religious figures were tailoring the project of republican independence to fit the language to traditional Protestant religion."[24] Likewise, Darsey noted, "The Whigs were able to present rebellion as an act of virtue, meaning not only that the act was praiseworthy, but that failure to act would constitute moral degeneracy."[25] Perhaps Whitefield was glad he was dead, being a publicly loyal subject of the king, since, owing to him, the curse was recalled for military use. Whitefield helped to blend the vocabularies and meanings, had a hand in shaping the thought that permitted its existence, and articulated the precise arguments that were used to energize rebellion. The curse's use against Tories, the British Parliament, and the Crown was practically inevitable, as was their construal of the British as God's enemies.

Yet this religious impulse extended well beyond New England, especially into areas further inland. While many of America's Founding Fathers may have been genuinely motivated to support independence by secular reasons, numerous historians are beginning to question Jon Butler's assertion that, "at its heart, the Revolution was a profoundly secular event."[26] While church membership records of traditional denominations were not impressive, and colonial leaders distanced themselves from New Light affiliations, Gordon Wood insists that a strictly secular view of the Revolution is a retrospective "optical illusion" caused by looking for religion in the wrong places. Arguing that Whig ideology was not able to displace the religious beliefs from which "ordinary people explained the world and made it meaningful," Wood reasoned:

> After all, the period preceding the Revolution experienced such a vast outpouring of religious passion that later commentators could only call it a Great Awakening, and the period following the Revolution outdid even that initial explosion of evangelical religious feeling to become the Second Great Awakening. Could religion during the Revolutionary decades have simply dropped out of sight? Was popular religion like a raging river that suddenly went underground only to reemerge downstream with more force and vigor than ever?[27]

Wood constructs an account that posits a "popular Christianity," an expression of faith that evolved out of the Awakening that combined orthodox doctrine with popular beliefs and increasingly met the spiritual needs of multiple communities of colonists. Nontraditional New Light–inspired sects experienced a phenomenal growth in the decades immediately prior to the Revolution. These communities of believers had been splintered and physically separated from the authority structures of traditional denominations, establishing new congregations led by Yale and Harvard graduates from underprivileged backgrounds who formed loose affiliations among the expanding inland populations. Accommodating Butler's research, Wood concluded, "One kind of American religion may have declined during the Revolution, but it was more than replaced by another kind."[28]

Perceptive political leaders understood the implications of Protestant theology upon this constituency that adhered to popular Christianity and employed it for their own revolutionary ends, and likewise, the religious communities clearly saw their own advantage in maintaining colonial political autonomy. Prior distinctions between religion and politics increasingly began to blur as their religious and republican vocabularies—as well as beliefs—merged together. Furthermore, the independence-minded leaders openly worked hand in hand with ministers. As the Revolution drew near, colonial leaders called on the likes of Gilbert Tennent and William Henry Drayton to itinerate into the backcountry, preaching up Whig propaganda in order to "break the hold of the Tories."[29] According to J. C. D. Clark, "By 1776, religious revivalism had inspired in a minority of the most frenzied colonists a vision of an imminent millennium, in the majority a heightened sense of the colonies' place in an international moral drama."[30]

If one were to follow Aristotle's sage advice regarding the art of persuasion, the best arguments are those the majority of the audience is most likely to believe, not necessarily the most logically rigorous ones. From first to last, successful propaganda is an audience-centered activity, seeking to influence the perceived majority of an audience leading up to a point of democratic decision. Departing from what people already believe to be true, the polemicist builds a case in a logical direction that those preexisting beliefs will warrant. Throughout history, such practices have often been labeled as "sophistry" in cases where deception and ulterior motives on the part of the rhetor were apparent. But "virtuous" orators also employ the audience-centered approach. Even upon a cursory reading, arguments founded upon religious beliefs step forth from the writings of America's foremost Revolutionary propagandists.

## Samuel Adams: America's Thoroughgoing Polemical Voice

On the self-evident grounds that successful persuasion is audience centered, we shall consider the writings of Samuel Adams and Thomas Paine. The rhetoric of these master polemicists reveals much about their perceived audiences, evidencing their belief that they were addressing people who were effectively persuaded by arguments drawn from religious fields. Blended with the republican concepts of vice and virtue, liberty and slavery, their religious appeals brought immediacy and passion to stimulate political activism.

Educated at Harvard, trained in the classics, fluent in Locke and other enlightened writers, Samuel Adams was perfectly prepared for the polemical side of politics. Adams' diverse career provided the insight needed to speak as a clergyman, lawyer, or merchant, and his life in the trenches of Boston imbued his mind with a consubstantial knowledge and experience of American life. Not only did he know how and what Americans thought, Adams was able to vividly articulate a public consciousness that people could adopt. With "a burning zeal for the doctrine of liberty, and religious fervor for the tenets of Puritanism," Adams could, without guile, proclaim the evils of arbitrary power that rose against the church or the New England polity.[31] Beginning in 1763, writing under at least twenty-five pseudonyms, Adams untiringly supplied the colonial press with editorials and articles that voiced coherent and consistent opposition to British policies. And from Samuel Adams' writings, the rhetorical analysis expands our view into the perceived mind of his intended audience. One who knew Americans so intimately also pragmatically understood what kinds of rhetoric it would take to successfully persuade them.

"Candidus," a man who would speak candidly and one of Adams' favorite voices, wrote an editorial published in the *Boston Gazette* in 1771, offering the opinion of a citizen regarding Parliament's obnoxious legislation. Within the article, Adams reminds New Englanders of the Israelite king Jeroboam, who under the pretense of calling the nation to worship God, made sacrifices to idols, causing the entire nation to sin. Adams labels this act "*treason against the people*," obviously using the biblical case to analogically criticize New England's current Tory leaders.[32] His republican perspective is supported by the biblical story. Attacking the Anglicans and the governor, Adams writes, "There is no question but the priests were the *viceregents* of the Governor, or his *heralds to publish his impious proclamations to the people*." Herein Adams makes a charge against the Anglican ministers who were assisting the British government in prosecution of their tyranny. The bishop issue had not been settled in 1771, although it was being replaced by a more potent antipapism, which provided the Whig propagandists with better arguments for unification. So, missing no bases, Adams manages to slip in a thinly veiled connection with Roman Catholicism:

Even in these enlightened times, the people in some parts of the world are so bewitched by the enchantments of *priest-craft* and *king-craft*, as to believe they sin against their own consciences, in compliance with the instruction of the one, or in obedience to the command of the other.

In New England, with Salem tainting its recent past and papism threatening its future, Adams' employment of the terms "bewitched," "*priest-craft*," and "*king-craft*" carried potent and explicit accusations that the Church of England and the king were satanically inspired, that they were secretly working with the Roman Catholics to lead the British back to papal control. Adams continues by using another biblical story to criticize Tory leadership, wherein Israel foolishly rejected God's ordained form of government and chose to follow a man instead, instituting the monarchy:

For they grew weary of their liberty in the days of Samuel the prophet, and exchanged that civil government which the *wisdom of heaven* had prescribed to them, for an absolute despotic monarchy; that they might in that regard be like the nations round about them.

Here Adams suggests that the monarchy was the human choice for government, in contrast to a theocracy as administered through a succession of judges (the position held by the biblical prophet Samuel at the time of the change). Adams questions his audience—whether they will follow a man who will lead them into slavery and sin, or follow God, who will lead them to freedom and piety. After speculating and arguing about where the wrong choice will lead, Adams concludes the editorial by saying:

To *complement* a great man to the injury of *truth* and *liberty*, may be in the opinion of a very degenerate age, the part of a *polite* and *well-bred* gentleman—Wise men however will denominate him a *Traitor* or a *Fool*. But how much more aggravated must the folly and madness of those, who instead of worshipping God . . . can utter a lie TO HIM!!—in order to render themselves acceptable to a man who is a worm or to the son of a man *who is a worm*.

Adams' final phrase in the above quote is taken from Scripture, the metaphor "worm" being a common biblical trope that emphasized

human frailty in light of God's sublimity.[33] Adams couches his conclusion in the form of a question, having a logically obvious answer.
If a reader has not rejected a premise earlier in the argument, then
it becomes difficult to disagree with his conclusion and articulate a
rejoinder to his question. Would American colonists sin against God
in order to remain obedient to illegal laws instituted by an impious
government—colonists who had embraced religion more seriously in
increasing numbers?

A year later, Adams explicitly repeated an argument intermingling
the notions of tyranny, slavery, freedom, and liberty with their spiritual
corollaries of virtue, vice, ignorance, and knowledge. "Valerius Popli-
cola" argued that the king exercised arbitrary power and also accused
the king's "British Ministers" (echoing Joseph Galloway's complaint
regarding pensioned judges) of stealing America's wealth: "An awakening Caution to Americans! Lest by tamely submitting to be plundered,
they encourage their Plunderers to grasp at all they have." Although
the term "Great Awakening" had not been invented at this point, ministers and writers were using the term "awakening" to metaphorically
describe the series of revivals. So Adams' insertion of that term into
his discourse invokes recognition and choice. After making his case
that the king's "hirelings" were robbing the people and trampling their
liberties, Adams prays: "Merciful God! Let not the iron Hand of Tyranny ravish our Laws and seize the Badge of Freedom, nor avow'd
Corruption and the murderous Rage of lawless power be ever seen
on the sacred Seat of Justice!"[34] Following his prayer, which eloquently
summarizes his complaint against the king and his ministers, Adams
asks Americans to act:

> Is it not High Time for the People of this Country explicitly to declare,
> whether they will be Freemen or slaves? . . . For wherever Tyranny is
> establish'd, Immorality of every Kind comes in like a Torrent. It is in the
> Interest of Tyrants to reduce the People to Ignorance and Vice. For they
> cannot live in any Country where Virtue and public Liberty of a People
> are intimately connected. . . . For this Reason, it is always observable, that
> those who are combin'd to destroy the People's Liberties, practice every
> Art to poison their Morals. . . . Let us then act like wise Men. . . . Let us
> converse together upon this most interesting Subject. . . . Let Associa-
> tions & Combinations be everywhere set up to consult and recover our
> just Rights.[35]

There is no mistaking Adams' connection of piety with liberty, and sin with tyranny. He skillfully interweaves religious and republican concepts, liberally quoting or alluding to the Bible while suggesting analogies between biblical figures and modern politicians. Even his anaphoric use of the phrase "Let us. . ." in the quote above echoes the style of an inspirational biblical passage.[36] More significantly, Adams simply asserts the above premises without offering any arguments that the premises are true. He sensed that his audience needed no preparatory argumentation; Adams simply solicits these premises as accepted preexisting beliefs.

Throughout the discourse Adams positions good against evil, the tyranny of Britain against the freedom of Americans. Obviously, since tyranny is "evil" as proved by its deeds, the Americans are "good" and, consequently, Americans are "us" while the Britons are "them." Adams has no qualms about American identity, referring continually to "Americans," "the People of this Country," and "American interests." But where Adams used the ministerial persona and its accompanying eloquence perhaps judiciously or sparingly, usually presenting political and economic arguments, another colonial propagandist did not hesitate to adopt a full ministerial persona to voice a forceful point in the Revolutionary period's most powerful piece of polemic writing.

## Donning a Minister's Robe: Thomas Paine's *Common Sense*

In January 1776 Thomas Paine released *Common Sense*, adding his voice for public consideration over the deteriorating British-American situation. The sheer volume of issues alone attests to the pamphlet's demand and suggests a significant impact on colonial thought. Reprinted over fifty times before the year was out, accounting for over five hundred thousand copies, *Common Sense* was certainly the most widely published of the Revolutionary literature as one of our nation's first best sellers, not to mention that newspaper reprints increased its distribution.

The immediate effect of *Common Sense* was to break a deadlock between a minority of colonial leaders who wished to form an independent American state and the majority of leaders who sought reconciliation with the British. J. Michael Hogan and Glen Williams bluntly claim that Paine's ideas "radically impacted colonial thought"[37] and Arthur Schlesinger opined that Paine influenced "the public as well as the delegates themselves to adopt the fateful step."[38] When the proposal for independence was subsequently debated in the Continental Congress in July 1776, only New York voted against it. In all likelihood many reconciliationists kept their views increasingly private as the notion of independence gained momentum, but the ideological reorientation evidenced in the vote count was remarkable.

We must keep in mind that *Common Sense* climaxed a series of influential pamphlets analyzed above, completing a collective rhetorical effort in the movement toward independence. No single text worked in isolation, but all were cast into the public sphere and interacted with sermons, newspapers, songs, cartoons, and broadsides to influence the American community. In light of the progression of resistance to parliamentary rule and the dissatisfaction with the British legal system, "Loyalty to the King," a Saxon tradition affirmed even by Jefferson, emerged as a stubborn bond between English colonists and the mother country that twenty years of argumentation failed to loosen.[39] Even from Whitefield's and Mayhew's perspective, reconciliationists felt George III should either reform his ways or be replaced with a "good" king and all would be well again.

Loyalty to the king was manifest in two distinct doctrines, both originating from, and warranted by, Christian doctrine: (1) the *divine right to rule*, which asserted that all kings were appointed by God, and to oppose that king—whether he was good or evil—was to oppose God, and (2) *hereditary succession*, which vested that right to rule in the king's son.[40] Whitefield, Mayhew, Samuel Adams, and others had been questioning these doctrines for decades, causing the interpretation of the doctrines to change. The notion of divine right, according to Clark, underwent a necessary transformation in the century leading up to the Revolution, shifting meanings from the right of hereditary succession to the right of Providence to select the king.[41] But this transformation in the doctrine still did not condone a republican-fueled rejection of the current king. Consequently, since the British legal system had been undermined, since Parliament's powers had been argued into limitation, and since Americans had a traditional right of emigration, the belief that God had ordained George III to rule remained as a significant roadblock to the collective embrace of independence by colonial religious communities.

*Common Sense* addressed the colonial-authority controversy with a clear sense that Americans and Britons were distinct and that Americans were settling their own sense of national identity. By the time

*Common Sense* was published and disseminated, violent tactics had commenced on both sides, and the issue, as it had evolved, demanded a choice between (1) the preservation of English liberties and colonial autonomy within voluntary loyalty to the king, or (2) severing political ties and declaring independence. Reconciliationists argued that Christianity required loyalty to the British monarchy. *That belief constituted a critical reservation for religiously influenced colonists* (as well as the established church), who composed the rank and file of the colonial armies. Thus, Paine's rhetorical challenge was to undermine this notion of loyalty to the king before he could instigate practical arguments on the advantages and likelihood of successful independence.

With the intent of breaking through the barrier of prejudice in his readers' minds, Paine introduces a theme that will recur throughout the pamphlet: "A long habit of not thinking a thing wrong, gives it a superficial appearance of being right."[42] At each transition in the essay, Paine reminds his readers of the perils of prejudging his claims. Paine gets right to the point after warning of bias and prejudice. In the second paragraph, Paine argues that not only do Americans object to the acts of Parliament, but their complaint also implicates the king:

> As the king of England hath undertaken in his own right, to support the parliament in what he calls theirs, and as the good people of this country are grievously oppressed by the combination, they have an undoubted privilege to inquire into the pretensions of both, and equally to reject the usurpations of either.

Thus, Paine foreshadows his intent to critique and attack the king, suggesting that the king's inattention to grievances delineated by Jefferson constituted complicit cooperation with Parliament in the oppression. By the phrase, "rejecting the usurpations," Paine empowers his American audience with republican notions of self-rule.

But before moving forward with the argument, Paine provides a narrative of the facts necessary to comprehend his case. He tells his version of the origin and theory of government and thus provides a context for his readers, many of whom were ignorant of English history and its political system. He concludes the narrative section by saying:

> I know it is difficult to get over local or long standing prejudices, yet if we will suffer ourselves to examine the component parts of the English

constitution, we shall find them to be the base remains of two ancient tyrannies, compounded with some new republican materials.

Paine politely reminds his readers to withhold judgment (even while he does not withhold his), employing the word "tyranny" to describe two of the three components of the British government: the monarchy and the aristocracy. By this term "tyranny" Paine directly implies that kingship is evil, as he will take care to explain in section two. From here, Paine elucidates the internal inconsistency of the English Constitution, showing the "absurdity" of setting up a House of Commons to check the power of an untrustworthy king, then giving power to the king to override their decisions. Paine then cites the Tory explanation of this situation:

> Some writers have explained the English constitution thus; the king, say they, is one, the people another; the peers are an house in behalf of the king; the commons in behalf of the people; but this hath all the distinctions of an house divided against itself.

Many political theorists up to this point had revered England's three-part government as elegant, effective, and protective against excessive tyranny. Paine recognized the necessity of breaking down the prejudice in audiences who favored the British arrangement and perceived no better political system. His mention of "an house divided" was borrowed from a saying of Jesus in reference to the devil's kingdom, clearly expressing that Paine considered the British government to be thoroughly corrupt. Paine employs antithesis to simplify a potentially confusing arrangement, and it is in this device that the title of the pamphlet, *Common Sense*, epitomizes how Paine is able to make sense of American affairs. By oversimplifying affairs, options are clarified and choices become self-evident.[43] Paine closes the section by showing how the current constitution could not have been established by God: "*How came the king by a power which the people are afraid to trust, and always obliged to check?* Such a power could not be the gift of a wise people, neither can any power, *which needs checking*, be from God." Again, the people are empowered in this statement and their foolishness displayed for giving away their power to the king. Thus, Paine has portrayed the American situation as a structural paradox—a problem that needed solving.

Deist and republican that he was, one might expect Paine to address this sensitive issue from a more enlightened perspective. But he does not. To effectively persuade the "sober dissenters" of New England required arguments from the epistemological source that they respected most: the Bible. Consequently, the prudent Paine effectively draws upon Protestant beliefs to construct his argument; essentially, that a pious Christian is not opposing God by supporting independence. Despite Paine's beliefs (and as a Deist, Paine did not reject Christianity—he consistently claimed a respect for God and religion), his argument reveals a pragmatic understanding of the Protestant portions of his audience.[44] Regarding the character of kings in general, Paine asserts, "[A] thirst for absolute power is the natural disease of monarchy." The natural inclination of a king will be toward corruption, immorality, and other evils, making him unfit to lead a pious nation. This argument echoes the doctrine of the "depravity of man," as the Calvinists taught it.

Mayhew, in his attempt to refute belief in the divine right of kings, reinterpreted the very scriptures used to justify the doctrine, concluding that one may oppose a tyrannous rule. Yet in Mayhew's view, the argument remains that a good ruler is to be obeyed, and his view does not negate the need for a king in general. In contrast, Paine uses an argument that avoids any hermeneutical haggling with Tories, rising above arguments that support *divine right* and *hereditary succession* by undercutting their scriptural authority:

> As the exalting one man so greatly above the rest cannot be justified on the equal rights of nature, so neither can it be defended on the authority of scripture; for the will of the Almighty, as declared by Gideon and the prophet Samuel, expressly disapproves of government by kings.

We immediately recognize a repeat of Samuel Adams' case from 1772. This argument had been in circulation to a certain extent, giving at least some in America a familiarity with it. But where Adams only gave it a paragraph, Paine develops the argument fully, devoting to it 21 percent of the text of *Common Sense*. No other argument in the pamphlet received this level of explanation and support, signifying that Paine believed it was critical to advancing his case.

Paine argues that the Scriptures provide no authoritative warrant for kingship, claiming that the first monarchy of Israel constituted a concession God made in response to their rejection of the theocratic government instituted through the Mosaic law. Nor does the Bible obligate Christians to specifically respect the monarchy or English system of government. Quoting Jesus, Paine states, "Render unto Caesar the things which are Caesar's is the scriptural doctrine of courts, yet it is no support of monarchial government, for the Jews at that time were without a king, and in a state of vassalage to the Romans." In supporting these arguments, Paine exclusively employs scriptural warrants. Undoubtedly, Paine is attempting to appeal to religiously minded colonists by warranting his argument in this manner. Enlightened Americans such as Franklin or Jefferson needed little convincing on this issue. For them, divine right was not an obstacle to supporting independence. Paine is appealing to what he felt was a sizable Christian audience who respected Scripture and still thought that supporting independence was rebellion against God's ordained government. In closing the argument, Paine repeats the essence of his position by making his appeal to scriptural authority:

> These portions of scripture are direct and positive. They admit of no equivocal construction. That the Almighty hath here entered his protest against monarchial government is true, or the scripture is false. And a man hath good reason to believe that there is as much of kingcraft, as priestcraft in withholding the scripture from the public in Popish countries. For monarchy in every instance is the Popery of government.

For the active Protestant of that day, Scripture certainly was not false. Any theological arguing about how to interpret St. Paul's injunction to "submit to the governing authorities" (a central argument of pacifists and reconciliationists) was transcended by Paine's argument that such an authority is of corrupt human origin, not divine, and is based in a misunderstanding of the Scriptures. In addition to his religious appeal, Paine makes another rhetorical move in the above excerpt. Drawing upon this now deep propaganda tradition, Paine claims that the monarchy itself is a product of papal origin. In this case, Paine maintains that the hegemonic, authoritarian method of Roman Catholic governance, connections which the English rejected and severed over two hundred years earlier, was organizationally reified in the British monarchial system—a lamentable situation that recent British policies in America seemed to support. Regardless of whether or not

Paine stretched the truth, Protestant colonists had their deepest fears pricked, and they responded.

Next, Paine tackles the notion of hereditary succession, extending his logical arguments and citing the doctrine of original sin, showing its expression in the history of the British monarchy:

> [B]ut of a family of kings for ever, hath no parallel in or out of scripture but the doctrine of original sin, which supposes the free will of all men lost in Adam; and from such comparison, and it will admit of no other, hereditary succession can derive no glory. For as in Adam all sinned, and as in the first electors all men obeyed; as in the one all mankind were subjected to Satan, and in the other to Sovereignty; as our innocence was lost in the first, and our authority in the last; and as both disable us from reassuming some former state and privilege, it unanswerably follows that original sin and hereditary succession are parallels. Dishonorable rank! Inglorious connection! Yet the most subtle sophist cannot produce a juster simile.

Paine points out congruencies of the kingdom of darkness with the kingdom of Britain. The deictic parameters of virtue and vice, good and evil, that undergird Paine's logic need not be expounded in the argument. Thomas Paine knew his audience, knew what kind of people they were, and knew what arguments and notions would be likely to persuade them. In this case, he is clearly appealing to profound religious sentiments. For its rhetorical force, the argument requires auditors immersed in distinctions between right and wrong, demarcating their world in dualistic structures where God's kingdom rivals the work of the devil. This was an audience originally shaped by George Whitefield and the other leading ministers during the previous three decades. Even ministers who eschewed the Awakening enthusiasm promoted the same conceptual system. The hard work was already complete; Paine merely needed to build upon common beliefs by demonstrating that the king and Parliament were at work against God's kingdom. Paine builds his case upon a religious as well as natural epistemology, citing biblical injunctions against evil and drawing upon the palpable policies of recent British legislation that were perceived as oppressive and demeaning.

His rhetoric functions in the interior spaces of the mind, connecting King George's actions to the kingdom of darkness. Yet the dual thrust of his discursive assault defies separation into discreet parts. Republicanism and reformed Protestantism shared intellectual space in the colonial world and constructed meaning to activities in both the religious and political spheres. Paine's republican arguments bolster his authoritative scriptural proof, and his biblical assertions prescribe conversion to republican ideals. His logic leads to the logical conclusion that to fight a revolution in opposition to God would be a futile endeavor, but to challenge an evil tyranny becomes the Christian's duty.

Paine's effort to convince colonists that opposition to George III was not sinful was an essential step in garnering popular support of the Revolution from people identified together in the "body of Christ," people who would bear martial hardships. For active Protestants, Paine's other arguments for the inescapability of declaring independence at some point and the likelihood of America's successful engagement in war with a more powerful enemy, necessitate "permission from God" to make war in the first place. Paine's argument did not just remove God's blessing from the British monarchy and associate the king with evil; he transferred that blessing over to the colonists. For Protestants, his pamphlet applied civil millennialism as an inventional rhetorical topic to this situation and transformed the proposed revolution from a rebellion against God's sovereign and established government to a religious war against a satanic, tyrannical oppressor with God supporting the American colonists. Lambert understates the scope of the colonists' conceptual system when he suggests that Americans understood the religious resistance of sin metaphorically to mean resisting British hegemony.[45] Such resistance was not simply a figure of speech; it reveals the blended ideologies of colonial affairs.

In section three, Paine evaluates the current state of affairs with Great Britain and observes that reconciliation with Great Britain has been the goal of both sides up to this point, though Britain has used "force" and the American's "friendship" to achieve this end. Again, the antithetical actions of each side suggest who is good and who is evil, implying a "correct" position on the issue. Paine argues that Americans owe no special loyalty to Great Britain, and he promotes a complete separation as the only viable long-term solution to the dispute—the needed solution to the people's political paradox. In this section, Paine also confronts the most repeated arguments against independence, refuting each in turn with practical reasoning and commonplace evidence.

John Adams indicated that Paine would have been better off to end *Common Sense* at this point. He criticized the pamphlet publicly because of Paine's naive suggestions for constructing a government.[46] Nevertheless, recognizing that more experienced politicians might have a wiser plan, Paine posits his suggestions for a republican form of government that could function without a monarchy. Keep in mind that Paine illuminated and simplified a currently unknown path (government without a king) for the people—a trajectory where its unknown character could inhibit political adoption. Thus, his recommendations for the nature of a republican government were essential for showing colonists that there could be life after a king and that a manageable government with built-in mechanisms to prevent arbitrary power was possible.

Finally, in section four, Paine discusses America's practical ability to wage a successful war with Great Britain. He cleverly turns each American weakness into a strength. And though his arguments may be oversimplified, most Americans would not have known what it would really take to win anyway. Having provided theoretical reasons, pragmatic reasons, the cost, and a concrete plan, Paine presses his audiences for a decision: "[U]ntil an independence is declared, the continent will feel itself like a man who continues putting off some unpleasant business from day to day, yet knows it must be done, hates to set about it, wishes it over, and is continually haunted with the thoughts of its necessity."[47] Such an allusion appealed to the Puritan work ethic that abhorred procrastination and added significant punch to the religious arguments that Paine emphasized in section two.

No writer before Paine had so completely undermined *divine right* and *hereditary succession* or successfully disseminated their arguments to so wide an audience. By founding critical arguments in his pamphlet on an epistemological resource that his readers respected, Paine's rhetorical efforts were accelerated. His foregrounding of religious arguments against the king evidences that colonists held deep respect for religious truth. Paine did not employ such arguments necessarily because he personally believed them or ascribed to the same Awakening conceptual system, but because he understood that his audience would be most efficaciously persuaded by such arguments.[48] As Ernest

Wrage taught, since rhetorical pamphlets are "designed in the main for the popular mind, conversely and in significant ways they bear the impress of the popular mind." Rhetorical discourses must stand upon "prevalent beliefs" that reflect the "tone and temper of audiences" and in this way they function as "useful indices" for understanding the thinking of people to whom the rhetoric was directed.[49]

One might ask how Paine, who had recently arrived from Great Britain, was able to ascertain the nature of his audience. John Adams supplied some insight for us, noting that upon Paine's arrival he "got into such company as would converse with him, and ran about picking up what information he could concerning our affairs, and finding the great question was concerning independence, he gleaned . . . the common-place arguments."[50] Essentially, he was polling his audience. Interestingly, modern marketing and PR firms are beginning to employ similar techniques—getting in and among people by means of cool-hunting—to augment their quantitative polling and market research. Recall, too, that Paine had once considered becoming a minister and that the Awakening had touched England through Whitefield and the Wesleys where he previously lived, familiarizing him with Awakening thought. Moreover, Paine befriended and occasionally resided with Benjamin Franklin, who knew Whitefield, the colonists, and the times as well as anyone in the British Empire.

Whether or not Paine's use of scriptural arguments should be viewed as disingenuous may be a question never fully answered. Yet Paine revealed to John Adams his attitude toward his arguments in *Common Sense*. Adams recalled a candid conversation between the two men shortly after its publication. Adams, the staunch Puritan, wrote:

> I told him further, that his reasoning from the Old Testament was ridiculous, and I could hardly think him sincere. At this he laughed, and said he had taken his ideas in that part from Milton; and then expressed a contempt of the Old Testament, and indeed of the Bible at large, which surprised me.[51]

Paine, ever the polemicist, apparently adopted a ministerial persona in critical sections of *Common Sense*—a rhetorical disguise that created the perfect voice to catch the ears of Protestant colonists. Thus, Paine donned the rhetorical robes of George Whitefield for portions of *Common Sense* (as Samuel Adams often did) and appealed to his audience by producing arguments drawn from scriptural warrants. Within months colonists were convinced that it was not a sin to rebel against a king—especially a tyrant. Paine's arguments tipped the balance in favor of war, converting a large block of the public from reconciliationists to patriots.

# CHAPTER 9

## THE LEGACY OF WHITEFIELD

At a structural level, the parallels between religious patterns of thought disseminated by Whitefield in the 1740s and the political ideology of the 1770s are striking. Republican notions of virtue and liberty were deeply rooted in Reformation and revival theology that redefined the concepts for the church. Subsequently, the new logic underneath the new definitions operated as inventional topics to empower republican ideas and afford them a rapid acceptance in the people. Not all of the Revolutionary propagandists employed specific themes drawn from New Light rhetoric, as did those who cited the curse of Meroz, but they did draw upon the Awakening conceptual system to distinguish Americans from the British, to define slavery and liberty, and to condemn injustice and tyranny. The argument fields of the Revolutionary propagandists reveal the beliefs and character of their audiences! Natural-rights ideology is able to establish the primacy of the citizens over the king within its own logic. Yet the Revolutionary polemicists found it necessary to undermine the monarchy with religious arguments that privileged the relationship of the people to God over a community's right to choose its preferred form of government. This fact suggests that Lockean liberalism or republicanism ideals were not as profoundly embedded, or at least as widespread, in the minds of colonists.

Religion, republicanism, and liberalism did not compete with one another for intellectual ascendancy. Each of these components of the American conceptual system blended together to construct the dominant ideology, appropriating arguments or premises interchangeably as needed to support specific claims. It is beyond the scope of this study of Whitefield's rhetorical practices to explore the integration of these perspectives, and others have already begun that task. This study has been primarily focused on the circulation of religious discourse and the shifts in the conceptual systems of colonists that Whitefield's

243

alterations facilitated. The central themes of the Awakening—conversion, agency, choice, common privileges, the role of the Spirit, and a framework for judgment—invited its audiences to be something, birthed out of deeply held values and beliefs, redefining and articulating those beliefs. Without the religious community and a corresponding conceptual system in place, enabling colonists to interpret accurately what the Revolutionary polemicists were trying to say, the pamphlets' identity assertions regarding "us" and "them" would not have been fully intelligible, and indeed, the Revolutionary polemicists *could not have produced* these arguments. They, with a few exceptions, were as enmeshed in the conceptual system as their audiences and were constrained to argue within the limits of what they understood as well as what their audiences understood!

The rhetoric of community did not revolutionize the American churches; it worked from within them for reform, splitting the existing groups into New Light– and Old Light–type factions that ultimately made peace and, in the case of the Presbyterians, consolidated back into one unified denomination. After the aggressive Whitefield of 1740 goaded ministers into either the New Light or Old Light camps, the mature peacemaking Whitefield of 1745, through "another spirit," reached out to the offended clergy, asked their pardon, and included them in the community of genuine believers. His inclusion was a genuine testament to his ecumenical outlook on the church, downplaying the role of denominations and the differences between separatist, dissenting, and episcopal divisions of Christianity at large.

By 1744 Whitefield began distancing himself from radical revivalists who had encouraged separations, aligned himself with moderate New Lights, and reaffirmed the position of the status quo, legitimating the Old Light denominations. In the end it was the intellectual and enthusiastic cooperation of elements within the New Light and Old Light camps that enabled a successful Revolution. As Perry Miller observed, the "pure rationalism" of the Liberal [Old Light] clergy contributed to the intellectual notion of American independence, "but it could never have inspired them to fight for it."[1] Bonomi has argued that the preponderance of piety and church attendance was more extensive and uniform than Butler had stated, suggesting the profundity of the Awakening conceptual system. Wood has suggested the presence of a perspective he calls "popular Christianity" found in people who fundamentally believed in the essentials of Christianity while adding their own idiosyncrasies of spiritualism to their lives. Ostensibly, people holding both orthodox and popular views enthusiastically stepped forward when called to arms. As exemplified by Whitefield's martial sermons and assistance to specific martial causes, the inspiration to fight was a task taken up by preachers. In the Revolutionary generation, ministers like Israel Putnam and Joseph Bellamy in Connecticut, who traveled the communitarian and rhetorical trails blazed by Whitefield, adopting his rhetoric of community with its tolerance of ambiguity and unifying tendencies, and preached themes like the curse of Meroz to encourage and compel support from colonists.

Successful constitutive rhetoric requires an audience "already constituted with an identity and within an ideology," otherwise the call for unity cannot be intelligible.[2] Yet little scholarship has theorized on precisely how disparate groups develop shared identities and standardized ideological values. Hence, this study asked the question, "So how did American colonists develop a sufficient sense of identification with one another in order for the constitutive rhetoric of Revolutionary-era leaders to be intelligible on a widespread scale?" Historians, not without much debate, seem to conclude that the Awakening was a key part of that process, identifying Whitefield as the key figure of the Awakening. But their research too often only examined the broader themes of religious thought as connected to the political sphere, making an intellectual leap from religion to politics across a chasm filled with unanalyzed discourse, seldom stooping to describe the process of precisely how we got from "there to here" in terms of a discourse that did the dirty work. What was needed was further rhetorical analysis of pre-Revolutionary literature to continue to fill the chasm of our ignorance and show all the steps taken by evolving and blending ideologies that helped colonial Americans to merge the religious and political spheres. This study has only begun that task.

## FILLING THE CHASM

As the intellectual transformation progressed throughout the eighteenth century, the overt movement from religion into politics was impelled by civil millennialism, and then republican reasoning was put in service to advance religious causes as the Revolution approached.[3] Whitefield was at the heart of shifts in public discourse in both oral and written media, facilitating the dissemination of rhetoric that enabled each step. From a larger perspective, this study has taught how religious belief and consequent identity were integrated into political and national ideology, complete with its own prescribed identity, through a "rhetoric of community." This rhetoric successfully promoted a common conceptual system among the disparate colonists, establishing their "we-ness," their sense of identity within a community of revived religious converts. Moreover, we have uncovered the elemental units (at the linguistic level of deictic parameters) of this rhetoric and followed its evolution from one rhetorical sphere into others as Whitefield crafted definitions of "us" and "them." From the religious sphere, through the social-structuring ability of religious thought, uniquely American senses of identity and community emerged as other constraints (war and economic oppression) supplied a common threat to the freedoms of American colonists.

This study has examined the multiple communities that existed in the colonies prior to 1740 and has shown how many were susceptible identity-shaping conditions. Whitefield's rhetoric told them exactly who they were and who they ought to be, supplying a religious answer to any identity ambiguities they may have held. Upon his arrival into this identity exigence, Whitefield displayed a consummate oratorical practice and a sophisticated deployment of all his media options to disseminate his rhetoric to a diverse and scattered population. Whitefield promoted this message with performative eloquence and passion, arguing within the guidelines of theological and Enlightenment rules, warranting his claims with sacred Scripture and natural reason. His message saturated the colonial culture, allowing his followers and even his detractors (especially after he included them in the community) to affirm its implicit assumptions about how the world was. Whitefield's religious rhetoric simplified and solidified the theology of Edwards, providing a vocabulary that made it both comprehensible and accessible, facilitating the spread of forces that impelled the pre-Awakening revivals.

As the Awakening faded and political affairs resumed their place on the front pages of colonial newspapers, the Awakening conceptual system, expressed through Whitefield's "rhetoric of community," provided a grammar and vocabulary able to amalgamate with growing republican sentiments as well as Lockean liberalism, producing an ideology capable of rebellion that emerged fully formed through notions of religious self-understanding. It empowered Whig ideologies through its democratic impulse and ensured that a majority of

American settlers developed into supporters of the Whig movement. Evidence of the Awakening conceptual system permeates the pamphlets of the American Revolution, providing discursive links between religious rhetoric and ideological rhetoric intended to rally Anglo-Americans around opposition to British oppression and ultimately around the movement for independence. And while certain secular constraints each provided their own impetus in developing the American spirit, it has not been the goal of this study to explore these constraints in depth, as has adequately been done elsewhere.

## IMPLICATIONS FOR RHETORIC AND HISTORY

With regard to American self-understanding, this study provides a fine-grained explanation for how emerging conceptions of personal identity in America were influenced by religious thought. Awakening preaching, among other things, served to break down the form of community expressed through traditional religion. In the traditional scheme, one's identity and religion were by-products of national/religious heritage. In other words, if our church is, let's say, Dutch Reformed and serves as a symbol of our national identity, then "we are all Christians." The revivalists said, "No, true religion is personal, and each one must choose Christianity personally." The genuine believers became a community having more in common with the other newly born converts down the road than relatives next door. Yet old identifications could not be discarded outright; they were merely subordinated to, and subsequently complemented by the identity that grew out of the new birth. As ties of nationality faded, the religious ties of a citizenship in the kingdom of God served to bind people into a more inclusive community with a reason and will for increasing the amount of intercolonial contact. Consequently, believers from different national backgrounds could converse with a common vocabulary that transcended any cultural or political differences. Individuals gained a sense of unity and fellowship with other colonists where before there had been various levels of division or indifference.

Moreover, at a societal level, this study suggests that the intellectual identification required for the successful constitutive political rhetoric of the American Revolution developed in part from the implied doctrines of colonial Protestantism. As a codified reflection of culture, religion is primal, and from it are generated the assumptions (first principles) that underpin other human institutions. As shown in this study's introductory section, religious belief stood (at least in the eighteenth century) as the controlling factor that structured belief about wider issues. We must take care not to read history through today's lenses. The scientific worldview had not yet achieved its preeminence in 1740, and even by 1776 it only shared the stage with religion. Only after Enlightened American intellectuals continued to chart the ideological development of the new nation did notions of liberty begin to divorce themselves from the religious sphere and the Protestant epistemological influence begin its slow steady decline. Yet, as Alan Heimert wrote, "Whether the enlightened sage of Monticello knew it or not, he had inherited the mantle of George Whitefield."[4]

The "straight-line" theory of influence posited by Heimert holds that the New Light challenge to the authority of the established church exerted a direct and widespread influence among people who subsequently challenged the authority of Parliament and the British king. In contrast, this study affirms an indirect influence supplemented by other nascent ideologies. The New Lights, by and large, were loyal to the king and promoted rigid authoritarian organizational structures that would overtly tend to affirm political authority. New Lights did not become rebellious and independent by nature. In fact they sought out and cherished authority figures. What changed were the expectations they placed on leaders as well as their willingness to reject leaders who did not meet their recently raised standards. Rather than overt patterns of resistance that survived until the Revolutionary period, the "us" and "them" of religious experience set an implicit pattern for understanding. That pattern was able to invent the "good British Protestants" who defended the colonies against "evil French Catholics" in the war for the empire. Later this pattern of understanding invented the good Whig Americans who defended the natural rights of Englishmen to live free lives against the evil Tory Britons who were trampling those rights. Then, with the willingness to replace corrupt leaders, political revolution became possible. Perhaps these primal shifts in self-understanding provide the source of John Adams' infamous observations:

> But what do we mean by the American Revolution? Do we mean the American war? The Revolution was effected before the war commenced. The Revolution was in the minds and hearts of the people; a change in their religious sentiments of their duties and obligations.[5]

Along with directly involving the change of religious sentiments in causes of the Revolution, Adams lucidly discusses the transformation in the filial conception between the colonies and England:

> The people of America had been educated in an habitual affection for England, as their mother country; and while they thought her a kind and tender parent, (erroneously enough, however, for she never was such a mother,) no affection could be more sincere. But when they found her a cruel beldam, willing like Lady Macbeth, to "dash their brains out," it is no wonder if their filial affections ceased, and were changed into indignation and horror.

As has been discussed above, the family metaphor forms a common theme in almost every polemic of the period. As Breen has demonstrated, the American identity tension was clearly at the heart of the Revolution. Upon recognizing that the British family was disinheriting Americans, the family of God remained upon which they could reconstruct their familial understanding and embrace the American identity that independence offered.

Echoing Whitefield's "deep laid plot" and Jefferson's "systematical plan," Adams also refers in the letter to a "formal plan to raise revenues" from America and cites several figures already discussed in this study who initiated their polemic efforts in response. Stephen Hopkins, Samuel Adams, and Jonathan Mayhew, among others, began to express these uniquely American sentiments. While Adams does not mention Whitefield by name, this is precisely the period when Whitefield was helping explicitly to characterize the British authority structure (represented by the Anglican Church) as the new "them" who were expressing "arbitrary" tendencies. Whitefield's role was more concealed at this point, limited to redefining the nature of British Anglicans. Moreover, his most influential tasks had been completed by 1746—it was the rhetoric he placed into circulation that was influential more so than his own personal charm. And as the rhetorical analyses of this study have demonstrated, the argument fields employed by each subsequent activist were either drawn from first-stage rhetorical topics of Whitefieldian rhetoric or inspired by the identity crisis Americans faced over British family membership.

The present study has built a case that much of the momentum for this change in sentiments, to which Adams refers, originated in a preconstitutive rhetoric that enabled colonists to understand and respond to Otis, Hopkins, and Mayhew. The possibility that White-field's rhetoric could implement an impact can be located in his patriarchal relationship to the society. One writer has asserted that Whitefield was the "Forgotten Founding Father."[6] But it might be more accurate to assert that Whitefield merely personified an idea and promoted a rhetoric. While this study necessarily focused on the life of an individual, the secondary object of analysis has been a rhetoric, which has a life and a reach far beyond the realm of any individual. And this rhetoric of community, as I have labeled it, helped bridge the gulf between the Awakening generation and the Revolutionary generation. While issues that demanded zealous activity continually shifted in the pre-Revolutionary decades, the Revolutionaries became the Founding Fathers of our nation with a political fervor equal to the day. Their sense of mission was similarly profound, but that zeal was directed primarily at the faces of arbitrary power that threatened their society in contrast to the religious apostasy that had threatened their ancestors.

Secondly, this study affirms the valuable contributions the field of rhetoric offers to the study of humanity. We have observed how wide-spread social change occurs through evolving conceptual systems that develop a message able to translate ideas across societal institutions. The Awakening conceptual system empowered the growth of the Whig political ideology in colonial America. Knowledge or ideologies cross disciplines and argument spheres through an inventional system of topical logics as propelled by arguments that take ideas or principles from one sphere and utilize them in the other.[7] Through new perspectives enabled by first-stage inventional topics, as they are applied to new discursive fields, principles and perspectives travel across spheres to generate new knowledge, often with profound or insightful results. Once established, the implied doctrines, operating as inventional topics, have an indeterminate range of application and deep cultural reach for any who choose to co-opt them!

What follows is an agential model of widespread social change characterized by the cooperation of six critical elements. Every aspect of the Whitefield case study contributes to the articulation of this model. I will briefly mention the elements of the model here, referring back to the study itself rather than recounting evidence. Initially, the model requires:

1. *A potent set of messages* capable of insinuating themselves into and subsequently shaping the society's dominant conceptual system. Edwards, Whitefield, and a tradition of religious leaders created the messages of conversion and community that generated a new conceptual system for those who would adopt it.

2. *At least one eloquent spokesperson* or a faction of spokespersons articulating a somewhat consistent message who have access to, and the ears of, the society. Here Whitefield moves to the fore, promoting this conceptual system and creating a rhetoric that other itinerants adopted and began to spread.

3. *An effective means of dissemination* to carry this message to all members of the society. Itinerancy and the print medium proliferated simultaneously to provide an effective means of dissemination through their cutting-edge mass media technology.

4. *Periodic adjustments in the messages* distributed consistently to the society that respond to changing external conditions. Whitefield provided critical and timely adjustments in the message in response to specific challenges, adjustments that were picked up and disseminated by others as well.

5. *A receptive context* in place that creates an exigency, a need for "something" such messages are designed to fill. America was faced with identity challenges from a variety of sources.

6. Changes in the conceptual system must proceed from *a central institution* capable of influencing the entire society through the structuration process. Religious ideas interacted with growing intellectual and political movements to support this emerging conceptual system.

Lastly, and most importantly for this study, we have filled some gaps about George Whitefield and his enterprise. His ministry played an instrumental role in shaping American thought by introducing and promoting central elements of the Awakening conceptual that provided a central force contributing to fundamental change. Only an effective energetic, committed orator, tolerant of ambiguity, able to survive public criticism, and possessing the personality to maintain relationships with multiple communities could have succeeded at the overwhelming task of disseminating that rhetoric to an emerging nation. Whitefield, by persistent travel and reinforcement of the Awakening conceptual system among the colonists, encouraged and nourished this ecumenical spiritual community, which he did not distinguish from the coalescing national community. In time, Whitefield, the public man, was transformed into an icon of the American experience around which an intercolonial identity founded in the new birth could coagulate.

An idea requires circulation, in one form or another, to permeate a culture. Some historians mistakenly divorce the notion of the new birth from Whitefield, as if it possessed and controlled the Awakening ministers without his efforts. Although the term did find its own legs as an ideograph, the new birth required Whitefield's promotion as much as Whitefield relied upon it for the potency of his rhetoric. Moreover, little scholarship has examined Whitefield's rhetorical contributions: "regeneration," "indwelling," "common privilege," "almost and altogether Christians," his prescriptions for judging and responding to leadership, his early warnings about the danger of arbitrary power, the curse of Meroz, and his conflict with Anglican leaders. Without his itinerating and popularity, these concepts would have remained local, circulating throughout the colonial society at a much slower rate, if at all, and never instigating the cultural motion of discourse that coaxed people into the Awakening conceptual system.

## *HOMO RHETORICUS*

We have also learned something about George Whitefield's "secret," which has been ascribed to several different sources by modern scholars—to his uncompromising ethos, to bringing drama into the pulpit, and to his unprecedented marketing skills. We can add to these accounts another aspect of Whitefield's enterprise and personality. Borrowing the positive meaning of Richard Lanham's term, Whitefield was *homo rhetoricus*: the man who thought rhetorically, who was "an actor; his reality public, dramatic, . . . centered in time and concrete local event," assuming a "natural agility in changing orientations."[8] Understanding Whitefield as *homo rhetoricus* transcends earlier views and portrays him in a genuine light. Whitefield operated chiefly in the oral sphere where he argued rhetorically, making claims and supporting them with reasons he felt would most likely move his particular audience, reasons that would change *depending on the nature of the audience*. Whitefield could see both sides of issues and produce "positions" without contradicting his statements to other communities.

As *homo rhetoricus*, Whitefield was a man flexible enough to alter his views in response to exigencies, a man who could negotiate the fine line between divergent positions. Whitefield could speak in the market language of British commoners or cross pens with England's best ecclesiastical minds in struggles to influence the lower classes. Whitefield was the Anglican who ministered to Dissenters. He was funded by aristocrats but struggled for the rights of common people to dissent from the Church of England, as well as have a stronger hand in self-governance.[9] As an aristocratic chaplain, he ultimately promoted an ideology that legitimated Whig attacks on Tories. The finesse he had to maintain was astounding. Here was a man who attracted the lower classes to field sermons by day and spoke to Britain's highest classes in Lady Huntingdon's drawing room by night, with bishops—some of whom he publicly attacked—sneaking in to hear him. It is simply amazing that Whitefield was able to castigate his own bishop of Gloucester as well as the archbishop of Canterbury in print and retain his Anglican priesthood. If nothing else, this accomplishment alone is a tribute to his rhetorical skill founded in a *phronesis* that emerged from his commoner's upbringing shaped by an Oxford education. In appreciating Whitefield as *homo rhetoricus* in the tradition of "Periclean instructive rhetoric," we can add a missing part of the puzzle to the previous Whitefield biographical scholarship. This view provides a framework for his ethos, dramatic skills, marketing skills, his aesthetic eloquence, his passion-laden sermons, his political involvement, his public conflicts—in short every aspect of his enterprise finds its niche to form the larger picture.

When the American Founding Fathers opened the Constitution of the United States with "We the people," they referenced a people who had been in various stages of existence for nearly three decades. To label "We the people . . ." a speech act of "fabulous retroactivity," as the philosopher Derrida has done, largely ignores the historical record that charts the emergence of this people from colonial settlers to national citizens.[10] To claim that the Revolution was predominantly founded upon economic interests ignores that historical record with equal fervor. Although Whitefield was almost six years dead by the time independence was declared, one can trace the implied doctrines that formed the colonial conceptual system back through Whitefield and his rhetoric to the Puritans. And as the analyses of American war propaganda consistently demonstrate, over two centuries after George Whitefield's death, a rhetoric empowered by religious theology predictably surfaces when Americans are threatened.

# NOTES

## Chapter One

*Alexis de Tocqueville, *Democracy in America*, ed. Richard D. Heffner (New York: New American Library, 1956), 1.

[1] Michael Warner, "What's Colonial About Colonial America?" in *Possible Pasts: Becoming Colonial in Early America*, ed. Robert St. George (Ithaca: Cornell University Press, 2000), 49–70.

[2] Sydney Ahlstrom, *A Religious History of the American People* (New Haven: Yale University Press, 1972), 344.

[3] Tocqueville, 17.

[4] See Michael Silverstein, "The Improvisational Performance of Culture in Real-time Discursive Practice," in *Creativity in Performance*, ed. Keith Sawyer (London: Ablex, 1997), 265–312; See also George Lakoff and Mark Johnson, *Metaphors We Live By* (Chicago: University of Chicago Press, 1980), 3.

[5] John Corrigan, *The Prism of Piety: Catholick Congregational Clergy at the Beginning of the Enlightenment* (New York: Oxford University Press, 1991), 131.

[6] I am specifically drawing upon Structuration Theory as explained by Anthony Giddens, *New Rules of Sociological Method: A Positive Critique of Interpretative Sociologies* (New York: Basic Books, 1976).

[7] Arthur Benedict Berthold, *American Colonial Printing as Determined by Contemporary Cultural Forces, 1639–1763* (New York: Burt Franklin, 1934).

[8] Ruth Bloch, "Religion and Ideological Change in the American Revolution," in *Religion and American Politics: From the Colonial Period to the 1980s*, ed. Mark A. Noll (New York: Oxford University Press, 1989), 44–61.

[9] Carl Bridenbaugh, *Mitre and Sceptre: Transatlantic Faiths, Ideas, Personalities, and Politics, 1689–1775* (New York: Oxford University Press, 1962).

[10] Alan Heimert, *Religion and the American Mind: From the Great Awakening to the Revolution* (Cambridge, Mass.: Harvard University Press, 1966).

[11] Alan Heimert and Perry Miller, eds., *The Great Awakening: Documents Illustrating the Crisis and its Consequences* (New York: Bobbs Merrill, 1967), lxi.

[12] See Edmund S. Morgan, review of Heimert, *Religion and the American Mind*, in *William and Mary Quarterly* 24 (1967): 454–59; see also Sidney E. Mead, "Through and Beyond the Lines," review of Heimert, *Religion and the Mind*, in *Journal of Religion* 43 (1968): 274–88. Both Morgan and Mead criticize Heimert for reading "not between the lines [of the historical record], but, as it were, through and beyond them" to sup-

port his thesis. Essentially they were criticizing him for performing rhetorical criticism of primary historical data.

[13] Bernard Bailyn, *The Ideological Origins of the American Revolution* (Cambridge, Mass.: Harvard University Press, 1992), 19.

[14] Bailyn, *Ideological Origins*, 34.

[15] See Cushing Strout, *The New Heavens and New Earth: Political Religion in America* (New York: Harper & Row, 1974), 44.

[16] Patricia U. Bonomi, *Under the Cope of Heaven: Religion, Society, and Politics in Colonial America* (New York: Oxford University Press, 1986).

[17] J. C. D. Clark, *The Language of Liberty, 1660–1832: Political Discourse and Social Dynamics in the Anglo-American World* (Cambridge: Cambridge University Press, 1993), 362–65.

[18] Nathan O. Hatch, *The Sacred Cause of Liberty: Republican Thought and the Millennium in Revolutionary New England* (New Haven: Yale University Press, 1977), 26.

[19] Jon Butler, *Awash in a Sea of Faith: Christianizing the American People* (Cambridge, Mass.: Harvard University Press, 1990), 2.

[20] Charles L. Cohen, "The Post-Puritan Paradigm of Early American Religious History," *William and Mary Quarterly* 54 (1997): 712.

[21] Gordon S. Wood, "Religion and the American Revolution," in *New Directions in American Religious History*, ed. Harry S. Stout and D. G. Hart (London: Oxford University Press, 1997), 174.

[22] Harry Stout, "Religion, Communications, and the Career of George Whitefield," in *Communication and Change in American Religious History*, ed. Leonard I. Sweet (Grand Rapids: Eerdmans, 1993), 109. See also Wood, "Religion," 175.

[23] Perry Miller, "From the Covenant to the Revival," in *The Shaping of American Religion, Religion in American Life*, vol. 1, ed. James W. Smith and A. Leland Jamison (Princeton: Princeton University Press, 1961), 340.

[24] At a practical level, Stout defends Heimert's reading of primary texts, which amounts to an ideological method of rhetorical criticism. Harry Stout, "Religion, Communications, and the Ideological Origins of the American Revolution," *William and Mary Quarterly* 34 (1977): 523.

[25] I refer to Marshall McLuhan's oft-quoted maxim, "The medium is the message."

[26] Mark A. Noll, *America's God: From Jonathan Edwards to Abraham Lincoln* (New York: Oxford University Press, 2002).

[27] Berthold, 26–27.

[28] See Christopher Looby, *Voicing America: Language, Literary Form, and the Origins of the United States* (Chicago: University of Chicago Press, 1996). Looby's claim is supported by Jay Fliegelman, *Declaring Independence: Jefferson, Natural Language and the Culture of Performance* (Stanford, Calif.: Stanford University Press, 1993).

[29] Stout, "Ideological Origins," 520.

[30] David Hume, "Of Eloquence," in *The Philosophical Works*, ed. Thomas H. Green and Thomas H. Gross (London: Scientia Verlag Aalen, 1964), 3:165.

[31] Thomas Sheridan, *A Discourse: Being Introductory to His Course of Lectures on Elocution and the English Language* (Los Angeles: William Andrews Clark Memorial Library, 1969), 25.

[32] Jay Fliegelman, *Declaring Independence*. Fleigelman's book recounts the problems and responses in oratorical practice at the time of the Revolution, showing the impact that elocutionists were having on writers such as Thomas Jefferson as well as society in general.

[33] See Benedict Anderson, *Imagined Communities: Reflections on the Origin and Spread of Nationalism* (London: Verso, 1983), 6.

[34] Heimert and Miller, xxiv.

[35] There is general agreement among religious historians on this point. See Winthrop Hudson and John Corrigan, *Religion in America* (New York: Macmillan, 1992), 69; Darrett B. Rutman, *The Great Awakening: Event and Exegesis* (New York: Wiley & Sons, 1970), 35; J. M. Bumstead, ed., *The Great Awakening: The Beginnings of Pietism in America* (London: Blaisdell, 1970), 62; Cedric B. Cowing, *The Great Awakening and the American Revolution: Colonial Thought in the 18th Century* (Chicago: Rand McNally, 1971), 59; Alice Baldwin, *New England Clergy and the American Revolution* (Durham, N.C.: Duke University Press, 1928), 56.

[36] Stout, "Ideological Origins," 520.

[37] Frank Lambert, *Pedlar in Divinity: George Whitefield and the Transatlantic Revivals, 1737–1770* (Princeton: Princeton University Press, 1994), 131; and Stout, "Career of George Whitefield," 108–25.

[38] Charles Chauncy wrote, "A Number of Ministers, in one Place and another, were by this Time formed into Mr. Whitefield's Temper, and began to appear and go about preaching, with a Zeal more flaming, if possible, than his" (*A Letter . . . to Mr. George Wishart* [Edinburg, 1742], 10). Cowing supports the view that Whitefield initiated a practice and theology that others took up and propagated: "More often Whitefield was effective indirectly. Preachers inspired by his New Light did the followup counseling in the wake of the Awakener or carried God's sovereignty and the new birth into the hinterlands" (62).

[39] Edwin Black, "The Second Persona," *Quarterly Journal of Speech* 56 (1970): 119.

[40] John Angus Campbell, "Between the Fragment and the Icon: Prospect for a Rhetorical House of the Middle Way," *Western Journal of Speech Communication* 54 (1990): 346–76. See also John Angus Campbell, "Rhetoriography: An Essay in Method," paper presented at the National Communication Association Convention, Chicago, November 1999.

[41] Campbell, "Rhetoriography." See also Michael Leff, "Things Made by Words: Reflections on Textual Criticism," *Quarterly Journal of Speech* 78 (1992): 223.

[42] See Michael Silverstein, "Indexical Order and the Dialectics of Sociolinguistic Life," in *SALSA III: Proceedings of the Third Annual Symposium about Language and Society*, ed. R. Parker and others (Austin: University of Texas, 1996), 266.

[43] See Silverstein, "Indexical Order," 267.

[44] T. H. Breen and T. Hall, "Structuring Provincial Imagination: The Rhetoric and Experience of Social Change in Eighteenth-century New England," *American Historical Review* 103 (1998): 1412–13.

[45] Walter Jost and Michael Hyde, eds., *Rhetoric and Hermeneutics in Our Time: A Reader* (New Haven: Yale University Press, 1997), 13.

[46] Wood describes a progressive drift toward "popular Christianity" that began in the Awakening period and continued through the early decades of the Republic.

He summarizes it as "a proliferation and splintering of sects, a complete separation between church and society, a weakening of clerical authority and a strengthening of lay control, a growing tendency toward Arminianism in the process of conversion, a blurring of theological distinctions and doctrines, and an increased emphasis on activist and progressive postmillennialism" ("Religion," 198).

[47] T. H. Breen, "Ideology and Nationalism on the Eve of the American Revolution: Revisions Once More in Need of Revising," *Journal of American History* 84 (1997): 19.

[48] Bonomi bluntly states that "[r]ecent estimates suggest that a majority of adults in the eighteenth-century colonies were regular church attenders" (87). This statement contrasts with the opinions of other historians but is supported by the rhetorical evidence of the present study.

[49] Thomas Clap, *The Declaration of the Rector and Tutors of Yale-College in New-Haven, Against the Reverend Mr. George Whitefield, His principles and Designs, in a letter to him* (Boston: T. Fleet, 1745), 8.

[50] Bonomi, 153.

[51] Maurice Charland, "Constitutive Rhetoric: The Case of the Peuple Québécois," *Quarterly Journal of Speech* 73 (1987): 134.

[52] Tocqueville, 150–51.

[53] Edwin Charles Dargan, *A History of Preaching* (New York: Burt Franklin, 1912), 2:291.

## Chapter Two

[1] Unless otherwise noted, biographical quotations are from George Whitefield, *George Whitefield's Journals* (Meadow View, England: Quinta Press, 2000), 42–78.

[2] John Gillies, a contemporary of Whitefield, provides the source for this otherwise obscure fact, noting that his squint was "occasioned either by the ignorance or carelessness of the nurse who attended him in the measles, when he was about four years old" (*Memoirs of the Life of the Reverend George Whitefield* [Meadow View, England: Quinta Press, 2000], 211).

[3] Butler, *Awash in a Sea of Faith*, 188.

[4] The "body as text" is discussed by Karlyn K. Campbell and Kathleen Hall Jamieson, "Form and Genre in Rhetorical Criticism: An Introduction," in *Form and Genre: Shaping Rhetorical Action*, ed. Karlyn K. Campbell and Kathleen Hall Jamieson (Falls Church, Va.: Speech Communication Association, 1978), 9–32.

[5] Gillies, 44.

[6] Quintilian, *Institutes of Oratory*, vol. 4 (Loeb Classic Library Series. Cambridge, Mass.: Harvard University Press, 1979), X.II.I. See also Cicero, *De Oratore* (Loeb Classic Library Series. Cambridge, Mass.: Harvard University Press, 1979), 2:xxii.

[7] Harry Stout, *The Divine Dramatist: George Whitefield and the Rise of Modern Evangelicalism* (Grand Rapids: Eerdmans, 1991), 5.

[8] Servitors were lower-class students who attended Oxford with a tuition scholarship for which they "served" the gentlemen class of students who paid their own way and often endowed the university while still undergraduates. Whitefield cleaned, cooked, and did laundry for such students and became a favorite of several of the upper

class. See Douglas Macleane, *A History of Pembroke College Oxford Anciently Broadgates Hall* (Oxford: Oxford Historical Society, 1897), 360–61.

[9] See Whitefield, *Journals*, 47–48, 50. Stout uses the characterizations "young rake" and "Oxford odd-fellow" to characterize the sections of Whitefield's life in the early chapters of his study. The terms, though, are Whitefield's.

[10] At this time "Methodists" as a denomination did not yet formally exist. But as a practice, it was labeled such and flourished under Charles and John Wesley as a popular movement within the Church of England.

[11] Henry Scougal, *The Life of God in the Soul of Man* (London: T. Dring & J. Weld, 1691).

[12] L. S. Sutherland and L. G. Mitchell, *The Eighteenth Century*, vol. 5, *The History of the University of Oxford* (Oxford: Clarendon, 1986), 469.

[13] Wilbur Samuel Howell, *Eighteenth-century British Logic and Rhetoric* (Princeton: Princeton University Press, 1971), 22. See also Thomas Conley, *Rhetoric in the European Tradition* (New York: Longman, 1990), 212.

[14] Howell, 13.

[15] Some of these other works were John Wallis's *Institutio Logicae* and Richard Crankthorp's *Logicae Libri Quinque*, cited by Howell as influential texts. Howell, 15–16, 22–41.

[16] Sutherland and Mitchell, 479, 471, 472.

[17] Sutherland and Mitchell, 479.

[18] Macleane, 357.

[19] Stout, *Divine Dramatist*, 29.

[20] Wakeley records a revealing anecdote about Whitefield's persona. Upon climbing onto a scaffold to preach to a London crowd, Whitefield lost heart and was about to stop. "Hairy chests, cauliflower ears and broken noses were not pretty sights to a man timid at heart. Hearing ferocious and horrid imprecations and menaces, his courage began to fail. He felt a tug on his gown and looked down. Elizabeth [Whitefield's wife] had her eyes firm upon him. 'George,' she called. 'Play the Man for God!'" Whitefield got back up and delivered a strong sermon. J. B. Wakeley, *Anecdotes of the Rev. George Whitefield* (Meadow View, England: Quinta Press, 2000), 100.

[21] Stout, *Divine Dramatist*, 277.

[22] Whitefield's friendship with Benjamin Franklin began as a business arrangement in 1740 wherein Franklin was employed to print Whitefield's journals and sermons. Though Franklin never embraced evangelicalism, near the end of Whitefield's life Franklin proposed they found a new colony in Ohio, a fact that offers a glimpse into their relationship. For more on their friendship, see David T. Morgan, "A Most Unlikely Friendship: Benjamin Franklin and George Whitefield," *Historian* 47 (1985): 208–18; See also Stout, *Divine Dramatist*, 220–33.

[23] Francis John McConnell, *Evangelicals, Revolutionists, and Idealists: Six Contributors to American Thought and Action* (London: Kennikat, 1942), 79.

[24] George Whitefield, *The Works of the Rev. George Whitefield, M.A. Late of Pembroke College, Oxford, and Chaplain to the Rt. Hon the Countess of Huntingdon, Containing All His Sermons and Tracts Which Have Been Already Published with a Selected Collection of Letters*, ed. John Gillies (Meadow View, England: Quinta Press, 2000), 1:124.

[25] Until noted, biographical quotations are from Whitefield, *Journals*, 81–105.

[26] Stout, *Divine Dramatist*, 44.

[27] Stuart Henry, *George Whitefield: Wayfaring Witness* (New York: Abingdon, 1957), 180.

[28] Reported in the *Pennsylvania Gazette*, 15 November 1739, 2.

[29] Whitefield, *Journals*, 219.

[30] Whitefield, *Journals*, 230.

[31] These sermonic themes consisted of a single argument, perhaps even a story, limited to a particular topic. Perhaps constituting one to seven minutes of preaching time each, such themes can be linked together in argument chains to form a complete sermon. For example, Whitefield could produce a memorized argument supporting "the depravity of man" to strengthen this belief in an audience not particularly disposed to Calvinism. Other themes might be used to produce a certain emotional effect. Whitefield had "terror" themes to produce a fear of the Lord, invitational themes to encourage repentance, anti-Papist themes to warn of Roman Catholic hegemony, or grieving themes designed to produce tears in his audience. Such themes are referred to as topoi by homileticians but are not to be confused with the inventional topoi from rhetorical theory.

[32] Whitefield, *Journals*, 330–33.

[33] Until noted, biographical quotations are from Whitefield, *Journals*, 232–43.

[34] Lambert, *Pedlar in Divinity*, 97.

[35] Stephen Mansfield, *Forgotten Founding Father: The Heroic Legacy of George Whitefield* (Nashville: Cumberland House, 2001), 79.

[36] Norman Pettit, *The Heart Prepared: Grace and Conversion in Puritan Spiritual Life* (New Haven: Yale University Press, 1966).

[37] Cornelius Winter, *Memoirs of the Life and Character of the late Reverend Cornelius Winter*, ed. William Jay (Bath, England: M. Gye, 1808), 81–82.

[38] This famous attribution to Hume does not appear in Whitefield's or Hume's own writings, but every Whitefield biographer takes care to point it out. The earliest American occurrence of it is from Sarah Edwards's letter (a primary source) to her brother James Pierpont, dated 1740. The story is cited by Whitefield biographers Stout, Lambert, and Henry. Until someone argues otherwise, I shall accept his citation of Hume as factual. See Sarah Pierpont Edwards, "A letter to her brother James dated October 24, 1740," in David S. Lovejoy, *Religious Enthusiasm and the Great Awakening* (Englewood Cliffs, N.J.: Prentice Hall, 1969), 33–34. Edwards's letter has been widely reprinted.

[39] Gillies, 211, 214.

[40] Eugene White, "Whitefield's Use of Proofs During the Great Awakening in America," *Western Speech* 14 (1950): 6.

[41] Whitefield, *Works*, 6:88.

[42] Garrick was known for his quick wit and appreciation of comedy, so I cannot but suspect that his statement is exaggerated. Nevertheless, exaggerative humor requires a "reality" of some sort in order to be effective. See Sarah Edwards, 33–34. See also Wakeley, 151.

[43] Wakeley, 151.

[44] Foote is quoted in Henry Angelo, who also noted that "many who went with

the serious intention to benefit by Whitefield's pious exhortations, on listening to the freedom, not to say levity, with which he handled scripture, and the indecorous familiarity with which he frequently spoke of sacred things, making the preacher more of the zany than the priest, quitted the tabernacle in disgust" (*Reminiscences of Henry Angelo* [New York: Benjamin Blom, 1904], 1:259–60).

[45] Gillies, 215.

[46] Heimert, *Religion and the American Mind*, 288.

[47] Alexander Richardson, "Grammatical Notes," *Logicians School-Master* (London, 1657), 15.

[48] John Charles Adams, "Linguistic Values and Religious Experience: An Analysis of the Clothing Metaphors in Alexander Richardson's Ramist-Puritan Lectures on Speech, 'Speech is a Garment to Cloath our Reason,'" *Quarterly Journal of Speech* 76 (1990): 66.

## Chapter Three

[1] Breen explains that "assertions of Britishness did not transform Irish Protestants into Englishmen." The Scots received much the same treatment from the English. See Breen, "Ideology and Nationalism," 25–28.

[2] Warner, "What's Colonial," 58, 64–67.

[3] Cohen, "The Post-Puritan Paradigm," 697.

[4] Patrick Griffin, "The People with No Name: Ulster's Migrants and Identity Formation in Eighteenth-century Pennsylvania," *William and Mary Quarterly* 58 (2001): 589.

[5] See Breen, "Ideology and Nationalism." The latter portions of the essay explain the development of British identity in America and its subsequent crisis in the years just preceding the Revolution.

[6] J. Hector St. John de Crèvecoeur, *Letters from an American Farmer and Sketches of Eighteenth-Century America* (New York: Penguin Books, 1981), 69–70.

[7] Nearly 100,000 Germans had settled in Pennsylvania by the outbreak of the Revolution. Louis Wright, *The Cultural Life of the American Colonies: 1607–1763* (New York: Harper & Row, 1957), 58.

[8] David D. Hall, *Worlds of Wonder, Days of Judgment: Popular Religious Belief in Early New England* (Cambridge, Mass.: Harvard University Press, 1989), 19.

[9] Jonathan Edwards, *Sinners in the Hands of an Angry God* (Boston: Kneeland & Green, 1741).

[10] Samuel Adams, *The Writings of Samuel Adams*, ed. Harry Alonzo Cushing (New York: Octagon Books, 1968), 2:337.

[11] See Rutman, 43–44. Whitefield reports in his journal preaching to four thousand in Middletown, Connecticut on October 23, 1740. Whitefield, *Journals*, 481.

[12] Samuel Davies, *The State of Religion among the Protestant Dissenters in Virginia* (Boston: Kneeland & Green, 1751).

[13] Crèvecoeur, 72.

[14] Carl Bridenbaugh, *Cities in Revolt: Urban Life in America, 1743–1776* (New York: Capricorn Books, 1964), 3.

[15] Lambert, *Pedlar in Divinity.* See also T. H. Breen, *The Marketplace of Revolution: How Consumer Politics Shaped American Independence* (New York: Oxford University Press, 2004).

[16] Perry Miller, "Crisis and Americanization," in Rutman, 143.

[17] See Lovejoy, *Religious Enthusiasm*, 4; Wright, 91; Richard Bushman, "A Psychological Earthquake," in Rutman, 159; and Harry Stout, "The Great Awakening in New England Reconsidered: The New England Clergy," *Journal of Social History* 8 (1974): 26.

[18] Breen, "Ideology and Nationalism," 28–29.

[19] Lambert, *Pedlar in Divinity*, 46–49.

[20] Wright, 98–99, 114.

[21] Lambert, *Pedlar in Divinity*, 138.

[22] Andrew Eliot in a letter to Thomas Hollis, January 29, 1769, cited in Bridenbaugh, *Mitre and Sceptre*, 192.

[23] Isaiah Thomas, *The History of Printing in America, with a Biography of Printers and an Account of Newspapers* (Albany, N.Y.: J. Munsell, 1874).

[24] Lambert, *Pedlar in Divinity*, 99, 56.

[25] Benedict Anderson defined the nation as an "imagined political community—and imagined as both inherently limited and sovereign" (6).

[26] Lambert explains the function of Prince's *Christian History* as a periodical crucial to encouraging the title "Great Awakening" to the series of revivals. Frank Lambert, *Inventing the "Great Awakening"* (Princeton: Princeton University Press, 1999), 9.

[27] Bonomi, 15.

[28] William Shurtleff, "A Letter to those of his brethren in the Ministry who refuse to admit the Rev. Mr. Whitefield into their Pulpits," in Heimert and Miller, 357.

[29] Butler takes this particular example from England, but as his book is about America, it is undoubtedly characteristic of American preaching as well. Butler, *Awash in a Sea of Faith*, 20.

[30] For a general assessment see Solomon Stoddard, "Defects of Preachers Reproved," a sermon preached at Northampton, May 19, 1723, in *The Great Awakening: Documents on the Revival of Religion*, ed. Richard L. Bushman (London: The University of North Carolina Press, 1969), 15.

[31] See Michael Warner, "New English Sodom," *American Literature* 64 (1992): 19–47.

[32] Sweet, 273, 277.

[33] See Jon Butler, "Enthusiasm Described and Decried: The Great Awakening as Interpretive Fiction," *Journal of American History* 69 (1982–1983): 305–25. See also Timothy D. Hall, *Contested Boundaries: Itinerancy and the Reshaping of the Colonial American Religious World* (Durham, N.C.: Duke University Press, 1994).

[34] Charles Lloyd Cohen, *God's Caress: The Psychology of Puritan Religious Experience* (London: Oxford University Press, 1986), 15.

[35] Noll, 7–8.

[36] Cohen, *God's Caress*, 14.

[37] Cohen, *God's Caress*, 76.

[38] Noll, 21. For an overview of Puritan theology, see Cohen, *God's Caress*, 79–86.

[39] Pettit, 17.

[40] Pettit, 19.

[41] Pettit, 17.

[42] Ernest G. Bormann, *The Force of Fantasy: Restoring the American Dream* (Carbondale: Southern Illinois University Press, 1985), 67.

[43] Bormann, 67–68.

[44] Strout, *New Heavens*, 33. See also Ahlstrom, 298, 351. Edwards explains the role of sensations and affections in great detail in Jonathan Edwards, *The Works of Jonathan Edwards* (London: Henry G. Bohn, 1871), 1:266–67.

[45] Edwards described his own conversion experience as follows: "I walked abroad alone, in a solitary place in my father's pasture, for contemplation. And as I was walking there, and looking up on the sky and clouds, there came into my mind so sweet a sense of the glorious majesty and grace of God, that I know not how to express. I seemed to see them both in a sweet conjunction; majesty and meekness joined together. . . . After this my sense of divine things gradually increased, and became more and more lively, and had more of that inward sweetness. The appearance of every thing was altered; there seemed to be, as it were, a calm, sweet cast, or appearance of divine glory, in almost everything. God's excellency, his wisdom, his purity and love, seemed to appear on every thing; on the sun, moon, and stars; in the clouds, and blue sky; in the grass, flowers, trees; in the water, and all nature" (*Works*, 1:lv).

[46] Edwards, *Works*, 1:609.

[47] Edwards, *Works*, 1:354.

[48] Corrigan, 89.

[49] Hudson and Corrigan point out that ultimately, "Evangelicalism was formed as a compound of an emotional experience of 'rebirth' and a commitment of obedience to God's law." I have abbreviated the evolution of evangelicalism somewhat. What is critical here is the final form that Whitefield and other colonial ministers agreed upon and taught. For a fuller story, see Hudson and Corrigan, 80–81.

[50] Bormann, 73.

[51] Heimert confirms the "new birth" as Whitefield's "primary contribution to the thought and vocabulary of American Evangelicalism" (*Religion and the American Mind*, 37).

[52] Noll, 57.

[53] Francis Fukuyama, *Trust: The Social Virtues and the Creation of Prosperity* (New York: Free Press, 1995), 286.

[54] See Heimert, *Religion and the American Mind*, 43.

[55] Harvey Yunis, *Taming Democracy: Models of Political Rhetoric in Classical Athens* (Ithaca: Cornell University Press, 1996), 85. Yunis maintains that Athenians ideally practiced a "Periclean Instructive Rhetoric" wherein the rhetor understood sound policy, was able to explain it, was devoted to the polis, and was incorruptible. The power of this rhetoric was rooted in the rhetor's "recognized devotion to the common good, and on his political intelligence." See pages 72–74.

[56] Bormann explained how the Puritans organized their world into a bifurcation of relevant aspects, divided into "matters of spirit and of flesh, into worlds of light and of darkness, of the host of God and the hosts of the devil, of the elect and the damned, of saints and sinners" (35).

[57] While certainly all the itinerant ministers to follow Whitefield were not clones, his message, itinerancy, and preaching style influenced many of them in various ways. For example, Tennent was encouraged by Whitefield to itinerate, and even Tennent's famous sermon condemning unconverted ministers derived its inspiration from conversations with Whitefield. See Milton J. Coalter Jr., *Gilbert Tennent, Son of Thunder: A Case Study of Continental Pietism's Impact on the First Great Awakening in the Middle Colonies* (New York: Greenwood Press, 1986), 64. Additionally, Pilcher attributes parts of Samuel Davies's preaching style, as well as other New Light ministers', to Whitefield's influence. See George William Pilcher, *Samuel Davies: An Apostle of Dissent in Colonial Virginia* (Knoxville: University of Tennessee Press, 1971), 82.

[58] Benjamin Franklin, *The Works of Benjamin Franklin*, ed. John Bigelow (New York: G. P. Putnam's Sons, 1887), 1:210.

[59] Wakeley, 80.

## Chapter Four

[1] Whitefield, *Journals*, 337–42. See also Timothy Hall, *Contested Boundaries*, 17.

[2] George Whitefield, "The Good Shepherd," in *Works of George Whitefield: Additional Sermons* (Meadow View, England: Quinta Press, 2000), 243–44.

[3] Arnold A. Dallimore, *George Whitefield: The Life and Times of the Great Evangelist of the Eighteenth Century* (Wheaton, Ill.: Crossway Books, 1990), 69.

[4] See Frank Lambert, "Subscribing for Profits and Piety: The Friendship of Benjamin Franklin and George Whitefield," *William and Mary Quarterly* 50 (1993): 529–54.

[5] Whitefield, *Journals*, 51.

[6] Whitefield, *Journals*, 375.

[7] *The Nature and Necessity of Our New Birth in Christ Jesus* was the original name for the sermon, published under this title twice in London and once in Boston. It was later published under the title *On Regeneration*. Three editions of *On Regeneration* were printed in America and fifteen in Great Britain. It is included in six sermon collections, four printed during the height of the Awakening (1738–1740), one in 1745, and the last in Whitefield's *Works*. See Richard Owen Roberts, *Whitefield in Print: A Bibliographic Record* (Wheaton, Ill.: Richard Owen Roberts, 1988), 41.

[8] Unless otherwise noted, all quotes in the rhetorical analysis of *On Regeneration* are from Whitefield, *Works*, 6:262–76.

[9] Perhaps "inoculation theory" has only been identified lately, and even its articulators would admit to its existence at an earlier date. See William McGuire and D. Papageorgis, "The Relative Efficacy of Various Types of Prior Belief-defense in Producing Immunity Against Persuasion," *Journal of Abnormal and Social Psychology* 62 (1961): 327–77.

[10] See Jerome Mahaffey, "Whitefield as Rhetorician: A Textual Analysis of Whitefield's 'Marriage of Cana,'" paper presented at the National Communication Association Convention, Chicago, November 1999.

[11] Black, 119.

[12] Whitefield, *Journals*, 377–79.

[13] Benjamine Franklin, *The Works of Benjamin Franklin, 1706–1744*, ed. John Bigelow (New York: G. P. Putnam's Sons, 1887), 1:206. This label "half beast and half

devil" is quoted from Whitefield's sermon *Indwelling*, which was also preached in Philadelphia.

[14] Franklin, *Works*, 1:206.

[15] Recorded in Stout, *Divine Dramatist*, 40.

[16] Sarah Edwards, 33–34.

[17] Gillies, 214.

[18] See Robin Lakoff, *Language and Women's Place* (New York: Harper & Row, 1975). See also Cheris Kramarae, *Women and Men Speaking: Frameworks for Analysis* (Rowley, Mass.: Newbury House, 1981).

[19] Michael W. Casey, "The First Female Public Speakers in America (1630–1840): Searching for Egalitarian Christian Primitivism," *Journal of Communication & Religion* 23 (2000): 10–11.

[20] See Catherine A. Brekus, *Strangers and Pilgrims: Female Preaching in America, 1740–1845* (Chapel Hill: University of North Carolina Press, 1998).

[21] Stout, *Divine Dramatist*, 158–60, 276.

[22] See Stephen H. Browne, *Angelina Grimké, Rhetoric, Identity, and the Radical Imagination* (East Lansing: Michigan State University Press, 1999), 34.

[23] Whitefield, *Journals*, 421.

[24] Whitefield, *Journals*, 422.

[25] Alexander Garden, "To the Inhabitants of the Parish of St Philip, Charles-Town, Nov 24, 1740," in Heimert and Miller, 57.

[26] Throughout *The Second Treatise of Civil Government*, John Locke employs the terms "common" and "rights" (e.g., IV.22, V.26, V.27) as he constructs his foundation for a governmental system. These common rights are granted to humans, in Locke's view, by "God, who hath given the world to men in common" (V.26). In *The First Treatise of Civil Government*, Locke contends that humans form governments by voluntary submission to a chosen political system for their own interests, that people are willing to freely give up certain rights to protect others. In fact, according to Thomas Cook, Locke wrote the two *Treatises* in defense of the 1688 revolution; Locke argued that William "freed the people of England from tyranny and safe guarded the natural rights which belonged to them as individuals" (*Two Treatises of Government*, ed. Thomas I. Cook [New York: Hafner, 1947], ix). In Whitefield's co-opting of Locke's principles, he replaces the term "right" with "privilege," presumably for theological reasons. His Calvinist beliefs would never support the notion that humans have a "right" to salvation, but that God grants it to whom he chooses. But upon being chosen, the benefits of God indeed become a "privilege" for that individual. These benefits could not be reserved for any special class of people since all are equal in the sight of God. Whitefield clearly promoted "equality of the believers" by his ecumenical and tolerant approach to Christianity. Providing the rationale for Whitefield's view, which was definitely not typically Anglican, John Locke argued, in *A Letter Concerning Toleration*, that no religion is better or more orthodox than another. Within this treatise Locke applies his utilitarian system to establish equality among Protestant religions, demonstrates the impossibility of proving other religions heretical before God, and delineates the appropriate roles of government and religion in administrating the behavior of citizens. Locke's arguments provided the first-stage rhetorical topics Whitefield needed and used to defend the infant Methodism against Anglican hegemony.

[27] Charles Chauncy, "Enthusiasm Described and Caution'd Against," in Heimert and Miller, 231.

[28] *Indwelling* was aimed at Anglican clergy. It is likely that he freely substituted those under attack depending upon his venue.

[29] Whitefield, *Journals*, 397.

[30] Whitefield, *Journals*, 504.

[31] Whitefield, *Journals*, 504–5. Stout provides a fuller account of the incident supplemented by local newspaper accounts, Stout, *Divine Dramatist*, 119–20.

[32] Whitefield, *Journals*, 506.

[33] Whitefield, *Journals*, 534.

[34] Ahlstrom records that Whitefield persuaded Tennent to begin itinerating and that Davenport (a later contributor to the revival) adopted Tennent and Whitefield as his heroes, Ahlstrom, 284–85. There is no record of Frelinghuysen traveling outside of his own parishes, but only to New York to visit his ecclesiastical superiors. Edwards traveled to neighboring parishes by invitation during 1736 but did not travel outside of the Connecticut Valley. See Hudson and Corrigan, 68.

[35] Ahlstrom, 293.

[36] Heimert, *Religion and the American Mind*, 95.

[37] Butler, *Awash in a Sea of Faith*, 164–65. See also Butler, "Enthusiasm Described."

[38] See Lambert, *Inventing the "Great Awakening."*

[39] Bonomi, 85.

[40] Gillies, 213.

[41] Whitefield, *Journals*, 351.

[42] Chauncy, *Wishart*, 6.

[43] Wigglesworth is quoted in Baldwin, 61–62.

[44] Data complied from Roberts, 3–55.

[45] Population data is sketchy for colonial America. I calculated an adult population figure (including slaves) of 616,000 in 1740 extrapolated from a Connecticut demographic from 1774 that showed 68 percent over age ten.

[46] Gillies, 214.

[47] Bonomi, 157.

[48] For other examples, see Jonathan Dickinson, *The Nature and Necessity of Regeneration* (Philadelphia, 1743) and Samuel Quincy's *Regeneration* (1745) outlined in this volume. The term "regeneration" was not Whitefield's original invention, but again, as with the term "new birth," Whitefield was its agent of widespread promotion.

[49] *The Oxford English Dictionary*, 2nd ed. (Oxford: Clarendon, 1989), 7:900.

[50] Aristotle, *Rhetoric*, trans. W. Rhys Roberts (New York: Modern Library, 1954), 1355a.

[51] Fukuyama, 270.

[52] See Stout, "Ideological Origins," 525–27.

[53] Fukuyama, 270.

[54] Jennifer Rose Mercieca, "Choice, Loyalty, and Safety in the Construction of a Distinctly American Imagined Nationalism," *Rhetoric & Public Affairs* 9 (2006): 281.

[55] Fukuyama, 270, 289.

[56] We have already noted that the relationship between religion and politics is one of mutual influence. Certainly the English civil war (1640–1644) was founded

upon religious tensions that worked hand in hand with political alignments. William Laud, archbishop of Canterbury and chief adviser to King Charles I, exasperated many Englishmen with his authoritarian approach to leadership and unpopular goals, seeking uniformity in worship styles and religion. Laud suppressed Puritan preaching, extended the influence of church courts into daily life, and enforced harsh, even "savage," sentences against preachers who criticized the government. The civil war that followed was divided along class and religious lines; the "Roundheads," aligned with Puritans and the lower classes, against the "Cavaliers," aligned with Anglicans and the upper classes. In subsequent years, fears of encroaching Roman Catholicism would be added to the political and religious power struggles in England. Walter P. Hall and Robert G. Albion, *A History of England and the British Empire* (Boston: Ginn, 1946), 339–40.

[57] Hudson and Corrigan, 42.

[58] See Tocqueville, 17.

[59] See John T. McNeill, "The Democratic Element in Calvin's Thought," *Church History* 18 (1949): 153–71; and Winthrop S. Hudson, "Theological Convictions and Democratic Government," *Theology Today* 10 (1953): 230–39.

[60] Jerome Mahaffey, "George Whitefield's Rhetorical Art: Neo-Sophism in the Great Awakening," forthcoming in *Homiletic* 31 (2006).

## Chapter Five

[1] Bonomi, 157.

[2] Nancy Ruttenburg, "George Whitefield, Spectacular Conversion, and the Rise of Democratic Personality," *American Literary History* 5 (1993): 443.

[3] Stout, "Career of George Whitefield," 116.

[4] Whitefield, *Journals*, 42.

[5] Whitefield, *Journals*, 97.

[6] Stout, "Career of George Whitefield," 116.

[7] Whitefield, *Journals*, 157.

[8] Whitefield, *Journals*, 169.

[9] Whitefield's letter to Wesley went through five editions by 1742.

[10] Though the journals clearly deserve a close analysis in their own right, we will have to defer that task to another study and be content with knowing that they intimately created the "public" man who brought the message.

[11] Stout fully develops the story in more detail than necessary in the present work. Stout, *Divine Dramatist*, 136–39.

[12] Whitefield, *Works*, 1:301.

[13] British antipapism began in earnest in 1678 over questions of succession of the British throne. The duke of York, brother of Charles II, converted to Catholicism. He held a legitimate claim to the throne were his brother to die or abdicate. The frenzy over "popish plots" originated with the false testimony of an informer, Titus Oates, who revealed a Jesuit plot to assassinate the king, burn London, seize control of England with French troops, massacre all Protestants who would not turn Catholic, and set Place James on the British throne. The unrest over the supposed plot gave rise to the Whigs and serendipitously contributed to the abdication of James II and ascension

of William. See J. C. D. Clark, *English Society, 1660–1832: Religion, Ideology, and Politics during the Ancient Regime* (New York: Cambridge University Press, 2000), 70–78.

[14] See Mansfield, 99–100. Stout provides a fuller account that characterizes the marriage as a practical matter that they both might more effectively be involved in ministry. Stout, *Divine Dramatist*, 168–70.

[15] Whitefield, *Works*, 2:55.

[16] For a more robust account of the violence and ecclesiastical opposition against the Methodists and Whitefield, see Stout, *Divine Dramatist*, 70.

[17] Whitefield describes many such instances that occurred in 1743 in letters to his friends. Whitefield, *Works*, 2:36–39.

[18] Whitefield, *Works*, 4:117, 120.

[19] Whitefield describes the trial in great detail in a letter dated March 12, 1744. Whitefield, *Works*, 2:57–61. He also recounts the story in pamphlet form. *Works*, 4:111–21.

[20] Whitefield, *Works*, 4:138.

[21] Whitefield, *Works*, 4:141.

[22] All quotes in the analysis of *A Letter, &c. to the Right Reverend the Bishop of London, &c.* are from Whitefield, *Works*, 4:140–52.

[23] Whitefield tells the story in two letters dated June 1744 in Whitefield, *Works*, 4:62–64.

[24] Coalter, 64.

[25] Davenport and his supporters, on one occasion at New London, collected their "heretical" books, "ministerial vestments," wigs, and other worldly items and burned them in a large bonfire. Gilbert Tennent condemned the act as "horrid" and "ridiculous," and even Davenport later admitted he was missing the point of the revival as a movement to reform the inner man, rather than outer appearances. Heimert and Miller, 258.

[26] Roberts, 203.

[27] Chauncy, "Enthusiasm Described," 55.

[28] Stout, *Divine Dramatist*, 184.

[29] Hudson and Corrigan, 82.

[30] Ryan points out that speeches of *apologia* always respond to specific questions about the rhetor's character, questions that are normally articulated in a speech of *kategoria*, or accusation. Thus, within the apologia, the accusation is challenged by counterarguments that seek to absolve, vindicate, explain, or justify the rhetor's actions. Halford Ross Ryan, "Baldwin vs. Edward VIII: A Case Study in *Kategoria* and *Apologia*," *Southern Speech Communication Journal* 49 (1984): 125–34.

[31] Whitefield, *Works*, 2:79.

[32] Heimert, *Religion and the American Mind*, 11.

[33] Almost all the weekly editions of the *Boston Evening-Post* from November 1744 to March 1745 contained multiple anti-Whitefield editorials or excerpted tracts and letters, including lengthy sections of Chauncy's sermon on enthusiasm in several editions.

[34] *Boston Evening-Post*, November 19, 1744. See also *Boston Evening-Post*, December 4, 1744: "I know it is the Thought of some, that this Gentleman is not come with another

spirit;" and *Boston Evening-Post*, April 29, 1745: "In order to which, it was given out, that he was now come with another Spirit, and would labour to heal our Divisions."

[35] Throughout his career, Whitefield was subjected to implications that his relationships with the women who co-labored in the Methodist movement involved sexual activity. A particular cartoon depicted a woman at a Whitefield sermon saying, "I wish his spirit was in my flesh." See Myra Jehlen and Michael Warner, *The English Literatures of America: 1500–1800* (New York: Routledge, 1996), 598. In a similar vein, Samuel Foote, in his play *The Minor*, cast a matronly convert of Whitefield's Tabernacle ministry in London as running an escort service when she was not in church. See Samuel Foote, *The Works of Samuel Foote, Esq.* (London: Sherwood, Gilbert & Piper, 1830).

[36] Coalter, 59.

[37] Charles Chauncy, *Seasonable Thoughts on the State of Religion in New England* (Hicksville, N.Y.: Regina Press, 1975), 36–37.

[38] *Boston Evening-Post*, November 19, 1744.

[39] Chauncy, *Seasonable Thoughts*, 140–41.

[40] Gillies, 65.

[41] Harvard College, *The Testimony of the President, Professors, Tutors and Hebrew Instructor of Harvard College in Cambridge, against the Rev. Mr. George Whitefield and his conduct* (Boston: T. Fleet, 1744), 8–9.

[42] Chauncy, *Seasonable Thoughts*, 242.

[43] Chauncy, *Seasonable Thoughts*, 77.

[44] *Boston Evening-Post*, February 11, 1745.

[45] Chauncy, *Seasonable Thoughts*, 242, 141–42, 246.

[46] Clap, *Declaration of Rector*, 8.

[47] Hall, *Contested Boundaries*, 41.

[48] Chauncy, *Seasonable Thoughts*, 47, 51, 150, 144.

[49] Clap, *Declaration of the Rector*, 10–12. See Thomas Clap, *A Letter from the Rev. Mr. Thomas Clap, rector of Yale College at New Haven, to a friend in Boston . . . that the Rev. Mr. Edwards told him, that the Rev. Mr. Whitefield said in his hearing, that it was his design to turn the generality of minister in the country out of their places and resettle them with ministers from England, Scotland, and Ireland* (Boston: T. Fleet, 1745). For Edwards's response to Clap, see Jonathan Edwards, *An expostulatory letter from the Rev. Mr. Edwards to the Rev. Mr. Clap, Rector of Yale College* (Boston: Kneeland & Green, 1745). The entire exchange is described in Edwards, *Works*, cxix–cxx.

[50] From 1661 to 1665 the "Cavalier Parliament" passed a series of acts known as the Clarendon Code. In particular the Conventicle Act "imposed savage penalties" for attending meetings where anything but Anglican services were held. The Test Act of 1673, specifically designed to exclude Catholics (and possibly Dissenters) from public office, prevented anyone who would not take the sacraments according to the Church of England from holding a civil or military post under the Crown during the reign of Charles II, after Cromwell and the Puritans were out of power. See Hall and Albion, 380, 386–87.

[51] Whitefield, *Journals*, 581.

[52] George Whitefield, *A Letter to the Reverend Dr. Chauncy* (Philadelphia: W. Bradford, 1745), 6–7.

[53] An advertisement for a publication published by Kneeland and Green appeared in the Boston papers on December 11, 1744: *An account of money Received and Distributed for the Orphan House, 1740–1742*. There is no corresponding work in Roberts's bibliography of Whitefield. The closest publication is a sixteen-page document dated 1745: George Whitefield, *A brief account of the rise, progress and present situation of the Orphan-House in Georgia, in a letter to a friend* (Philadelphia: W. Bradford, 1745). These are probably the same works published in different locations.

[54] George Whitefield, *A Letter to the Reverend, the President, and Professors, Tutors, and Hebrew Instructor of Harvard College in Cambridge In answer to a Testimony Published by them against the Reverend Mr. George Whitefield, and his Conduct.* (Boston: Kneeland & Green, 1745), 14.

[55] Whitefield, *Letter to Chauncy*, 17.

[56] Whitefield, *Letter to . . . Harvard College*, 11–12. See also Whitefield, *Letter to Chauncy*, 21–23.

[57] Whitefield, *Letter to Chauncy*, 26–29.

[58] Whitefield, *Letter to . . . Harvard College*, 5.

[59] Whitefield, *Letter to Chauncy*, 31–32.

[60] Whitefield, *Letter to Chauncy*, 10.

[61] Whitefield, *Letter to . . . Harvard College*, 21–22.

[62] Whitefield, *Letter to Chauncy*, 20–21.

[63] Whitefield, *Letter to Chauncy*, 20.

[64] Gillies, 117.

[65] Hatch, 40.

[66] Shurtleff, 356–63.

[67] *Boston Evening-Post*, August 19, 1745. Though the writer casts a suspicious eye to the upcoming meeting, I believe it is significant that the report is in the *Evening-Post* and not the pro-Whitefield paper.

[68] See *Convention of New England Ministers: The Testimony of a Number of New England ministers met at Boston Sept. 25, 1745. Professing the ancient faith of these churches; inviting others who hold it, to unite in profession and maintaining the same; reciting and recommending an excellent Act concerning preaching lately made by the General Assembly of the Church of Scotland* (Boston: Kneeland & Green, 1745).

[69] Lambert also recognizes the existence of both radicals and moderates who supported a "multidimensional" revival. According to Lambert, the moderate party included Jonathan Edwards, Benjamin Colman, William Cooper, Thomas Prince, Jonathan Dickinson, Gilbert Tennent, Samuel Blair, and Ebenezer Pemberton. Lambert, *Inventing the "Great Awakening,"* 244, 246.

[70] Whitefield, *Works*, 3:383.

[71] Hatch, 40.

[72] Whitefield, *Works*, 5:123.

[73] Whitefield, *Works*, 2:100.

[74] Bonomi, 84.

[75] Gillies, 118.

[76] Whitefield, *Works*, 2:90.

*Chapter Six*

[1] Whitefield, *Works*, 3:152.

[2] Whitefield, *Works*, 3:178.

[3] Noll, 83.

[4] The Jacobites were supporters of James VII (1633–1701) after he was deposed in 1688. The term is from "Jacobus," Latin for James, a pejorative use of the name alluding to the deception of the biblical character Isaac by his son Jacob. They retained an older definition of divine right as by hereditary succession as a chief difference with the Whigs who welcomed and supported the Hanoverian line as justified by providential divine right. From either perspective a king had the right to rule, their ideological quarrel was over which king and by what justification.

[5] Narrative compiled from Basil Williams, *The Whig Supremacy: 1714–1760*, vol. 9, *The Oxford History of England* (Oxford: Clarendon, 1962), 251–56.

[6] See Charles Evans, *American Bibliography* (Chicago: Blakely Press, 1905).

[7] Griffin, 606.

[8] Clark, *English Society*, 87.

[9] *Boston Gazette*, September 16, 1746.

[10] All quotes, unless otherwise noted, in the rhetorical analysis of *Britain's Mercies and Britain's Duties*, are from Whitefield, *Works*, 5:91–105.

[11] Griffin, 589.

[12] Ahithophel was King David's advisor who defected to his son Absalom during a coup in Jerusalem as recorded in 2 Samuel 15–17.

[13] See the editorial by "Methodistus" in the *Boston Gazette*, September 23, 1746.

[14] Clark, *English Society*, 47.

[15] Hatch, 76.

[16] Whitefield, *Works*, 2:107–8.

[17] Whitefield, *Works*, 2:111.

[18] *Boston Gazette*, September 23, 1746.

[19] Hatch, 22–23.

[20] Hatch, 54.

[21] Hatch, 46–47.

[22] Clark explains that the concept of "arbitrary power" was clearly linked with "popery" in the discourses of British society as early as 1670. Clark, *English Society*, 68.

[23] Whitefield, *Works*, 2:97.

[24] Whitefield, *Works*, 2:107.

[25] *Boston Gazette*, August 18, 1747.

[26] Whitefield, *Works*, 2:122.

[27] Whitefield, *Works*, 2:128.

[28] Whitefield, *Works*, 2:147.

[29] James Patterson Gledstone, *George Whitefield, M.A.: Field Preacher* (Meadow View, England: Quinta Press, 2000), 227.

[30] Henry, 84–86, 143.

[31] Whitefield, *Works*, 2:174.

[32] Despite their common ground, Mayhew would continue to decry enthusiasm and accuse Whitefield of its practice. See Jonathan Mayhew, *Christian Sobriety* (Boston: Richard & Samuel Draper, 1763).

[33] Bernard Bailyn, *Pamphlets of the American Revolution: 1750–1776*, vol. 1, ed. Bernard Bailyn (Cambridge, Mass.: Harvard University Press, 1965), 206.

[34] All quotes in the analysis of Mayhew's sermon taken from Jonathan Mayhew, *A Discourse Concerning Unlimited Submission and Nonresistance to the Higher Powers* (Boston: D. Fowle, 1750), 21–28.

[35] Here Mayhew uses the rhetorical figure "apostrophe" as Whitefield often did. But the difference between their uses is revealing. Whitefield directs his comment to God: "Be astonished, Oh heavens, at this," while Mayhew directs it at "everybody." It seems that Mayhew is proposing a shift in authority, at least in his mind, from God to the people to judge outrageous acts.

[36] John Adams, *The Works of John Adams: Second President of the United States*, vol. 10, ed. Charles Francis Adams (Boston: Little, Brown, 1856), 288.

[37] Heimert, *Religion and the American Mind*, 241.

[38] Bailyn, *Pamphlets*, 209.

[39] Henry, 90.

[40] Gillies, 163.

[41] Davies, 10. Morris is quoted in Davies' account.

[42] Henry, 91.

[43] Whitefield, *Works*, 3:144.

[44] Whitefield, *Works*, 3:152.

[45] Whitefield, *Works*, 3:506.

[46] Heimert, *Religion and the American Mind*, 324.

[47] See Evans, *American Bibliography* for the year 1756. *William and Elizabeth Fleming, A Narrative of the Sufferings and Surprizing Deliverances of William and Elizabeth Fleming*.

[48] All quotes in the rhetorical analysis of *A Short Address to Persons of all Denominations, Occasioned by the Alarm of an Intended Invasion, in the Year 1756* taken from Whitefield, *Works*, 4:265–74.

[49] Judg 5:23 KJV.

[50] Heimert, *Religion and the American Mind*, 332.

[51] Neither Davies nor Finley is listed in the *American Bibliography* for the year 1756.

[52] James Darsey, *The Prophetic Tradition and Radical Rhetoric in America* (New York: New York University Press, 1997), 47.

[53] Heimert, *Religion and the American Mind*, 334.

[54] Gillies, 168. Gillies is quoting from the Glasgow Courant, Edinburgh, September 9, 1756.

[55] Tennent is quoted in Heimert, *Religion and the American Mind*, 326.

[56] The engraving was first published in the *Pennsylvania Gazette*, May 9, 1754. Early Americans believed that if a snake that had been cut in two was rejoined before sunset, it would live.

[57] Whitefield, *Works*, 4:268. Foote's play is not entirely about Whitefield. A single reference is made to Dr. Squintum, and a minor character in the play refers to him in two other places. However, Foote used to impersonate Whitefield in the monologue

before the play, an act that was quite popular with audiences.

⁵⁸ The campaign to establish an American bishop began in earnest on March 30, 1763. Bridenbaugh, *Mitre and Sceptre*, 220.

⁵⁹ Bridenbaugh, *Mitre and Sceptre*, 208.

⁶⁰ Bridenbaugh, *Mitre and Sceptre*, 215.

⁶¹ All quotes in the sermon analysis are from Ezra Stiles, "A Discourse on Christian Union," in Heimert and Miller, 593–608.

⁶² Heimert, *Religion and the American Mind*, 135.

⁶³ Stiles, 596–97.

⁶⁴ Bernard Bailyn supposes Joseph Galloway to be the author. Bailyn, *Pamphlets*, 247.

⁶⁵ See Bailyn, *Pamphlets*, 249.

⁶⁶ Breen, "Ideology and Nationalism," 32.

⁶⁷ All quotes in the analysis are taken from Joseph Galloway, *A Letter to the People of Pennsylvania, &c* (Philadelphia, 1760), 3, 33–36.

⁶⁸ Greg Urban, *Metaculture: How Culture Moves through the World* (Minneapolis: University of Minnesota Press, 2001).

⁶⁹ Bridenbaugh, *Mitre and Sceptre*, 207.

## Chapter Seven

¹ Bridenbaugh, *Mitre and Sceptre*, 230.

² All quotes in the rhetorical analysis of *Observations on Some Fatal Mistakes, In a Book Lately Published, and Entitled, "The Doctrine of Grace"* are taken from Whitefield, *Works*, 4:303–22.

³ Whitefield, *Works*, 3:293.

⁴ Bridenbaugh, *Mitre and Sceptre*, 294.

⁵ Heimert, *Religion and the American Mind*, 367. See also Henry, 144.

⁶ Whitefield, *Works*, 3:317.

⁷ Whitefield is quoted by Samuel Langdon in Bridenbaugh, *Mitre and Sceptre*, 244.

⁸ Bridenbaugh, *Mitre and Sceptre*, 245.

⁹ Adams, *The Works of John Adams*, 10:288.

¹⁰ Stephen Hopkins, *The Rights of Colonies Examined* (Providence, R.I.: W. Goddard, 1765), 3–24.

¹¹ Darsey, 46.

¹² Heimert, *Religion and the American Mind*, 354.

¹³ Whitefield, *Works*, 3:329.

¹⁴ Whitefield, *Works*, 2:255.

¹⁵ Whitefield, *Works*, 3:36, 3:357, 3:485, 4:348.

¹⁶ Adams, *Writings of Samuel Adams*, 1:26. There is no extant letter to Mason or a J____ M____ in Whitefield's writings.

¹⁷ Adams, *Writings of Samuel Adams*, 1:31.

¹⁸ Quotes are from Adams, *Writings of Samuel Adams*, 1:34–38.

¹⁹ Joseph Galloway, *Historical and Political Reflections on the Rise and Progress of the American Rebellion* (London: G. Wilkie, 1780), 54–55.

²⁰ Heimert, *Religion and the American Mind*, 346.

[21] These events occurred on August 14, 1765. See Edmund S. Morgan and Helen M. Morgan, *The Stamp Act Crisis: Prologue to Revolution* (New York: Collier Books, 1963). See also Philip Davidson, *Propaganda and the American Revolution 1763–1783* (New York: W. W. Norton, 1973), 149–50.

[22] Quoted in Davidson, 195. Excerpted from a sermon titled *A Discourse, Addressed to the Sons of Liberty, At a Solemn Assembly, near Liberty-Tree, in Boston, February 14, 1766.*

[23] Gordon S. Wood, "Rhetoric and Reality in the American Revolution," *William and Mary Quarterly* 23 (1966): 25.

[24] Benjamin Franklin, "His Examination Before the House of Commons" (1766), in *The World's Famous Orations*, ed. William Jennings Bryan (New York: Funk & Wagnalls, 1906), 42.

[25] Gillies, 189.

[26] See Nathaniel Whitaker, *A Funeral Sermon* (Boston, 1771), 34.

[27] Davidson, 41.

[28] See Stout, *Divine Dramatist*, 263–65.

[29] Charles Chauncy, quoted in Bridenbaugh, *Mitre and Sceptre*, 257.

[30] Bridenbaugh, *Mitre and Sceptre*, 305.

[31] From an editorial signed "The Puritan," *Boston Gazette*, April 4, 1768.

[32] *Boston Gazette*, May 9, 1768.

[33] Whitefield, *Works*, 3:366.

[34] Whitefield, *Works*, 3:486.

[35] Lambert eloquently explained this point in *Pedlar in Divinity*, 214.

[36] Whitefield, *Works*, 4:340.

[37] Whitefield, *Works*, 4:349.

[38] Bridenbaugh, *Mitre and Sceptre*, 299.

[39] Carl F. Kaestle, "The Public Reaction to John Dickinson's Farmer's Letters," *American Antiquarian Society Proceedings* 78 (1969): 329–59.

[40] Forrest McDonald, ed., *Empire and Nation* (Indianapolis: Liberty Fund, 1999), xiii.

[41] Hall and Albion, 465.

[42] McDonald, xi.

[43] Jonathan Dickinson, "Letters from a Pennsylvania Farmer: Letter I," in *Empire and Nation*, ed. Forrest McDonald (Englewood Cliffs, N.J.: Prentice Hall), 4.

[44] Dickinson, "Letters," Letter II, 6.

[45] Dickinson, "Letters," Letter II, 7.

[46] Dickinson, "Letters," Letter III, 20.

[47] Dickinson, "Letters," Letter II, 14.

[48] Dickinson, "Letters," Letter V, 33.

[49] Stephen Browne, "The Pastoral Voice in John Dickinson's First 'Letter from a Farmer in Pennsylvania,'" *Quarterly Journal of Speech* 76 (1990): 54.

[50] Browne, "Pastoral Voice," 48.

[51] Whitefield, *Works*, 3:421.

[52] Whitefield, *Works*, 3:425.

[53] Whitefield, *Works*, 3:428.

[54] Whitefield, *Works*, 3:428.

[55] See Lambert, *Pedlar in Divinity*, 224.

[56] Whitefield, *Works*, 3:429.

[57] Mansfield, 30–31.

[58] Butler, *Awash in a Sea of Faith*, 188.

[59] Heimert, *Religion and the American Mind*, 362.

[60] *Boston Gazette*, May 30, 1785.

## Chapter 8

[1] Hatch refers to him as the first "religious celebrity." Nathan Hatch, "Foreword" to Stout, *Divine Dramatist*, x.

[2] Heimert, *Religion and the American Mind*, 354.

[3] Recall that Patrick Henry's speech before the Virginia legislature in 1765 brought charges of treason.

[4] Breen and Hall specifically posit a common underlying conception of shifting rules as a structurating force in colonial views on choices in both religion and the use of paper currency. Breen and Hall, 1438.

[5] Adams, *Writings of Samuel Adams*, 352.

[6] Davidson, 123–28.

[7] Davidson, 128.

[8] Hatch, 75.

[9] See McCloskey, in James Wilson, *The Works of James Wilson*, ed. Robert G. McCloskey (Cambridge, Mass.: Belknap Press of Harvard University Press, 1967), 8.

[10] Wilson, 3. All quotes in this section are from Wilson, *The Works*.

[11] Browne, "Jefferson's First Declaration," 250.

[12] Stephen Lucas, *Portents of Rebellion: Rhetoric and Revolution in Philadelphia, 1765–76* (Philadelphia: Temple University Press, 1976).

[13] Fliegelman, *Declaring Independence*, 5.

[14] All quotes in the analysis of "A Summary View" are from Thomas Jefferson, *The Life and Selected Writings of Thomas Jefferson*, ed. Adrienne Koch and William Peden (New York: Random House, 1944), 298–303.

[15] Stephen Browne, "Jefferson's First Declaration of Independence: A Summary View of the Rights of British America Revisited," *Quarterly Journal of Speech* 39 (2003): 236.

[16] Browne, "Jefferson's First Declaration," 245.

[17] Hudson and Corrigan, 96.

[18] Oliver is cited in Hudson and Corrigan, 96.

[19] Samuel Peters, *A General History of Connecticut* (London: J. Bew, 1781), 414–18. Peters, once a governor of Connecticut, carefully distinguished between these "Sober Dissenters" and a "drunken mob" described a page later. This was an incredible size for a Connecticut militia, but Peters cited the army's size twice, writing it out in full as "forty-thousand." His account is a primary source published only seven years after the fact.

[20] *Historical Statistics of the United States: Colonial Times to 1970*, United States Department of Commerce, 1169.

[21] Heimert, *Religion and the American Mind*, 438.

[22] Clark, *Language of Liberty*, 276.

[23] Nathaniel Whitaker, *An Antidote Against Toryism or, The Curse of Meroz, in a discourse on Judges 5th 23* (Newburyport: J. Mycall, 1777).

[24] Noll, 85.

[25] Darsey, 49.

[26] Butler, *Awash in a Sea of Faith*, 195.

[27] Wood, "Religion," 175.

[28] Wood, "Religion," 177.

[29] Davidson, 25.

[30] Clark, *Language of Liberty*, 274.

[31] Davidson, 4.

[32] Quotes by "Candidus" are all from Adams, *Writings of Samuel Adams*, 2:271–72.

[33] Job 25:6 KJV.

[34] Adams, *Writings of Samuel Adams*, 2:334, 336.

[35] Published in the *Boston Gazette*, October 5, 1772. See also Adams, *Writings of Samuel Adams*, 336–37.

[36] Heb 10:22-25 KJV. This section is often called the "Lettuce Patch."

[37] J. Michael Hogan and Glen Williams, "Republican Charisma and the American Revolution: The Textual Persona of Thomas Paine's Common Sense," *Quarterly Journal of Speech* 86 (2000): 6.

[38] Arthur M. Schlesinger, *The Birth of the Nation: A Portrait of the American People on the Eve of Independence* (Boston: Houghton Mifflin, 1968), 176.

[39] As Schlesinger has noted, the English monarchy stood as the "one link with the Empire which . . . [even] the patriots continued to acknowledge" (240).

[40] "Divine right" and "hereditary succession" provided a topic for many sermons since as early as 1740. The New England minister Jared Eliot (1738) asserted that Englishmen must obey God rather than men in regard to a government inconsistent with the principles of God. See Alice Baldwin, *New England Clergy and the American Revolution* (Durham, N.C.: Duke University Press, 1928), 42–43.

[41] Clark, *English Society*, 87–91.

[42] All quotes in the rhetorical analysis of *Common Sense* are taken from Thomas Paine, *Common Sense*, ed. Isaac Kramnick (New York: Penguin Books), 63–83.

[43] See Michael Osborne, "Rhetorical Depiction," in *Form, Genre, and the Study of Political Discourse*, ed. H. W. Simons and A. Aghazarian (Columbia: University of South Carolina Press, 1986), 96.

[44] Although Paine's family was religious and his mother saw that he was indoctrinated in the Church of England, his mind began to question Christian notions at an early age, and he began to study science as a young man (Alfred Owen Aldridge, *Man of Reason: The Life of Thomas Paine* [New York: J. B. Lippincott, 1959], 7–28). Paine described himself as "one of those few, who never dishonors religion either by ridiculing, or caviling at any denomination whatsoever. To God, and not to man, are all men accountable on the score of religion" (59).

[45] Lambert, *Pedlar in Divinity*, 199.

[46] John Adams, *The Life and Work of John Adams*, vol. 2 (Boston: Charles C. Little and James Brown, 1850), 507–9.

[47] Paine, 113.

[48] One of his later works, *The Age of Reason*, identifies Paine as a Deist. Paine was not alone among the revolutionaries in his religious belief, joining elite company with Thomas Jefferson and Benjamin Franklin, among others. Hudson and Corrigan also number Paine among the Deists. Hudson and Corrigan, 92.

[49] Ernest J. Wrage, "Public Address: A Study in Social and Intellectual History," *The Quarterly Journal of Speech* 33 (1947): 453.

[50] Adams, *Life and Work*, 507.

[51] Adams, *Life and Work*, 508.

## Chapter Nine

[1] Miller, "From the Covenant to the Revival," 343.

[2] Charland, 134.

[3] Noll, 82.

[4] Heimert, *Religion and the American Mind*, 148.

[5] Adams, *Works of John Adams*, 10:282. Comments quoted in this paragraph and the next were made in an oft-quoted letter to Henry Niles in 1818.

[6] I am referring to the title of Stephen Mansfield's recent book, *Forgotten Founding Father*.

[7] Jerome Mahaffey, "The Rhetoric of Hermeneutics: Orality as a Rhetorical Topos in Biblical Interpretation," (Master's thesis, Syracuse University, 1997).

[8] Richard Lanham, *The Motives of Eloquence: Literary Rhetoric in the Renaissance* (New Haven: Yale University Press, 1976), 4.

[9] According to Mercieca and Aune, in the early years of the republic, "vernacular republicanism," a perspective and communication style, emerged as a dominant ideology. This perspective employs aggressive rhetorical critique, posits that public debate should be transparent; it rejects elite leadership and holds that liberty and republicanism stand for the "common good" rather than benefiting the few. It is also a perspective that demands immediate action to rectify discrepancies. Their view aptly describes the discursive practices and beliefs promoted by Whitefield in his ecumenical ministry to the lower classes. See Jennifer R. Mercieca and James Arnt Aune, "A Vernacular Republican Rhetoric: William Manning's Key of Liberty," *Quarterly Journal of Speech* 91 (2005): 119–43.

[10] Jacques Derrida, "Declaration of Independence," *New Political Science* 15 (1986): 10.

# BIBLIOGRAPHY

Adams, John Charles. "Linguistic Values and Religious Experience: An Analysis of the Clothing Metaphors in Alexander Richardson's Ramist-Puritan Lectures on Speech, 'Speech is a Garment to Cloath our Reason.'" *Quarterly Journal of Speech* 76 (1990): 58–68.

Adams, John. *The Life and Works of John Adams.* Vol. 1. Boston: Little, Brown, 1850.

———. *The Works of John Adams: Second President of the United States.* Edited by Charles Francis Adams. 10 vols. Boston: Little, Brown, 1856.

Adams, Samuel. *The Writings of Samuel Adams.* 4 vols. Edited by Harry Alonzo Cushing. New York: Octagon Books, 1968.

Ahlstrom, Sydney. *A Religious History of the American People.* New Haven: Yale University Press, 1972.

Aldridge, Alfred Owen. *Man of Reason: The Life of Thomas Paine.* New York: J. B. Lippincott, 1959.

Amos, Gary, and Richard Gardiner. *Never Before in History: America's Inspired Birth.* Dallas: Houghton, 1998.

Anderson, Benedict. *Imagined Communities: Reflections on the Origin and Spread of Nationalism.* London: Verso, 1983.

Angelo, Henry. *Reminiscences of Henry Angelo.* 2 vols. New York: Benjamin Blom, 1904.

Aristotle. *Rhetoric.* Translated by W. Rhys Roberts. New York: Modern Library, 1954.

Bailyn, Bernard. *The Ideological Origins of the American Revolution.* Cambridge, Mass.: Harvard University Press, 1992.

———. *Pamphlets of the American Revolution: 1750–1776.* vol. 1. Edited by Bernard Bailyn. Cambridge, Mass.: Harvard University Press, 1965.

Baldwin, Alice. *New England Clergy and the American Revolution.* Durham, N.C.: Duke University Press, 1928.

Berthold, Arthur Benedict. *American Colonial Printing as Determined by Contemporary Cultural Forces, 1639–1763.* New York: Burt Franklin, 1934.

Black, Edwin. "The Second Persona." *Quarterly Journal of Speech* 56 (1970): 109–19.

Bloch, Ruth. "Religion and Ideological Change in the American Revolution." In *Religion and American Politics: From the Colonial Period to the 1980s.* Edited by Mark A. Noll, 44–61. New York: Oxford University Press, 1989.

Bonomi, Patricia U. *Under the Cope of Heaven: Religion, Society, and Politics in Colonial America.* New York: Oxford University Press, 1986.

Bormann, Ernest G. *The Force of Fantasy: Restoring the American Dream.* Carbondale: Southern Illinois University Press, 1985.

Breen, T. H. "Ideology and Nationalism on the Eve of the American Revolution: Revisions Once More in Need of Revising." *Journal of American History* 84 (1997): 13–39.

———. *The Marketplace of Revolution: How Consumer Politics Shaped American Independence.* New York: Oxford University Press, 2004.

Breen, T. H., and T. Hall. "Structuring Provincial Imagination: The Rhetoric and Experience of Social Change in Eighteenth-century New England," *American Historical Review* 103 (1998): 1410–39.

Brekus, Catherine A. *Strangers and Pilgrims: Female Preaching in America, 1740–1845.* Chapel Hill: University of North Carolina Press, 1998.

Bridenbaugh, Carl. *Mitre and Sceptre: Transatlantic Faiths, Ideas, Personalities, and Politics, 1689–1775.* New York: Oxford University Press, 1962.

———. *Cities in Revolt: Urban Life in America, 1743–1776.* New York: Capricorn Books, 1964.

Browne, Stephen H. *Angelina Grimké, Rhetoric, Identity, and the Radical Imagination.* East Lansing: Michigan State University Press, 1999, 34.

———. "The Pastoral Voice in John Dickinson's First 'Letter From a Farmer in Pennsylvania.'" *Quarterly Journal of Speech* 76 (1990): 46–57.

———. "Jefferson's First Declaration of Independence: A Summary View of the Rights of British America Revisited." *Quarterly Journal of Speech* 39 (2003): 235–52.

Bumstead, J. M., ed. *The Great Awakening: The Beginnings of Pietism in America.* London: Blaisdell, 1970.

Bushman, Richard. "A Psychological Earthquake." In Rutman, *The Great Awakening: Event and Exegesis.* 157–65.

Butler, Jon. "Enthusiasm Described and Decried: The Great Awakening as Interpretive Fiction." *Journal of American History* 69 (1982–1983): 305–25.

————. *Awash in a Sea of Faith: Christianizing the American People*. Cambridge, Mass.: Harvard University Press, 1990.

Campbell, John Angus. "Between the Fragment and the Icon: Prospect for a Rhetorical House of the Middle Way." *Western Journal of Speech Communication* 54 (1990): 346–76.

————. "Rhetoriography: An Essay in Method." Paper presented at the National Communication Association Convention, Chicago, November 1999.

Campbell, Karlyn K., and Kathleen Hall Jamieson. "Form and Genre in Rhetorical Criticism: An Introduction." In *Form and Genre: Shaping Rhetorical Action*. Edited by Karlyn K. Campbell and Kathleen Hall Jamieson, 9–32. Falls Church, Va.: Speech Communication Association, 1978.

Casey, Michael W. "The First Female Public Speakers in America (1630–1840): Searching for Egalitarian Christian Primitivism." *Journal of Communication & Religion* 23 (2000): 1–28.

Charland, Maurice. "Constitutive Rhetoric: The Case of the Peuple Québécois." *Quarterly Journal of Speech* 73 (1987): 133–50.

Chauncy, Charles. *A Letter . . . to Mr. George Wishart*. Edinburgh, 1742.

————. "Enthusiasm Described and Caution'd Against." In Heimert and Miller, *The Great Awakening: Documents*, 228–56.

————. *Seasonable Thoughts on the State of Religion in New England*. Hicksville, N.Y.: Regina Press, 1975.

Cicero. *De Oratore*. 2 vols. Loeb Classic Library Series. Cambridge, Mass.: Harvard University Press, 1979.

Clap, Thomas. *A Letter from the Rev. Mr. Thomas Clap, rector of Yale College at New Haven, to a friend in Boston . . . that the Rev. Mr. Edwards told him, that the Rev. Mr. Whitefield said in his hearing, that it was his design to turn the generality of minister in the country out of their places and resettle them with ministers from England, Scotland, and Ireland*. Boston: T. Fleet, 1745.

————. *The Declaration of the Rector and Tutors of Yale-College in New-Haven, Against the Reverend Mr. George Whitefield, His principles and Designs, in a letter to him*. Boston: T. Fleet, 1745.

Clark, J. C. D. *The Language of Liberty, 1660–1832: Political Discourses and Social Dynamics in the Anglo-American World*. Cambridge: Cambridge University Press, 1993.

————. *English Society, 1660–1832: Religion, Ideology, and Politics during the Ancient Regime*. New York: Cambridge University Press, 2000.

Coalter Jr., Milton. *Gilbert Tennent, Son of Thunder: A Case Study of Continental Pietism's Impact on the First Great Awakening in the Middle Colonies.* New York: Greenwood Press, 1986.

Cohen, Charles Lloyd. *God's Caress: The Psychology of Puritan Religious Experience.* London: Oxford University Press, 1986.

———. "The Post-Puritan Paradigm of Early American Religious History." *William and Mary Quarterly* 54 (1997): 695–722.

Conley, Thomas. *Rhetoric in the European Tradition.* New York: Longman, 1990.

*Convention of New England Ministers: The Testimony of a Number of New England ministers met at Boston Sept. 25, 1745. Professing the ancient faith of these churches; inviting others who hold it, to unite in profession and maintaining the same; reciting and recommending an excellent Act concerning preaching lately made by the General Assembly of the Church of Scotland.* Boston: Kneeland & Green, 1745.

Corrigan, John. *The Prism of Piety: Catholick Congregational Clergy at the Beginning of the Enlightenment.* New York. Oxford University Press, 1991.

Cowing, Cedric. *The Great Awakening and the American Revolution: Colonial Thought in the 18th Century.* Chicago: Rand McNally, 1971.

Crèvecoeur, J. Hector St. John de. *Letters from an American Farmer and Sketches of Eighteenth-Century America.* New York: Penguin Books, 1981.

Dallimore, Arnold A. *George Whitefield: The Life and Times of the Great Evangelist of the Eighteenth Century.* Wheaton, Ill.: Crossway Books, 1990.

Dargan, Edwin Charles. *A History of Preaching.* 2 vols. New York: Burt Franklin, 1912.

Darsey, James. *The Prophetic Tradition and Radical Rhetoric in America.* New York: New York University Press, 1997.

Davidson, Philip. *Propaganda and the American Revolution, 1763–1783.* New York: W. W. Norton, 1973.

Davies, Samuel. *The State of Religion among the Protestant Dissenters in Virginia.* Boston: Kneeland & Green, 1751.

Derrida, Jacques. "Declarations of Independence." *New Political Science* 15 (1986): 7–15.

Dickinson, Jonathan. *The Nature and Necessity of Regeneration.* Philadelphia, 1743.

———. "Letters from a Farmer in Pennsylvania." In McDonald, *Empire and Nation.* 1–86.

Edwards, Jonathan. *An expostulatory letter from the Rev. Mr. Edwards to the Rev. Mr. Clap, Rector of Yale College.* Boston: Kneeland & Green, 1745.

———. *Sinners in the Hands of an Angry God.* Boston: Kneeland & Green, 1741.

———. *The Works of Jonathan Edwards.* London: Henry G. Bohn, 1871.

Edwards, Sarah Pierpont. "A letter to her brother James dated October 24, 1740." In Lovejoy, *Religious Enthusiasm and the Great Awakening*, 33–34.

Evans, Charles. *American Bibliography.* 14 vols. Chicago: Blakely Press, 1905.

Fleming, William, and Elizabeth Fleming. *A Narrative of the Sufferings and Surprizing Deliverances of William and Elizabeth Fleming.* Philadelphia: James Chattin, 1756.

Fliegelman, Jay. *Declaring Independence: Jefferson, Natural Language and the Culture of Performance.* Stanford, Calif.: Stanford University Press, 1993.

Foote, Samuel. *The Works of Samuel Foote, Esq.* London: Sherwood, Gilbert & Piper, 1830.

Franklin, Benjamin. *The Papers of Benjamin Franklin.* Edited by Leonard W. Labaree. New Haven: Yale University Press, 1959.

———. "His Examination Before the House of Commons (1766)." In *The World's Famous Orations*, edited by William Jennings Bryan, 37–52. New York: Funk & Wagnalls, 1906.

———. *The Works of Benjamin Franklin, 1706–1744.* Edited by John Bigelow. 10 vols. New York: G. P. Putnam's Sons, 1887.

Fukuyama, Francis. *Trust: The Social Virtues and the Creation of Prosperity.* New York: Free Press, 1995.

Galloway, Joseph. *A Letter to the People of Pennsylvania, &c.* Philadelphia, 1760.

———. *Historical and Political Reflections on the Rise and Progress of the American Rebellion.* London: G. Wilkie, 1780.

Garden, Alexander. "To the Inhabitants of the Parish of St Philip, Charles-Town, Nov 24, 1740." In Heimert and Miller, *The Great Awakening: Documents*, 46–61.

Giddens, Anthony. *New Rules of Sociological Method: A Positive Critique of Interpretative Sociologies.* New York: Basic Books, 1976.

Gillies, John. *Memoirs of the Life of the Reverend George Whitefield.* Meadow View, England: Quinta Press, 2000.

Gledstone, James Patterson. *George Whitefield, M.A.: Field Preacher.* Meadow View, England: Quinta Press, 2000.

Griffin, Patrick. "The People with No Name: Ulster's Migrants and Identity Formation in Eighteenth-century Pennsylvania." *William and Mary Quarterly* 58 (2001): 587–614.

Hall, David D. *Worlds of Wonder, Days of Judgment: Popular Religious Belief in Early New England.* Cambridge, Mass.: Harvard University Press, 1989.

Hall, Timothy D. *Contested Boundaries: Itinerancy and the Reshaping of the Colonial American Religious World*. Durham, N.C.: Duke University Press, 1994.

Hall, Walter P., and Robert G. Albion. *A History of England and the British Empire*. Boston: Ginn, 1946.

Harvard College. *The Testimony of the President, Professors, Tutors and Hebrew Instructor of Harvard College in Cambridge, against the Rev. Mr. George Whitefield and his conduct*. Boston: T. Fleet, 1744.

Hatch, Nathan O. *The Sacred Cause of Liberty: Republican Thought and the Millennium in Revolutionary New England*. New Haven: Yale University Press, 1977.

————. "Foreword" to Stout, *Divine Dramatist*.

Heimert, Alan. *Religion and the American Mind: From the Great Awakening to the Revolution*. Cambridge, Mass.: Harvard University Press, 1966.

Heimert, Alan, and Perry Miller, eds. *The Great Awakening: Documents Illustrating the Crisis and its Consequences*. New York: Bobbs Merrill, 1967.

Henry, Stuart. *George Whitefield: Wayfaring Witness*. New York: Abingdon, 1957.

*Historical Statistics of the United States: Colonial Times to 1970*. United States Department of Commerce, 1975.

Hogan, J. Michael, and G. Williams. "Republican Charisma and the American Revolution: The Textual Persona of Thomas Paine's Common Sense." *Quarterly Journal of Speech* 86 (2000): 1–18.

Hopkins, Stephen. *The Rights of Colonies Examined*. Providence, R.I.: W. Goddard, 1765.

Howell, Wilbur Samuel. *Eighteenth-century British Logic and Rhetoric*. Princeton: Princeton University Press, 1971.

Hudson, Winthrop S. "Theological Convictions and Democratic Government." *Theology Today* 10 (1953): 230–39.

Hudson, Winthrop S., and John Corrigan. *Religion in America*. New York: Macmillan, 1992.

Hume, David. "Of Eloquence." In *The Philosophical Works*, edited by Thomas H. Green and Thomas H. Gross. London: Scientia Verlag Aalen, 1964. 3: 163–73.

Jefferson, Thomas. "A Summary View of the Rights of British Americans." In *The Life and Selected Writings of Thomas Jefferson*, edited by Adrienne Koch and William Peden. New York: Random House, 1944, 298–303.

Jehlen, Myra, and Michael Warner. *The English Literatures of America: 1500–1800*. New York: Routledge, 1996.

Jost, Walter, and Michael Hyde, eds. *Rhetoric and Hermeneutics in Our Time: A Reader.* New Haven: Yale University Press, 1997.

Kaestle, Carl F. "The Public Reaction to John Dickinson's Farmer's Letters," *American Antiquarian Society Proceedings* 78 (1969): 329–59.

Kramarae, Cheris. *Women and Men Speaking: Frameworks for Analysis.* Rowley, Mass.: Newbury House, 1981.

Lakoff, George, and Mark Johnson. *Metaphors We Live By.* Chicago: University of Chicago Press, 1980.

Lakoff, Robin. *Language and Women's Place.* New York: Harper & Row, 1975.

Lambert, Frank. *Pedlar in Divinity: George Whitefield and the Transatlantic Revivals, 1737–1770.* Princeton: Princeton University Press, 1994.

———. *Inventing the "Great Awakening."* Princeton: Princeton University Press, 1999.

———. "Subscribing for Profits and Piety: The Friendship of Benjamin Franklin and George Whitefield." *William and Mary Quarterly* 50 (1993): 529–54.

Lanham, Richard. *The Motives of Eloquence: Literary Rhetoric in the Renaissance.* New Haven: Yale University Press, 1976.

Leff, Michael. "Things Made by Words: Reflections on Textual Criticism," *Quarterly Journal of Speech* 78 (1992): 223–31.

Locke, John. *Two Treatises of Government.* Edited by Thomas I. Cook. New York: Hafner, 1947.

Looby, Christopher. *Voicing America: Language, Literary Form, and the Origins of the United States.* Chicago: University of Chicago Press, 1996.

Lovejoy, David S. *Religious Enthusiasm and the Great Awakening.* Englewood Cliffs, N.J.: Prentice Hall, 1969.

Lucas, Stephen. *Portents of Rebellion: Rhetoric and Revolution in Philadelphia, 1765–76.* Philadelphia: Temple University Press, 1976.

Macleane, Douglas. *A History of Pembroke College Oxford Anciently Broadgates Hall.* Oxford: Oxford Historical Society, 1897.

Mahaffey, Jerome. "George Whitefield's Rhetorical Art: Neo-Sophism in the Great Awakening." Forthcoming in *Homiletic* 31 (2006).

———. "The Rhetoric of Hermeneutics: Orality as a Rhetorical Topos in Biblical Interpretation." Master's thesis, Syracuse University, 1997.

———. "Whitefield as Rhetorician: A Textual Analysis of Whitefield's 'Marriage of Cana.'" Paper presented at the annual convention of the National Communication Association, Chicago, November 1999.

Mansfield, Stephen. *Forgotten Founding Father: The Heroic Legacy of George Whitefield.* Nashville: Cumberland House, 2001.

Mayhew, Jonathan. *A Discourse Concerning Unlimited Submission and Nonresistance to the Higher Powers.* Boston: D. Fowle, 1750.

———. *Christian Sobriety.* Boston: Richard & Samuel Draper, 1763.

McConnell, Francis John. *Evangelicals, Revolutionists, and Idealists: Six Contributors to American Thought and Action.* London: Kennikat, 1942.

McDonald, Forrest, ed. *Empire and Nation.* Indianapolis: Liberty Fund, 1999.

McGuire, William, and D. Papageorgis. "The Relative Efficacy of Various Types of Prior Belief-defense in Producing Immunity Against Persuasion." *Journal of Abnormal and Social Psychology* 62 (1961): 327–77.

McNeill, John T. "The Democratic Element in Calvin's Thought." *Church History* 18 (1949): 153–71.

Mead, Sidney E. "Through and Beyond the Lines." Review of *Religion and the American Mind,* by Alan Heimert. *Journal of Religion* 48 (1968): 274–88.

Mercieca, Jennifer Rose. "Choice, Loyalty, and Safety in the Construction of a Distinctly American Imagined Nationalism." *Rhetoric & Public Affairs* 9 (2006): 279–302.

Mercieca, Jennifer R., and J. Aune. "A Vernacular Republican Rhetoric: William Manning's Key of Liberty." *Quarterly Journal of Speech* 91 (2005): 119–43.

Miller, Perry. "From the Covenant to the Revival." In *The Shaping of American Religion.* Edited by James Ward Smith and A. Leland Jamison. 322–68. Vol. 1: *Religion in American Life.* Princeton: Princeton University Press, 1961.

———. "Crisis and Americanization." In Rutman, *The Great Awakening: Event and Exegesis,* 139–55.

Morgan, David T. "A Most Unlikely Friendship: Benjamin Franklin and George Whitefield." *Historian* 47 (1985): 208–18.

Morgan, Edmund S. Review of *Religion and the American Mind: From the Great Awakening to the Revolution,* by Alan Heimert. *William and Mary Quarterly* 24 (1967): 454–59.

Morgan, Edmund S., and Helen M. Morgan. *The Stamp Act Crisis: Prologue to Revolution.* New York: Collier Books, 1963.

Noll, Mark A. *America's God: From Jonathan Edwards to Abraham Lincoln.* New York: Oxford University Press, 2002.

Osborne, Michael. "Rhetorical Depiction." In *Form, Genre, and the Study of Political Discourse.* Edited by H. W. Simons and A. Aghazarian, 79–107. Columbia: University of South Carolina Press, 1986.

*Oxford English Dictionary, The.* 2nd ed. Oxford: Clarendon, 1989.

Packer, J. I. "The Faith of the Protestants." In *Eerdmans' Handbook to the History of Christianity*. Edited by T. Dowley, 374–75. Herts, England: Lion, 1977.

Paine, Thomas. *Common Sense*. Edited by Isaac Kramnick. New York: Penguin Books, 1976.

Peters, Samuel. *A General History of Connecticut*. London: J. Bew, 1781.

Pettit, Norman. *The Heart Prepared: Grace and Conversion in Puritan Spiritual Life*. New Haven: Yale University Press, 1966.

Pilcher, George William. *Samuel Davies: An Apostle of Dissent in Colonial Virginia*. Knoxville: University of Tennessee Press, 1971.

Quincy, Samuel. *The nature and necessity of regeneration*. In *Twenty Sermons . . . preach'd in the Parish of St Philip, Charles-town, South Carolina* (Boston, 1475; rpt. 1750): 274–91.

Quintilian. *Institutes of Oratory*. Vol. 4. Loeb Classic Library Series. Cambridge, Mass.: Harvard University Press, 1979.

Richardson, Alexander. "Grammatical Notes." *Logicians School-Master*. London, 1657.

Roberts, Richard Owen. *Whitefield in Print: A Bibliographic Record*. Wheaton, Ill.: Richard Owen Roberts, 1988.

Rutman, Darrett B. *The Great Awakening: Event and Exegesis*. New York: Wiley & Sons, 1970.

Ruttenburg, Nancy. "George Whitefield, Spectacular Conversion, and the Rise of Democratic Personality." *American Literary History* 5 (1993): 429–58.

Ryan, Halford Ross. "Baldwin vs. Edward VIII: A Case Study in *Kategoria* and *Apologia*." *Southern Speech Communication Journal* 49 (1984): 125–34.

Schlesinger, Arthur M. *The Birth of the Nation: A Portrait of the American People on the Eve of Independence*. Boston: Houghton Mifflin, 1968.

Scougal, Henry. *The Life of God in the Soul of Man*. London: T. Dring & J. Weld, 1677.

Sheridan, Thomas. *A Discourse: Being Introductory to His Course of Lectures on Elocution and the English Language*. Los Angeles: William Andrews Clark Memorial Library, 1969.

Shurtleff, William. "A Letter to those of his brethren in the Ministry who refuse to admit the Rev. Mr. Whitefield into their Pulpits." In Heimert and Miller, *The Great Awakening: Documents*, 354–63.

Silverstein, Michael. "The Improvisational Performance of Culture in Realtime Discursive Practice." In *Creativity in Performance*. Edited by Keith Sawyer, 265–312. London: Ablex, 1997.

———. "Indexical Order and the Dialectics of Sociolinguistic Life." In *SALSA III: Proceedings of the Third Annual Symposium about Language and Society.* Edited by R. Parker and others. Austin: University of Texas, 1996.

Stiles, Ezra. *A Discourse on Christian Union.* In Heimert and Miller, *The Great Awakening: Documents,* 593–608.

Stoddard, Solomon. *Defects of Preachers Reproved,* a sermon preached at Northampton, May 19, 1723. In *The Great Awakening: Documents on the Revival of Religion.* Edited by Richard L. Bushman, 11–16. London: University of North Carolina Press, 1969.

Stout, Harry. "Religion, Communications, and the Ideological Origins of the American Revolution." *William and Mary Quarterly* 34 (1977): 519–41.

———. "The Great Awakening in New England Reconsidered: The New England Clergy." *Journal of Social History* 8 (1974): 21–47.

———. *The Divine Dramatist: George Whitefield and the Rise of Modern Evangelicalism.* Grand Rapids: Eerdmans, 1991.

———. "Religion, Communications, and the Career of George Whitefield." In *Communication and Change in American Religious History.* Edited by Leonard I. Sweet, 108–25. Grand Rapids: Eerdmans, 1993.

Stout, Harry, and D. G. Hart, eds. *New Directions in American Religious History.* London: Oxford University Press, 1997.

Strout, Cushing. *The New Heavens and New Earth: Political Religion in America.* New York: Harper & Row, 1974.

Sutherland, L. S., and L. G. Mitchell. *The Eighteenth Century.* Vol. 5. *The History of the University of Oxford.* Oxford: Clarendon, 1986.

Thomas, Isaiah. *The History of Printing in America, with a Biography of Printers, and an Account of Newspapers.* Albany, N.Y.: J. Munsell, 1874.

Tocqueville, Alexis de. *Democracy in America.* Edited by Richard D. Heffner. New York: New American Library, 1956.

Urban, Greg. *Metaculture: How Culture Moves through the World.* Minneapolis: University of Minnesota Press, 2001.

Wakeley, J. B. *Anecdotes of the Rev. George Whitefield.* Meadow View, England: Quinta Press, 2000.

Warner, Michael. "New English Sodom." *American Literature* 64 (1992): 19–47.

———. "What's Colonial About Colonial America?" In *Possible Pasts: Becoming Colonial in Early America.* Edited by Robert St. George, 49–70. Ithaca: Cornell University Press, 2000.

Whitaker, Nathaniel. *A Funeral Sermon.* Boston, 1771.

————. *An Antidote Against Toryism, or The Curse of Meroz, in a discourse on Judges 5th 23*. Newburyport: J. Mycall, 1777.

White, Eugene. "Whitefield's Use of Proofs During the Great Awakening in America." *Western Speech* 14 (1950): 3–6.

Whitefield, George. *A brief account of the rise, progress and present situation of the Orphan-House in Georgia, in a letter to a friend*. Philadelphia: W. Bradford, 1745.

————. *A Letter to the Reverend Dr. Chauncy*. Philadelphia: W. Bradford, 1745.

————. *A Letter to the Reverend, the President, and Professors, Tutors, and Hebrew Instructor of Harvard College in Cambridge In answer to a Testimony Published by them against the Reverend Mr. George Whitefield, and his Conduct*. Boston: Kneeland & Green, 1745.

————. *The Works of the Rev. George Whitefield, M.A. Late of Pembroke College, Oxford, and Chaplain to the Rt. Hon the Countess of Huntingdon, Containing All His Sermons and Tracts Which Have Been Already Published with a Selected Collection of Letters*. Edited by John Gillies. Meadow View, England: Quinta Press, 2000.

————. *George Whitefield's Journals*. Meadow View, England: Quinta Press, 2000.

————. *The Good Shepherd*. In *Works of George Whitefield: Additional Sermons*. Meadow View, England: Quinta Press, 2000, 243–44.

Williams, Basil. *The Whig Supremacy: 1714–1760*. Vol. 9. *The Oxford History of England*. Oxford: Clarendon, 1962.

Wilson, James. *The Works of James Wilson*. Edited by Robert G. McCloskey. Cambridge, Mass.: Belknap Press of Harvard University Press, 1967.

Winter, Cornelius. *Memoirs of the Life and Character of the late Reverend Cornelius Winter*. Edited by William Jay. Bath, England: M. Gye, 1808.

Wood, Gordon S. "Rhetoric and Reality in the American Revolution." *William and Mary Quarterly* 23 (1966): 3–32.

————. "Religion and the American Revolution." In Stout and Hart, *New Directions*, 173–205.

Wrage, Ernest J. "Public Address: A Study in Social and Intellectual History." *Quarterly Journal of Speech* 33 (1947): 451–57.

Wright, Louis. *The Cultural Life of the American Colonies: 1607–1763*. New York: Harper & Row, 1957.

Yunis, Harvey. *Taming Democracy: Models of Political Rhetoric in Classical Athens*. Ithaca: Cornell University Press, 1996.

# INDEX

Adams, John, 154, 164, 167, 190, 239–40, 248–49

Adams, Samuel, 15, 53, 189, 195–96, 198–99, 216, 232, 235, 240, 249; rhetoric of, 227–31, 235, 240

American Bishop, 7, 163, 165, 172, 176, 183, 188–89, 198, 201, 204, 210

American Revolution, 1, 3–10,12–13, 51, 102, 115, 148, 154, 164, 172, 209, 211, 213–17, 219–20, 226–27, 232, 238, 244–45, 247–49, 253

Angelo, Henry, 47

*Anglican Weekly Miscellany*, 86

Anglican, arbitrary power, 189, 202, 204, 249; British political influence, 133; conflict with Methodists, 124, 144, 185–86, 190; conversion, 27, 64–65; episcopacy in America, 6–7, 162, 176, 178, 185, 200, 204, 211, 218; opposition to Whitefield, 42, 52, 119; piety, 25; plot to assassinate Whitefield, 123; power of liturgy, 119; support of monarchy, 105

antirevivalists, 98, 109, 130, 138, 140, 171

*apologia*, 128

arbitrary power, 147, 150, 152, 156–58, 160, 166–83, 190, 194–95, 202, 207–8, 211, 216–17, 220, 222, 224, 228, 230, 239, 250, 252

Arminianism, 62, 65, 69, 79, 92, 106–7, 113–15, 131, 145, 177–78

Backus, Isaac, 178

Bellamy, Joseph, 225, 245

Bethesda orphanage, 94, 97, 130, 132, 135, 149, 168, 174, 202–3, 208, 211

*Boston Evening-Post*, 128–30, 134

*Boston Gazette*, 129, 134, 156, 158, 161, 201, 228

Broughton, Thomas, 36

Bunyan, John, 45, 84, 113

Calvin, John, 64

Calvinism, 17, 44, 64–70, 79–80, 92, 106–7, 114, 212, 140–42, 145, 172, 177, 180, 219, 235

Campbell, George, 11

Catholicism, 70, 105, 117, 139, 142–43, 147, 150, 154–55, 157–58, 160, 168–69, 173, 182, 185, 186, 200–01, 216–18, 220, 228–29, 236, 248

Charles Edward, 120, 148–49, 152, 154–57, 160, 166, 168

Chauncy, Charles, 12, 35, 86, 90, 95, 100, 106, 125–28, 130–35, 137, 140, 144, 149, 200